# Discipline and Debate

# Discipline and Debate

## The Language of Violence in a
## Tibetan Buddhist Monastery

———

Michael Lempert

UNIVERSITY OF CALIFORNIA PRESS

*Berkeley   Los Angeles   London*

University of California Press, one of the most distinguished university presses in the United States, enriches lives around the world by advancing scholarship in the humanities, social sciences, and natural sciences. Its activities are supported by the UC Press Foundation and by philanthropic contributions from individuals and institutions. For more information, visit www.ucpress.edu.

University of California Press
Berkeley and Los Angeles, California

University of California Press, Ltd.
London, England

Library of Congress Cataloging-in-Publication Data

Lempert, Michael.
    Discipline and debate : the language of violence in a Tibetan Buddhist monastery / Michael Lempert.
        p.  cm.
    Includes bibliographical references and index.
    ISBN 978-0-520-26946-0 (cloth, alk. paper)
    ISBN 978-0-520-26947-7 (pbk., alk. paper)
    Buddhist monasticism and religious orders—Education—India.
2. Buddhist monasticism and religious orders—Education—China—
Tibet Autonomous Region.   3. Liberalism (Religion—India.
4. Violence—Religious aspects—Buddhism.   5. Discipline—Religious
aspects—Buddhism.   6. Tibetans—India—Religion.   I. Title.
BQ7758.I4L46   2012
294.3'5697—dc22                                            2011027449

20   19   18   17   16   15   14   13   12
10   9   8   7   6   5   4   3   2   1

*For my grandparents*

CONTENTS

# ILLUSTRATIONS

## MAP

## FIGURES

## TABLES

# ACKNOWLEDGMENTS

I don't recall how the routine started, but its central prop consisted of a small cylindrical object, usually a AA battery, though a pencil or pen plucked from a nearby table would do. One of my monk friends from South India's Sera Monastery—my primary field site—would press the object toward my face, as if it were a microphone; mine was battery driven and had to be monitored constantly, which made AA batteries the perfect metonym for fieldwork stress. He would then rattle off questions about utterly quotidian aspects of my life (... Had I eaten dal and rice today? Was it true that I regularly wore sandals?...) but in a hushed, grave, reverential tone, at which point we'd all break down in laughter. I earned the sobriquet 'Interview' (*dri ba dris lan*) for having done one too many. The questions I posed often struck my interlocutors as odd, or obvious to the point of being inconsequential, and everyone thought it strange that I should wish to interview young monks—kids, really—rather than speak exclusively with the well-socialized and the learned. The monks' playful, table-turning mimicry reminds me of a real debt. My interlocutors were busy people. Most were in the throes of demanding classwork in Buddhist philosophical doctrine. Many had left everything and traveled to Sera at great personal risk, enduring the harrowing trek from Tibet into Nepal, just for a chance at a better future. I thank all of my Tibetan interlocutors for finding time to let me learn from them, and for doing so with a degree of patience, warmth, and humor that I still find remarkable.

I am grateful for support from a Fulbright-Hays fellowship, which funded the dissertation research on which this book is based. The University of Pennsylvania's Anthropology Department gave me funds to conduct valuable pre-dissertation fieldwork, and I wrote up my dissertation with the aid of a Charlotte W. Newcombe fellowship and a fellowship from the University of Pennsylvania's School of Arts and Sciences. During my early years of graduate training, I benefited from several years of Foriegn Language and Area Studies funding for the study of Tibetan. I thank the University of Michigan Office of the Vice President for Research for contributing a publication subvention.

The arc of my graduate studies ended up being longer than I anticipated. As my work evolved from the study of Buddhist philosophical texts to that of discursive interaction, I accumulated much intellectual debt, more than I can credit here. At the University of Pennsylvania, where I completed my degree in linguistic and sociocultural anthropology, I thank especially my dissertation committee members: Greg Urban, Stanton Wortham, and, above all, my adviser, Asif Agha, who added far more rigor and conceptual clarity to this project than it would otherwise have had. From my first days of graduate training in linguistic anthropology at Penn, I, like my peers, also felt the avuncular influence of Michael Silverstein, whose scholarship has inspired so many beyond his base at the University of Chicago. Farther back but no less influential were a couple of critical years of doctoral work at the University of Virginia's History of Religions program under David Germano and Jeffrey Hopkins. A self-styled apostate, I thought that in leaving religious studies for the social sciences I would end up in a different place. I now see that I have not strayed nearly as far as I imagined. I am still preoccupied with questions that arose in a paper I once labored over for a seminar with Jeffrey Hopkins during my first semester in graduate school. I still find myself puzzling over old issues about Buddhism and modernity, issues that are only half mine, which suggests how glacial intellectual preoccupations can be, and makes me appreciate what made "incarceration" such an alluring trope in the title of Donald Lopez's *Prisoners of Shangri-La: Tibetan Buddhism and the West.* Farther back still there is Hubert Decleer, a maverick scholar who introduced me to things Tibetan through the School for International Training's Tibetan Studies program and confirmed forever my instincts about the virtue of disciplinary irreverence.

I thank my former colleagues in Georgetown's Linguistics Department, especially Deborah Tannen, and present colleagues in the University of Michigan's Department of Anthropology. I am grateful to Francis Zimmermann and Michel de Fornel for the invitation to discuss this and other work at L'École des Hautes Études en Sciences Sociales in Paris in 2010. For comments on two chapters, I am indebted to a characteristically spirited Michicagoan faculty seminar in linguistic anthropology held in January 2011 (Richard Bauman, Susan Gal, Matthew Hull, Judith Irvine, Webb Keane, Alaina Lemon, John Lucy, Bruce Mannheim, Barbra Meek, Constantine Nakassis, Stephen Scott, Michael Silverstein, Robin Queen, and Kristina Wirtz). Several colleagues graciously read portions of the manuscript of this book: Sepideh Bajracharya, Anya Bernstein, Luke Fleming, Niklas Hultin, Judith Irvine, Webb Keane, Matthew Hull, Donald Lopez, Sabina Perrino, and Joel Robbins. A number of others fielded questions and offered advice, including Robert Barnett, José Cabezón, Geoff Childs, Melvyn Goldstein, Zeynep Gürsel, Sherap Gyatso, Lauran Hartley, Toni Huber, Charlene Makley, Amy Mountcastle, Erik Mueggler, Stephanie Roemer, Gray Tuttle, and Nicole Willock.

Several graduate research assistants provided help. Jermay Reynolds of Georgetown University's Linguistics Department assisted with aspects of the textual analysis in chapter 3, and Patrick Callier of the same department did prosodic work for me on chapter 4. In 2011, Charles Zuckerman of University of Michigan's Department of Anthropology provided technical, font-related help, and Jessica Krcmarik (University of Michigan, Class of 2012) did artist renderings of digital photos. I received fresh inspiration to finish this book in 2009–10 thanks to a yearlong interdisciplinary faculty seminar at the University of Michigan convened by Tomoko Masuzawa and Paul Christopher Johnson and entitled "Initiative on Religion and the Secular."

The list of Tibetans I wish to thank is too long to provide here, but more than length is the issue of anonymity, which I have tried to preserve in this book through the use of pseudonyms. Those who helped me know who they are and how grateful I am. As for Tibetans I hired as research assistants, I wish to acknowledge especially Lobsang Thokmey and Tenzin Dargye (pseudonym).

Portions of this book have appeared in the *Journal of Linguistic Anthropology, Language & Communication*, and *Text & Talk*. I am grateful to have had the opportunity to recheck transcriptions with a number of mother-tongue speakers since the time some of these articles were published, which in a few cases led to minor corrections. For chapter 2, Wiley-Blackwell allowed me to draw on my article "Denotational Textuality and Demeanor Indexicality in Tibetan Buddhist Debate," *Journal of Linguistic Anthropology* 15 (2) (2005):171–93. Chapter 4 draws on an article titled "Disciplinary Theatrics: Public Reprimand and the Textual Performance of Affect at Sera Monastery, India," *Language & Communication* 26 (1) (2006):15–33; Copyright Elsevier 2006. And for chapter 5, de Gruyter (see http://www.reference-global.com/) granted me permission to draw on "How to Make Our Subjects Clear: Denotational Transparency and Subject Formation in the Tibetan Diaspora," *Text & Talk: An Interdisciplinary Journal of Language, Discourse & Communication Studies* 27 (4) (2007):509–32.

Senior Editor Reed Malcolm of the University of California Press found excellent readers whose remarks improved this work, and his own frank editorial advice was invaluable.

# TECHNICAL NOTE ON TRANSCRIPTION
## AND RESEARCH METHODS

For students and scholars of literary Tibetan, I use orthographic transcription, specifically, the widely used romanized Wylie (1959) transliteration system. The variety of spoken Tibetan in this corpus is largely so-called Standard Spoken Tibetan (Tournadre and Rdo-rje 2003), a variety based on Central Tibetan in the Lhasa area. Of the many facets of spoken Tibetan not accurately represented by the standard orthography, the quotative clitic *-s* stands out as a special concern, since it figures into my analysis, especially in chapter 2 on debate. Some (e.g., Denwood 1999:118) suggest that the verb whose orthographic form is *zer* ('say'; /ser/) occurs in a reduced form, either as /sa/ (often with lengthening /sa:/) or as /-s/. /sa/ and /ser/ differ distributionally from -s, however. The latter can be framed by matrix clause verba dicendi (e.g., *zer* [ser] and *lab* [/lʌp/]):

e.g.,  drāshii-g͡ii c̲a tsābo d̲u̲ù {-s / *s̲a̲(:)} s̲er-gi   d̲u̲ù   Tashi says "the tea is hot."
       PN-ERG   tea hot   AUX-QT        say-NZR  AUX

The clitic /-s/ thus differs from *zer* (/ser/) and its reduced form (/sa/) on phonemic and morphosyntactic grounds. For this and other reasons, I use a combination of orthographic and phonemic transcription, especially for debate discourse in chapter 2 and reprimand discourse in chapter 4. In both chapters the following multi-tier transcription layout is used:

Line 1 orthographic transcription (in italics)   parallel free translation

Line 2 phonemic transcription

Line 3 item-by-item gloss

xiv

Line 1 is also used for indicating speech overlap, latching (lack of perceivable pause across a turn boundary), dysfluencies such as false-starts, and other details relevant to the analysis of discursive interaction (for theoretical and methodological reflections on transcription, see, for example, Ochs 1979; Edwards and Lampert 1993; Duranti 1997:137–54). For vocalizations such as filled pauses and backchannel cues, rough orthographic approximations are given, such as *a* for [ʌ:] and *'m* for [ʔmʔ]. In the debate transcripts in chapter 2, line breaks mark intonation unit boundaries, a unitization of discourse that is important for the study of interaction and for the analysis of phenomena like speech articulation rate.

For phonemic transcription in line 2, I have elected to use the simplified conventions found in Melvyn Goldstein's latest Tibetan-English dictionary (Goldstein, Shelling, and Surkhang 2001), in which tips on pronunciation can also be found. For simplicity, I do not represent the effects of phonological processes like vowel harmony, and while the transcription conventions from this latest dictionary are arguably not as helpful for linguists as those of the International Phonetics Alphabet or the Americanist conventions used in some of Goldstein's earlier dictionaries and in the classic work on Lhasa Tibetan phonology by Kun Chang and Betty Shefts Chang (1964, 1967), the improved accessibility seemed a worthwhile trade-off.

When I am not analyzing face-to-face interaction, I use orthographic transcription with free English translation, and when I mention Tibetan terms in the body of the text, I typically provide the orthographic form in italics after the English glosses. For proper names and for frequently used Tibetan terms, English approximations of Tibetan pronunciation are used (e.g., "Geluk" for *dge lugs*). The first time such names and terms are introduced, they are followed by their orthographic equivalent in parentheses or an endnote.

## TRANSCRIPTION ABBREVIATIONS AND SYMBOLS

| ABL | ablative |
|---|---|
| ACC | accusative |
| AGEN | agentive |
| ASR | assertoric mood |
| AUX | auxiliary verb |
| COND | conditional |
| CSQ | confirmation-seeking question |
| DAT | dative |
| DET | determiner |
| DIR | directive |
| DUBIT | dubitative mood |
| ERG | ergative |
| FCT | factive |

| | |
|---|---|
| GEN | genitive |
| HON | honorific |
| HON.A | addressee-focal honorific |
| IEV | imperfective evidential |
| IMP | imperative |
| INJ | injunctive mood |
| INS | instrumental |
| INT | interrogative mood |
| LOC | locative |
| NEG | negation marker |
| NH | non-honorific |
| NOM | nomic evidential |
| NP | noun phrase |
| NZR | nominalizer |
| OPT | optative |
| P | participant-indexing (auxiliary verb) |
| ~P | participant non-specific (auxiliary verb) |
| PEV | perfective evidential |
| PL | plural |
| PN | proper name |
| PRC | precative |
| PRP | participant role perspective |
| QT | quotative clitic |
| TOP | topicalizer |
| VLQ | volunteering question |
| WHQ | WH question |
| YNQ | yes/no question |
| {.../...} | paradigmatic contrast |
| [ ] | author's interpolations |
| : | lengthening |
| [line break] | intonational unit boundary (debate transcripts only) |
| / | vertical line termed *shad* in Tibetan, which typically marks clause and sentence boundaries |
| '' | latching (lack of perceivable pause between utterances; less than 1/10 of second) |

## STATEMENT OF METHODS

By necessity this work operates at the intersection of disciplines. I am indebted to and engage literature in Tibetan and Buddhist studies, but the book's home is anthropology, especially the subfield of linguistic anthropology. The chapters that follow may be considered, more specifically, essays in—perhaps, toward—an anthropology of interaction.

Why privilege face-to-face interaction? There is ample empirical motivation for this focus, since interaction is, after all, something Tibetans reflect on and care about, but this focus is also likely a reaction to the kind of textualism I experienced, and practiced, when I started doctoral work in Buddhist studies. At that time I found myself caught up in emerging critiques of the field mounted by those within it, critiques that targeted the field's textualism and supposed orientalism. It was in this period of ferment that works like Donald Lopez's (1998) *Prisoners of Shangri-La* appeared, followed by a string of volumes that announced a turn toward "practice" (e.g., Lopez's *Religions of Tibet in Practice* in 1997 and *Asian Religions in Practice* in 1999). Whatever field-specific purchase a notion like "practice" may have had, and arguably still has, it rarely seemed to mean, to put it crudely, what people "do"—at least not as studied through the craft of observation, recording, transcription, and analysis. (I should add that I harbor no positivist pretensions about transcription and analysis, as I hope will be apparent in the chapters that follow.) In privileging text-artifacts (Silverstein and Urban 1996) Buddhist studies appears to have remained methodologically textualist, listing either toward the "secular," historical-philological side or else toward the "religious," doctrinal-philosophical.

When it comes to interaction, anthropology has fared little better. Cultural anthropologists continue to rely—quite unreflectively, I should add—on interaction at every turn, from interviews to oral narratives to words culled from casual conversation. Though interaction is the empirical stuff from which ethnography is made, its pride of place is only rarely made explicit. What is more, there is a pernicious way in which folk ideologies of interaction and communication creep into arguments about the way macrosocial institutions and groups "interact." Even in linguistic anthropology, interaction remains a somewhat neglected area relative to linguistics and especially sociology; sociology's research tradition called "conversation analysis" has been extremely productive, to say nothing of the enormous influence of Erving Goffman's dramaturgical "micro"-sociology. While I work within linguistic anthropology, like many of my colleagues I draw liberally on adjacent research traditions such as interactional sociolinguistics, discourse analysis, and the ethnography of communication, even if none of these is quite expansive enough to accommodate the kinds of questions that concern contemporary anthropology.

Of all the reasons anthropologists use to justify their neglect of interaction, the most specious involves interaction's "scale." Entire research traditions (e.g., symbolic interactionism, conversation analysis, interactional sociolinguistics) have come into being with the aim of teasing out interaction's rules and regularities; they circumscribe interaction, making a neat domain of it. To be sure, many in response now wish to escape precisely these limits. They no longer want to treat "the interaction order" (Goffman 1983) as if it were some watertight chamber of activity insulated from the dynamics and pressures of macrosocial formations, yet in their rush to bridge "micro" and "macro" or to explore the supposed "dialectic" between the two, they continue to presume interaction's diminutive size. By leaving scale as an empirical question (Latour 2005; Lempert 2012b), not a problem to be solved in advance with the aid of prefabricated scalar distinctions (micro-, meso-, macro-), I aspire toward an anthropology of interaction more alive to interaction's "entanglements" (Maurer 2005).

Another reason some cite for this neglect of discursive interaction is not altogether unsound. Many feel that too much attention to the formal patterning of language use, coupled with an exaggerated faith in the fidelity of transcripts that borders on fetishization, encourages a blinkered aesthetics of sign behavior, perhaps even a kind of semiotic voyeurism. Marvel at the elegance and orderliness of signs, and you return to the rarefied heights of structuralism, confirming what many have long feared about semiotics: that it means the "autonomization of the sphere of meaning" (Latour 1993:62–63; see Ortner 1994; Parmentier 1997). For several decades now, linguistic and semiotic anthropologists have insisted that "semiotic mediation" (see Mertz and Parmentier 1985; Mertz 2007b) does *not* mean the study of some underlying, autonomous, immaterial "code" that is seamless and shared by a population. Still, if, in our writing, we dwell too long on transcripts and fail to experiment with integrating the analysis of these artifacts with other modes of writing, it becomes difficult to dismiss the criticism that we are, willy-nilly, severing discursive interaction from its surround and treating it as an autonomous domain.

Since this book is just as much a work in Tibetan and Buddhist studies—and in the small but emerging literature in the "anthropology of Buddhism"—as in linguistic anthropology, I recognize that many readers will be unfamiliar with methods for analyzing discursive interaction. As linguistic anthropologists have long argued, one cannot jump to function (what signs "do") without copious attention to form, but I have tried to strike a balance between the close, thick, transcript-centered description of language use and more familiar modes of narration, especially the ethnographic and occasionally the historiographic. For those impatient with transcripts, it is possible to skate around those sections of the book, which form the core of chapters 2 (on debate) and 4 (on public reprimand). In the interest of promoting exchange across fields, I have also tried to limit my engagement with linguistic-anthropological theory.

This book draws on over two and a half years of contact with and research on Tibetans in South Asia that stretch back over two decades, with the core of the fieldwork carried out in 1998 and 2000–2001. The corpus of fieldwork data includes video, audio, and textual material. In terms of Buddhist debate (the most intricate of the interaction rituals I examined), I recorded roughly 55 hours of video footage, consisting primarily of debates from Sera Monastery and monasteries in Dharamsala, including at the Institute of Buddhist Dialectics. At Sera and in Dharamsala, debates were originally selected based on several dimensions of expected variation, including (a) debate type (e.g., daily courtyard debate versus formal, indoor debates) and (b) relative status between interactants, reckoned in terms of age, seniority, and religious rank (recognized reincarnated lamas versus ordinary monks). For comparative purposes I recorded debates from nine other sites across India, six of which were monasteries of the Geluk sect (the sect to which Sera belongs); two were Geluk nunneries that offer debate; and one was a monastery of the Nyingma sect near Sera. In terms of audio data, approximately 170 hours were recorded, which include interviews, playback-elicitation sessions (where I asked monks to comment on recordings), narratives, and oral histories. I also collected a wide range of textual materials, including a five-volume published collection of public addresses in Tibetan by the Dalai Lama, extending over forty years (1959–2000), brochures and monastic histories in Tibetan, Tibetan-language newspapers and magazines from the late 1960s onward, and records kept at Sera that supply demographic facts about monks who join the monastery. Copious field notes were kept during every phase of my fieldwork.

I observed and transcribed many events but had to be extremely selective about which moments to include in the pages that follow. For purposes of exposition I chose to be faithful to the specificity of a few moments, to spend more time on their textures and qualities rather than race through many events in a bid to show how I "generalize." About the project's historical limits: This book stops at 2001, the year I returned from fieldwork. I do not address developments of the past decade. As with all fieldwork, this research consists of a series of moments in time and aspires to be nothing more, or less.

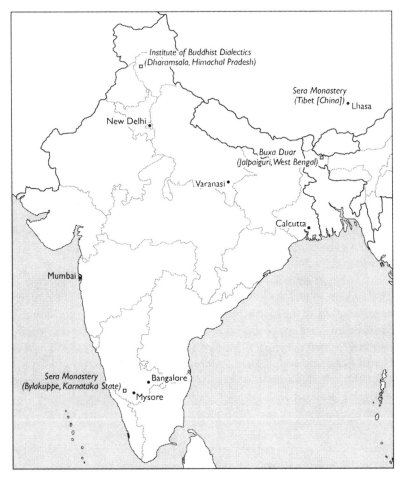

Primary monasteries and field sites discussed in this book

# Introduction

## Liberal Sympathies

Buddhist 'debate' (*rtsod pa*), a twice-daily form of argumentation through which Tibetan monks learn philosophical doctrine, is loud and brash and agonistic. Monks who inhabit the challenger role punctuate their points with foot-stomps and piercing open-palmed hand-claps that explode in the direction of the seated defendant's face. I was curious about the fate of this martial idiom in which monks wrangle, curious especially about its apparent disregard for ideals like nonviolence, compassion, and rights that Tibetans like the Dalai Lama have promoted. I came to Sera Monastery in India to study debate because Sera is one of the largest exile monasteries of the dominant Geluk sect and is renowned for its rigorous debate-based education. Founded in the early 1970s in Bylakuppe, some fifty miles west of Mysore in Karnataka State, South India, Sera presents itself as an avatar of its namesake in Tibet, the "original" Sera founded in 1419 and still in existence. India's Sera expanded from a community of a few hundred Sera monks who had fled Tibet into a massive settlement housing several thousand.

I had just settled in at Sera Mey, one of Sera's two monastic colleges, when Geshela, a senior Mey monk and frequent interlocutor of mine, told me what debate's centrality reveals about Buddhism as a whole. "Just belief, *that's* Christianity," he quipped. He uttered this uncharitable caption for Christianity in English, a language he used rarely. A frozen form, a shibboleth, the expression needed no explanation, and Geshe-la offered none. The point was obvious: Buddhism is unique among religions for its commitment to reason, a commitment he presumed I shared.

I nodded, sure that I had struck the edge of a familiar discourse about Tibet's religion. Following his dramatic flight from Lhasa to India in March 1959, the young, exiled Dalai Lama fashioned Tibetan Buddhism into a "modern" world religion, stressing its commitment to rational inquiry and its compatibility with empirical science. In addresses to Tibetans in India right from the start, in the early 1960s, he reminded his audiences of Buddhism's distinctiveness. Tibet's society may have been backward, but its religion was not. Unlike faiths such as Christianity and Hinduism, Buddhism offers a path of reason and does not discourage its votaries from debating its truth claims (e.g., T. Gyatso 2000a:vol. 1, pp. 234–35). He urged his fellow refugees to eschew the 'blind faith' (*rmong dad*) of other religions, because if Tibetans neglect to study Buddhist doctrine their practices will devolve into mere cultural habit, and they will lose their religious patrimony—as befell the Tamang of Nepal or the Mon of Myanmar, Buddhist peoples whose knowledge faded generation by generation till they were left with merely the trappings of religion, with just belief. And since Buddhism is an inner science on par with Western science, he argued, Tibetans must engage the latter, by learning from and even complementing it, which means that Tibetans should prepare themselves to part with doctrinal claims that are proven false, like the anachronistic belief in Mt. Meru, a mountain that sits at the center of the flat world in traditional Buddhist cosmology. In this and so many other respects, the Dalai Lama has become renowned as a chief architect and champion of a kind of "modern Buddhism" (Lopez 2002, 2008).

The affinity I perceived between Geshe-la's quip and the Dalai Lama's discourses on Buddhism began to break down fast. Geshe-la later told me that it would be disgraceful if a monk were to contradict his college's textbook in a debate; that scientists who dismiss the existence of Mt. Meru just don't have the karma to see it; that conception begins in men because consciousness starts in the sperm, not in contact between sperm and ovum, as they teach in school. The discrepancies between his sketch of Buddhism and the Dalai Lama's were nowhere more acute and unsettling than when Geshe-la railed against monastic reforms at Sera, such as attempts to curb corporal punishment—reforms invariably attributed to the Dalai Lama and loosely associated with liberal-democratic ideals.

The Dalai Lama's aspirations to modernity, which were always half addressed to a wider world and inseparable from his exile government's political struggles, have reciprocally affected the design of Buddhist institutions in India, including those of his own dominant Geluk sect.[1] This book examines this reflexive reanalysis of Geluk institutions, especially forms of ritualized violence in face-to-face interaction that are designed to make monks into educated, moral persons. In the early 1960s these institutions were in a parlous state and hence malleable to a degree unseen for centuries. Of the several thousand monks who escaped into India, Nepal, and Bhutan, those of the Geluk sect, whose three monastic seats of central Tibet (the Sera, Drepung, and Ganden monasteries) had figured prominently in the Lhasa-centered Dalai Lama–led theocratic state, were now scattered across the subcontinent. By 1960 about 1,200 Geluk monks were holed up in Buxa Duar, the hot, inhospitable former British cantonment and prison in West Bengal, near the Bhutanese border; about half that many settled on the cooler slopes of Dalhousie; many, many more had to set aside their monastic lives and were dispatched to undertake the grueling, sometimes fatal labor of road construction. It was not clear what shape Tibet's religious institutions in India would take, if they had a future at all.

As the Dalai Lama recast Buddhism as a religion of reason comparable to empirical science, he struggled to incorporate other Enlightenment ideals, ideals of liberal-democratic provenance. This appropriation began during the early years of exile in the 1960s, but in the late 1980s the Geluk sect's institutions came under heightened scrutiny in ways that incited new forms of self-consciousness. The Tibetan Government-in-Exile settled upon a new, self-consciously "international" campaign focused on lobbying the US Congress and building grassroots support. For the first time the Dalai Lama was put forward to present the Tibet issue to the world, the signature proposal of the period being the Five Point Peace Plan. The plan included calls for increased autonomy in Tibet, environmental protections, religious freedom, and above all human rights. The Dalai Lama became internationally renowned for making nonviolence, peace, and "universal compassion" Buddhism's essence, efforts that coincided with a political appeal: that the People's Republic of China (PRC) respect human rights in Tibet; that it turn back its policies of ethnic, cultural, and religious repression so that Tibet might enjoy, if not independence, then at least "genuine autonomy"—autonomy being a key concession to Beijing. The notion of universal human rights helped consolidate his government's message during this period. Human rights had been part of the Dalai Lama's appeal to the United Nations in 1959 and the early 1960s, yet Tibetans had been wary of this kind of appeal; they had wanted to frame their struggle in terms of sovereignty and the right to self-determination, but allies like the United States advised them against doing so. During the international campaign the exile government's stance on human rights was less ambivalent. As Vincanne Adams (1998) has suggested, the exile Tibetan appropriation of metropole rights discourse at times obliged Tibetans to take seriously the liberal-humanist ideals that underwrote this discourse, including belief in the individual, autonomous, rights-bearing subject (see also Frechette 2002). These ideals, together with the liberal, Enlightenment ideals of clarity, sincerity, and civility in speech, which had already entered Tibetan diasporic communities along several routes and whose genealogy stems from at least seventeenth-century England, were soon turned back upon refugee life in exile, including the monasteries.

Enlightenment ideals have often been felt to clash with Tibetan sensibilities about how to teach monks their vocation. Geshe-la, who was born in central Tibet and spent his early adolescent years at Lhasa's Sera Monastery, balked at many of these principles and the reforms tied to them, such as the idea that children have rights from birth, and the rejection of corporal punishment in favor of punitive measures that assume humans can control themselves naturally. A spry, jocular man in his early sixties, he reveled in being contrarian when our conversations touched on the topic of change in exile. He liked to provoke and had a hair-trigger readiness to shoot down pernicious stereotypes of Tibetan backwardness, stereotypes no doubt activated through conversations with me, a researcher from the States—all of which probably drove him toward rhetorical extremes. His preferred gambit was to wave in my face emblems of Tibetan backwardness. He would defend to the hilt every last inch of "traditional" Tibetan culture, the more seemingly anachronistic, the better. "Sky burials" in which you chop up the deceased's corpse, mix it with roasted barley flour, then offer it to vultures as a last act of giving? Much better than wasteful burials and cremations. Fraternities of pugilistic "punk monks" (*ldob ldob*) from pre-1959 monasteries like Sera, who would carry weapons, engage in sport, and get away with all sorts of high jinks? They've been sorely misunderstood. Though his positions may have been more moderate with Tibetan interlocutors, his ambivalence toward change was unmistakable and can be sensed among many monks of his generation.

His ambivalence also revealed something about Sera. It betrayed Sera's relatively conservative stance on pre-1959 monastic culture vis-à-vis other centers of learning within the field of Tibetan Buddhist education in India, like the self-consciously modern Institute of Buddhist Dialectics in upper Dharamsala, the town where the Dalai Lama resides. For people like Geshe-la, the locus of change in India, the veritable epicenter of Buddhist reform in the subcontinent, is unquestionably Dharamsala, a former British hill station in the Himalayan foothills where the Dalai Lama took up residence in April 1960, where the Tibetan Government-in-Exile stands (down the hill in Gangchen Kyishong), and where the Institute of Buddhist Dialectics presents itself as an alternative to "traditional" monasteries like Sera. Well traversed by foreign and Indian tourists and replete with objectified representations of Tibetan religion and culture, Dharamsala can feel like a town under glass (cf. Diehl 2002). It contrasts sharply with Sera, an isolated place seldom frequented by tourists due in part to the Protected Area Permits that the Government of India's Ministry of Home Affairs requires of foreign visitors. There is ambivalence—antipathy even—in Geshe-la's remarks about what he takes to be the Dalai Lama's Dharamsala-based reforms, reforms that often aspire to liberal-democratic ideals, and it is this ambivalence that I take as my point of departure.

I consider this ambivalence as it surfaces in and around face-to-face interaction between monks, especially in 'debate' (*rtsod pa*) but also in 'public reprimand' (*tshogs gtam*) and disciplinary practices like corporal punishment. Reprimands occur routinely in Sera's public gatherings and are issued by each monastic college's disciplinarian. They are loud and caustic and grate against the senses almost as much as debate, but the energy of reprimand is more diffuse, more "indirect." Rather than name names and point fingers, the disciplinarian works on dispositions through a kind of stinging morality play. He tells tales of errant monks whose portraits seem at once grotesque, like that of the derelict monk who shirks his duties and ends up reborn a hungry ghost, and naturalistic, where infractions are recounted in such detail—again, minus proper names—that wrongdoers squirm in their seats. Corporal punishment is meted out most often in public assemblies as well, for those who doze off or fool around. The disciplinarian's assistant, who burnishes a short leather whip, applies pain to the body with a swift stroke or two, the sound from which straightens spines across the room with the effortlessness of its echo. In each of these areas of male-monastic socialization, dissimulated, histrionic anger—virtuous anger, anger motivated by compassion—makes monks of men. It trounces pride, kindles humility, rights errant habits. So long as the anger required by this violence is not felt, so long as one's motivation is uncontaminated by it, it poses no karmic threat.

This book looks at how idioms of violence inscribed in the design of these rites of socialization help produce educated, moral persons but in ways that trouble Tibetans who aspire to modernity. For debate, what should be done with the challenger's histrionic "anger" when he pelts the seated defendant with taunts and uses blistering hand-claps that can explode inches from the defendant's nose? What of the practice's unequal "rights" of participation, like the fact that it's the challenger who regulates topic flow and gets to ask all the questions? Does that tip the balance and make the whole event look illiberal? Is the failure of Sera's disciplinarians to disclose the names of offending monks in public assemblies too "indirect," a failure to be clear? And what of the fundamental way that reprimand and corporal punishment figurate hierarchical relations between interactants and thus also shape moral dispositions in seemingly nonliberal ways? While I focus on debate and discipline at Sera Monastery in Bylakuppe, a bastion of traditionalism populated by some 4,500 monks, I draw out these tensions at times by comparing Sera with the self-consciously modernized Institute of Buddhist Dialectics in Dharamsala, home to the Dalai Lama and epicenter of Tibetan Buddhist modernism in India.

This self-scrutiny of ritualized face-to-face interaction takes place in the midst of interaction with hearers and overhearers. As an expanding network of advocacy, lobbying, and support groups took up the Tibet issue in the 1980s, the conversation, as it were, expanded for many Tibetans in exile. For Tibetans in contact with foreign sponsors and supporters, it was of course easy to feel that they were caught up in a "larger" conversation with far-flung social actors (some of whom, as Ann Frechette notes in her 2002 study of Tibetans in Nepal, made it quite clear what they expected in return for support: secular democracy).

The effects of these encounters, and their echoes, and the echoes of those echoes, made it possible for many other Tibetans in places like Dharamsala to feel as if they were in the midst of a more expansive interaction. And as Erving Goffman explored in his many ruminative essays on face-to-face interaction, when we are in the presence of others, we exhibit a kind of sensitivity and responsiveness, what conversation analysts call "recipient design": the "multitude of respects in which the talk by a party in a conversation is constructed or designed in ways which display an orientation and sensitivity to the particular other(s) who are the co-participants" (Sacks, Schegloff, and Jefferson 1974:727). We tailor our speech and behavior to others and to the occasion, shaping what we say and how we say it based on whom we take to be present.[2] Goffman restricted his attention to face-to-face interaction between copresent people, but virtual interlocutors can be copresent, too, even if, empirically speaking, they are ethereal—not voices you can see, hear, or record. Mikhail Bakhtin knew well how intrusive such voices can be. A conversation may feel haunted by an incorporeal god, taboo in-law, political constituency, or "collective consumer witnessing our wants and choices" (Warner 1993:242), to the point that these voices affect the design and content of speech.[3] In speech these virtual interlocutors materialize most commonly as named figures, many of which I encountered in my conversations with monks at Sera. A monk in charge of discipline at Sera Mey's school once told me candidly that he knows "the West" disapproves of the monastery's use of corporal punishment. He cited this figure—which sounded as if it haunted the monastery like a diffuse, generalized other—as a reason Tibetans at Sera were busy changing how they punish monks. In his public addresses to Tibetans in India, the Dalai Lama has often defended Buddhism against a host of distant critics, which include such named figures as "scientists," "foreigners," "Communist China," and "Mao Zedong." Under these conditions, the spatiotemporal envelope of interaction expands, the cast of interactants increases, and one begins to anticipate and react to new kinds of agents. This sense that the envelope of interaction has expanded, materializing new addressees and motivating new forms of recipient design, is partly what has fueled the mimesis and partial replication narrated in this book, where Tibetans find themselves calibrating their speech and demeanor with those of new interlocutors that stand in their communicative pathways. The Dalai Lama's scrutiny of monastic institutions suggests a sensitivity to these new interlocutors, including figurations of the liberal West and Communist China, both of which adopt what they understand to be a "modern," critical stance on "traditional" Buddhism.

Why should Tibetans bother recalibrating their behavior at all, beyond the basic impulse to countenance the presence of new addressees and overhearers? In the early years of exile, there was no shortage of motivation for liberal mimicry, for joining the chorus of voices that champion liberal-democratic ideals. To the extent that these ideals are grounded in self-evident truths and international law—they are not supposed to belong to any nation in particular—their universal scope obliged Tibetans to cast their local aspirations in equally expansive terms. In addition, while the Dalai Lama and his exile government charged China with human rights violations, the PRC countered that Tibet's old society had committed human rights violations against its own people before the People's Liberation Army arrived to "liberate" them. So who respected rights more? In some seventy pages of their 1960 report, the International Commission of Jurists' Legal Inquiry Committee on Tibet weighed the evidence, asking "(1) whether, before the entry of the Chinese forces in 1951, the Tibetans enjoyed fundamental rights; and (2) whether they enjoyed such rights after the arrival of the Chinese" (International Commission of Jurists [1952-], Legal Inquiry Committee on Tibet 1960:65).

As for the Five Point Peace Plan of the late-1980s, there was again the question of consistency in word and deed, and this time many more publics were watching. The exile community's visibility was more acute, and the potential for being monitored greater. Do the religious and cultural attributes ascribed to Tibetans in this plan—their environmentalist sensibilities, their deep commitment to nonviolence—match what you see among Tibetans in exile? Naturally, scrutiny was trained upon the place where the plan was crafted, Dharamsala, which had also been experiencing growth and a surge of tourism. If Tibetans, and the religion that shaped their habits, are one with contemporary environmentalism, and if the Dalai Lama wants China to respect Tibet's environment, then, some foreign tourists wondered, why is Dharamsala so, well, filthy? (see Huber 1995; Diehl 2002:43–44). (The Dalai Lama at times cited these concerns of foreign tourists in public addresses to Tibetans, which helped inspire changes like the addition of a Green Office in Dharamsala.) What of democracy in exile? The Dalai Lama has long championed democratic principles, institutions, and processes,[4] so why has progress in Dharamsala politics looked so painfully slow to foreign observers and Tibetan critics? Why hasn't he stepped down, where are the political parties, what of the seemingly antidemocratic patrimonialism surrounding his family (e.g., even in the decade following the Dalai Lama's renewed efforts at democratization in 1990, every cabinet had at least one member of his family) (Sangay 2003:125). As for freedom of speech and the great "fourth pillar" of democracy, a free press, the impressions seemed just as unsettling. So it has been with the issue of Tibet's commitment to nonviolence, embodied in the very person of the Dalai Lama. As Robert Barnett (2001:275) observed, professional politicians in Europe and the United States quickly understood that they could not maintain the notion that Tibetans are inherently peaceful, and by the 1990s began to opt for "more subtle, less essentialist phraseology about the 'path of nonviolent resistance.'" It is precisely under these conditions that "violence" springs to attention and demands an account, and for some, a cure.

## ELICITING SYMPATHY THROUGH LIBERAL MIMICRY

Worries about how debate and discipline look to others—others from whom support is sorely needed—may be described by recalling the dynamics of "sympathy." In a familiar sense, sympathy means attunement to another's feelings, to suffering especially, yet as philosophized by Scottish Enlightenment writers David Hume and Adam Smith sympathy is a more expansive communicative capacity. Hume, for instance, saw sympathy as a universal human faculty that permits us to sense and feel as our own the states of others—others' suffering being but a special case. This communicative capacity to read others' "inclinations and sentiments, however different from, or even contrary to our own" (Hume 2000:206), can be harnessed to form impartial moral sentiments and has consequences for moral action. Considerable philosophical speculation in eighteenth-century Europe was dedicated to sympathy and the sentiments, and in the past few decades these affective dimensions of modernity have been retrieved, by critics of Enlightenment rationality like the antifoundationalist philosopher Richard Rorty (1993), who has argued that human rights should not be defended with reasons but rather championed through acts of eliciting sympathy; by philosophers and intellectual historians who draw out neglected sentimentalist strains from the tangle of Enlightenment views (M. Frazer 2010); and by recent researchers on colonialism who have shown how the affective and sentimental dimensions of colonial rule were often just as power laden as appeals to rationality (Stoler 2004). Of special relevance here is Dipesh Chakrabarty's (2000a) essay tracing how a European-based natural theory of the sentiments, not unlike Hume's and Smith's, made its way into colonial India in the nineteenth century and appeared among Bengali writers who began to note and document the suffering of others, such as the plight of upper-caste Hindu widows, as if from afar, from the perspective of an observer of suffering in general.

While Hume and Smith thought of sympathy in interactional terms, as a kind of communication between self and other, both privileged one pole: that of the observer or spectator. It is the spectator who sympathizes. Chakrabarty (2000a:119) usefully distinguishes "between the act of displaying suffering and that of observing or facing the sufferer." In underscoring the two interactional poles of sympathy, he reminds us that both need attention, and that displays of suffering exhibit a kind of recipient design, to the extent that such displays court sympathy from others. For suffering subjects like "deformed beggars of medieval Europe or of contemporary Indian or U.S. cities," continues Chakrabarty, these displays may elicit sympathy but their addressivity is narrow; it is suffering styled for *particular* spectators, typically those in immediate visual range or earshot. The suffering's source is equally narrow and biographically specific; it does not invite the kind of "generalized picture of suffering" (Chakrabarty 2000a:119) that characterizes modern, disembodied sympathy. However, when it comes to eliciting sympathy so as to redress, say, human rights abuses, which Tibetans and foreign supporters have tried to get the world to redress, this typically requires documenting suffering and securing witnesses so that *any* soul can sympathize. As rights are natural, so their violation should *naturally* spur spectators to action. It is a commonplace of human rights activism that public outrage over rights abuses is something to elicit and cultivate through grassroots projects of "mobilizing shame" (Keenan 2004), where affective sympathies are pooled and canalized in a bid to shame perpetrators into compliance, to get them to stop.

What concerns me are the preconditions for sympathetic flow across the interactional proscenium. To elicit sympathy from a spectator in cases like that of trammeled rights, there is a logically prior, and pressing, semiotic problem: one must first persuasively communicate one's similarity. As Hume (2000:207) appreciated, "we find, that where, beside the general resemblance of our natures, there is any peculiar similarity in our manners, or character, or country, or language, it facilitates the sympathy." The "closer" the sufferer and sympathizing spectator, through ties of blood or faith or some other form of preexisting resemblance or contiguity, the greater the ease and intensity with which sympathy is said to flow. It is a truism that it is easier to feel for those who already seem like oneself. This bothered writers like Hume. For Hume, the faculty of sympathy was something to be improved and corrected so that one's capacity for fellow feeling would be expansive and not limited to preexisting bonds of friendship, blood, religion, and territory. We would say now that neither Hume nor Smith (their differences on sympathy notwithstanding) was sufficiently alive to the labor involved in producing and sustaining affinities that facilitate sympathetic communication, labor initiated by the agent seeking sympathy. Forms of resemblance and contiguity that help construct affinities between self and other are notoriously precarious semiotic achievements; they require work to make and face entropy and resistance. It is not easy to get others to recognize affinities and make that recognition last.

To be sure, Tibetans in exile have often felt enormous pressure to be *different,* an exotic, spiritual, pacific, nonviolent people—constructions familiar in Europe and the United States. Yet exile Tibetans have also felt obliged to show that they, too, believe in things like natural rights and individual autonomy. (After all, if Tibetans themselves do not respect rights, how can they ask the world to step in to make sure that China respects theirs?) The Dalai Lama's calibration of Buddhist and liberal discourses can be seen as a deft response to this challenge. One of his most memorable and resonant phrases, "universal compassion," for instance, is styled as Buddhist in provenance, as stemming from his very being, since he is Avalokiteśvara incarnate—the embodiment of Buddha's compassion. At the same time, the fact that such compassion is "universal" means that it harmonizes with liberal ideals. His appeal for people to feel compassion for others is generalized; it is a universal, natural capacity, as reminiscent of Hume and Smith as of the historical Buddha, which, crucially, suggests that those who hear his message should come to Tibet's aid, just as one should aid *any* human, or sentient being, who suffers.

To elicit sympathy a few resonant words and expressions like "universal compassion" will not suffice, though. Tibetans in exile may have appropriated a "language of rights" and even articulated whole doctrines that echo liberal values, but consider how much harder it is—and in some respects more vital—to materialize these abstractions through embodied practices, so that it becomes possible to see (literally) the liberal subject in action. If a disciplinarian at Sera Monastery shapes moral dispositions by striking a monk in a public assembly with a short leather whip, how could this evince the monk's "autonomy" and "rights"? If, rather, he were to *explain* the offense to him, clearly, "gently"—as the modernized Institute of Buddhist Dialectics' founder and principal once advised—would this not make it look like the disciplined subject had the capacity to reflect on and adjust his own behavior? Would this not suggest his fundamental "autonomy," the whole punitive practice thereby embodying another memorable liberal-Buddhist amalgam, "You are your own master," which the Dalai Lama repeats often and credits to the historical Buddha? Tibetan monastic reformers, in short, have had to worry about what it *looks like* to embody liberal attributes like autonomy, rights, critical rationality, clarity, and sincerity. They have had to adjust and selectively highlight qualities of face-to-face interaction—in particular, male-monastic rites of socialization, from reprimand to verbal argument—so that foreign spectators, real and imagined, may see some of their own aspirations reflected in these performances.

Note the coercive power ascribed to mimesis, where agents elicit sympathy by first trying to look a little like their spectators. "Sympathy," again, in a broadly Humean and Smithian sense, means the spectator-centered capacity to imagine and feel as one's own the state of another—the special case being that of another's suffering. To draw out the coercive, mimetic dimension of this communicative process of sympathy, whose vector runs from agent toward spectator, I want to recover a special sense of the word "sympathy" that is now unfamiliar to us, though it was not unfamiliar to Hume and Smith. The *Oxford English Dictionary* reminds us of this sense: "A (real or supposed) affinity between certain things, by virtue of which they are similarly or correspondingly affected by the same influence, affect or influence one another (esp. in some occult way), or attract or tend towards each other."[5] Consider, in particular, the modifier "sympathetic" in what writers like the Victorian anthropologist E. B. Tylor once called "sympathetic magic": "The Zulu," for instance, "may be seen chewing a piece of wood, in order, by this symbolic act, to soften the heart of the man he wants to buy oxen from" (Tylor 1913:118).[6] Anthropological literature on ritual communication has frequently shown how one aspect of ritual's effectiveness comes from the way it tacitly traces out a picture of what it aspires to "do," like the way the mastication of wood metaphorically mimics the successful act of "softening up" the trader's heart.[7] It is precisely this mimetic and instrumental dimension of "sympathy" that I highlight and focus on in this book, in order to explain how Tibetans try to make their interaction rituals take on some of the qualities of the liberal subject, so that this may in turn invite liberal subjects—plural—to feel for them and come to their aid. Paraphrasing Walter Benjamin, Michael Taussig has drawn out the instrumental, pragmatic side of this sympathy:

"to get hold of something by means of its likeness" (Taussig 1993:21).[8] This mimetic sense of "sympathy"—that of affinities that can be exploited to affect someone or something else—has been attested in English since the late sixteenth century but is now obsolete, the *Oxford English Dictionary* tells us, albeit with the caveat "except in history" (*Obs. exc. Hist.*).

## THE PRAGMATICS OF MODERNITY

Obsolete, indeed, for is this not how we typically narrate the fate of this mimetic, coercive function of sympathy? The belief that modeling things through signs can change the things modeled—the belief, that is, in sympathetic magic—is something the West supposedly shed when it became modern. So, as good modern subjects, if we are to explore the role of mimetic sympathy in the broader process of sympathetic communication, we need to look at this narrative more critically. Whatever else being "modern" means as a form of self-understanding, it has often meant a shift from viewing language, and signs generally, as naturally embedded in the world through resemblance and repetition, sympathy and similitude, to language conceived as a medium that stands apart from the world that it passively represents (cf. Foucault 1973). The narrative is one of pushing past old word-world confusions and occult affinities, like the primitive "sympathetic magic" so copiously catalogued by E. B. Tylor and J. G. Frazer, so that we recognize that language, and signs more broadly, are merely arbitrary and conventional. They stand for things but are not the things themselves. Yes, phenomena like "onomatopoeia" exist, but at its core, language has no natural connection to the world. And as an arbitrary, conventional medium, language has a purpose: to represent faithfully and describe precisely so that humans can communicate and inform each other well, so that science can progress, and statecraft with it. Some linguistic anthropologists have called this ideology of language "referentialist" for the way it privileges reference and predication—the capacity of utterances to convey information "about" the world—over the myriad ways in which speech is tied into and can change the context of which it is a part. As Webb Keane (2007) appreciates, language in this view is treated as a moral problem, part of a moral narrative of modernity in which a free, autonomous, clear-speaking subject can and should emerge.

That there never really was a *singular,* epochal word–world rupture in how people actually use signs—a rupture that distinguishes the modern West from its past, and the West from its various nonmodern others—scarcely deserves mention. A moment's reflection reveals that these semiotic modalities of sympathy have not gone away. For more than a half century now, linguistic anthropologists have in fact dedicated considerable energy to explaining and describing semiotic modalities that Charles Sanders Peirce famously termed "iconicity" (signs felt to exhibit what they represent, like so-called onomatopoeia or the way poetic patterns of form, like repetition and parallelism, allow discourse to diagram extralinguistic relationships) and "indexicality" (signs felt to indicate or point to features of context, like smoke to fire, a pointed index finger to the visual surround, a pronoun to the speaker or addressee of the utterance).[9] Indexical and iconic modalities operate together to explain the countless ways in which we try to influence things through imitation.

The narrative of an epochal word-world rupture is best viewed as an ideological one, a break that we and many in the non-West continue to replay in varied and often ambivalent ways. It was replayed among my Tibetan interlocutors in India when they contrasted the more traditional and conservative Sera Monastery in South India with the Institute of Buddhist Dialectics, suggesting that older, more opaque, and ritualized methods of disciplining monks at Sera were becoming more comprehensible and transparent at the institute, a development they credited to the Dalai Lama. Clear, direct "advice" at the institute replaces Sera's corporal punishment and indirect style of reprimand. Explicit, reflexive talk replaces the automaticity of ritual, just as the self-conscious understanding of Buddhist doctrine replaces rote religious practices, from prostrations to the lighting of butter lamps before images of Buddhist deities. The Protestant inflection of all this change will be familiar to students of Buddhist modernism, but the important thing to see is the effort to act out the narrative of a break.

This break looks familiar, does it not? In early modern England, for instance, John Locke, Royal Society member and storied contributor to liberal thought, narrated such a break with respect to language. He envisioned language as an autonomous and neutral medium for representation whose signs are wholly arbitrary: "Sounds have no natural connexion with our ideas, but have all their signification from the arbitrary imposition of men" (Locke 1959:105). Like others after him, Locke saw this orientation toward language as unequally distributed across kinds of people. Not everyone had it, or had it to the same degree, and his foils included the muddled speech of a familiar stock of others, especially women, children, laborers, and provincial folk (Bauman and Briggs 2003:39–48). In the Victorian anthropological imagination of Tylor, quoted above, the plane of social comparison was tilted vertically and redescribed in cultural-evolutionary terms. Who is it who still thinks you can affect things by modeling them? Vestiges of this preoccupation with natural resemblances were discovered in the "magic" of European children, provincial folk, and, most notoriously, "primitives." As in the case of Locke, the valorized qualities of communication my Tibetan interlocutors cited, such as "clarity" and "direct"-ness in speech, are not just about language use (language ideologies never are; see Woolard 1998; Irvine and Gal 2000); persons may be "clear" and "direct," too. This suggests that you can reform people by reforming speech, a mimetic slippage that promises—threatens—to flatten Sera's "traditional" monastic hierarchies between old and young, senior and junior, reincarnate lama and ordinary monk, into a level field of autonomous agents, each endowed with rights and entitled to speak his mind.

A new but familiar kind of subject seems to be in the works. In tracing various attempts in the Tibetan Buddhist diaspora in India to break with the past, I show how the fissures and clefts run along lines that look parallel to those associated with the modern liberal speaking subject—ideals like "clarity" and "sincerity" in communicative behavior, and the antihierarchical principles of individual "autonomy" and "rights" that these ideals seem to presuppose. A familiar figure appears, an autonomous speaking subject endowed with reason and rights, a liberal subject. Materializing this subject in monastic rituals of face-to-face interaction is no mean feat, though. While likenesses may seem plastic and labile, always capable of becoming something else, their substrates—like the interaction ritual of debate—are stubborn things. They come to us in material form, with formal properties of their own, and resist deformation. I consider how monks try to fix what these practices resemble and what affinities the practices possess, through scheduling and staging interaction in the built environment, as well as through reflexive talk about these rites, including a kind of slow-motion, fuguelike reverie that plays on the design of these interaction rituals, seeing in their qualities the qualities of other, more expansive events: *The defendant's poise before challengers in debate is "just like" the modern subject's autonomous, rational-critical evaluation of competing truth-claims; the disciplinarian's dominance over monks is "just like" the way illiberal authorities of old lorded over subjects without securing their consent.* Affinities like these, which link discourse to discourse, event to event (Agha and Wortham 2005), are not the reflex of underlying master tropes in people's heads, nor the output of "culture" or code, but precarious chains of situated associations—little links forged here and there—that, if assembled well and distributed widely, just may succeed in getting some observers, and some ritual participants, to recognize them. Through this labor of association, qualities already present in "traditional" interaction rituals become likened to qualities of this liberal subject, not because monastic rituals *need* to change; if anything, they just need to reconnect with Buddhism's true liberal roots. This suggests a compromise: Tibetans can be faithful to their past while being deferential toward the new institutions and ideals of their foreign supporters, even if the net result is a liberal subject that can look shifty and sometimes not even sufficiently "liberal" at all, as we shall see.

Two final clarifications. In tracing the career of the modern liberal subject in the Tibetan diaspora in India, I do not supply the kind of anthropological tale that is keen to demonstrate how globalizing ideals are locally inflected and assimilated by preexisting cultural frameworks. This is not a story of how the local triumphs over the global, or the global over the local. Nor is my interest in sorting out what belongs to whom, what is old and what new, as if modernity were best addressed in terms of questions of cultural-historical proprietorship. Many trackers of modernity have been preoccupied with such questions of circulation, change, and flow, of global convergence and divergence, whether modernity is one or many. My concern is more with the pragmatics of appropriation and partial emulation, the question of why Tibetans should bother to mimic facets of the liberal subject, and especially how their efforts play out in what Goffman (1967a) called "interaction ritual": relatively routinized forms of face-to-face behavior that are axiological, that invoke and try to stabilize sociocultural norms and values. It is the sympathetic dimensions of interaction that I bring to the study of modernity.

As Bjorn Wittrock (2000) and others suggested some time ago, modernity should not be reduced to a set of institutions (e.g., democratic governance, science, a liberal economy, etc.) that is spreading and being adopted globally, lest we concede the embarrassing fact that we cannot even speak of universally adopted institutions in the West until very recently, and even then only for parts of Europe. Such institutional projects, argues Wittrock, are also culturally constituted, premised on new cardinal ideas about human agency, reflexivity, and history. While others have made similar arguments about modernity in terms of self-understanding and ideology (e.g., Taylor 1989; Keane 2007), of special use in Wittrock's argument is the way he asks *how* such new forms of conceptualization get enacted in discursive interaction. Here he speaks of modernity as aspirational (cf. Karlström 2004), specifically, as a set of "promissory notes, i.e., a set of hopes and expectations that entail some minimal conditions of adequacy that may be demanded of macrosocietal institutions no matter how much these institutions may differ in other respects" (Wittrock 2000:55). Tibetans, for instance, can make appeals in various forums for human rights to be respected in Tibet. Promissory notes, writes Wittrock (2000:39, 37, respectively), are "based on" and "entailed" by the deep cultural underpinnings of modernity, such as fundamental ideas about human agency and reflexivity and history. But notice the distance he puts between what people believe, think, and know, and how they act. His argument is not about subjectivity per se (nor is mine), but about what we might broadly call the pragmatics of modernity. It is the act of holding and trying to redeem promissory notes that matters. "To be modern," summarizes Joel Robbins (2001:902), who extends Wittrock's argument to language, "it is enough merely to hold the promissory notes, to feel that one has a right to what they promise, and to struggle to redeem them through institutional experimentation with new kinds of exchange, of polity, and of knowledge seeking." These prospective, future-oriented, aspirational discourses become privileged reference points in public-sphere debates, and they inform the design of new institutional forms and affect the treatment of old ones, like Tibetan monks who worry about what to do with debate and discipline in an age of reason and rights.

Why, finally, should I revive an obsolete sense of "sympathy"—its old mimetic, instrumental meaning—to study the pragmatics of emulation, when there are du jour semiotic terms at our disposal, terms untainted by modernity's primitivism? At times, in the chapters that follow, I employ the metalanguage of Peircean semiotics, of icons, indices, and symbols, to describe the sign processes at work; why not employ this metalanguage throughout? Why disinter a dead sense of the word "sympathy" and use it to explain how Tibetans ritually model aspects of the liberal subject? I prefer to use "sympathy" rather than familiar semiotic terms like indexicality and iconicity (and amalgams like indexical-iconicity) to talk about coercive mimicry not because I intend this move as some belated rejoinder to the triumphalist narrative of a world-historical turn in the way humans think about signs, as if to counter that we have never been modern (Latour 1993). (Of course sympathy has never left us.) I prefer "sympathy" because it reminds us to be alive to the story of a break in conceptions of how signs work in the world (or apart from it). While linguistic anthropology has, in a sense, labored to restore to language all that the Enlightenment legacy has tried to purge, so much so that it has become part of linguistic anthropology's subdisciplinary identity, the objective cannot be to fix theory once and for all by welcoming back all the semiotic modalities exiled under a post-Enlightenment referentialist regime. The aim cannot be to escape the orbit of referentialist ideologies of language per se, where reference and modalized predication are privileged over indexical and iconic modalities, because the relations among these semiotic modalities *continue* to be ideologically significant in certain narratives of modernity, narratives that are very much at large. "Sympathy" is useful because of its perceived obsolescence; its distressed patina and the fact that it bears the traces of primitivism and its atavistic culture-evolutionist models of difference, as in Tylor's classic discussions of "sympathetic magic," remind us of a narrative that has *not* gone away, even if the actors who speak clearly and can distinguish word from world have changed upon each retelling. Put another way, the story of an epochal, modern break from sympathy to symbolism is a live script, part of a moral narrative of modernity that is being retold in and around Tibetan monasteries. It is the story about such a break that has been at large, and "sympathy" can remind us to follow this.

This book is thus about liberal sympathies and the interaction rituals that try to make these affinities real, and effective in eliciting the affective sympathies of others. Chapter 1 introduces Sera Monastery in India and provides a context for appreciating debate's ritualized violence and mimetic power. The chapter surveys congeries of discursive practices that conspire to fix what debate does, or should do, as a rite of institution. The chapters that follow alternate between the close, thick description of interaction rituals, primarily debate (chapter 2) and public reprimand (chapter 4), and discourses about and reforms of these practices (chapter 3 on debate, chapter 5 on reprimand) that take place beyond the perimeters of these rituals and must be understood in relation to an ethnonationalist project of courting affective sympathies from the West.

Debate and disciplinary practices have had very different fates in India. Debate has been promoted in India—to Buddhist nuns who never practiced it before and to monasteries and sects that either historically lacked it or were not known for it—because debate is a modern diasporic pedagogy. That is, arguing about doctrine helps Tibetan refugees cultivate an autonomous, critical rationality, a rationality that belongs to two genealogies at once: it is Buddhist in origin but akin to the storied faculty of reason in the West's Enlightenment. Other qualities of debate—its violence and asymmetrical design, the fact that challenger and defendant do not enjoy "equal" rights of participation, for instance—have been largely ignored and left intact. The challenger's ritualized violence passes undetected. For reprimand and corporal punishment the story is different. For some Tibetans, especially those at the Institute of Buddhist Dialectics in Dharamsala, these practices feel retrograde; the practices look too hierarchical and fail to presuppose that monks have autonomy and natural rights—hallowed attributes of the liberal subject. Comparing the fates of debate and disciplinary practices reveals how *different fractions* of the liberal subject—autonomy, rationality, clarity, sincerity—have been selectively taken up by Tibetans as they reflect on and try to adjust what their interaction rituals do, in effect differentiating aspects of Buddhist practice and thereby conditioning their treatment and possible future. All of this suggests how misleading it can be to even speak of a single, cohesive formation called "the liberal subject," and how unproductive it would be to narrate these processes of change as if we were witnessing an epic clash of cultures, codes, discourses, or ideologies. Close attention to how people interact, and how they reflect on and struggle to alter how they interact, offers a more nuanced story of how Tibetans struggle to create mimetic sympathies between self and other that facilitate affective sympathies.

To sympathies, then: those between Tibet's centuries-long history of logic and dialectics and the Enlightenment rationality that helped make modern science, between the Buddha's Enlightenment and the West's, the Dalai Lama and Locke, the Buddhist subject and the liberal subject. And to that which acts in between and spans the divide: interaction.

PART ONE

# Debate

# 1

# Dissensus by Design

How could fierce, stylized wrangling about centuries-old religious doctrine—by monks, no less—seem as if it involves the exercise of an autonomous, critical rationality, a faculty akin to the one celebrated in the European Enlightenment? To appreciate how debate can exhibit attributes of the liberal subject and become a diasporic pedagogy—a means by which Tibetan refugees can avoid blind faith and protect their religious patrimony from the challenges of exile—we must first appreciate what debate does within the confines of a monastery. At Sera Monastery in India, debate's drama, where the defendant tries to save Buddhist doctrine from challengers who threaten it, becomes a coherent ritual drama not just because it is crafted a certain way but by virtue of the way this practice has been "placed" within a complex assemblage of discursive and educational practices, which range from daily memorization routines to the habitual ways in which monks physically handle their books. This means that the very question of what debate does at Sera—to say nothing of what it does in the diaspora in India—demands a detour. Let us therefore postpone consideration of debate for the moment and work from the outside in, beginning, as I began, with a critical feature of Sera's landscape, its division into two monastic colleges: Sera Jey and Sera Mey.

## CORPORATE PANORAMAS

Visually and from afar, Sera Monastery in South India—a sprawl of buildings and residences located near a bend in the Cauvery River and the town of Bylakuppe—shrinks into a compact, scintillating gilt-roofed jewel. Encircled by a sea of maize and grass, it looks whole and pacific, or did to me. By auto-rickshaw I would snake

up the roads that extend from the neighboring towns of Bylakuppe or Kushalnagar, and pass into Sera's premises through a singular, ornamental gateway—suggestive, again, of a monastic settlement with a monolithic identity. Here, the visual
landscape conspires with the lexicon, for perhaps nowhere is Sera's cohesiveness
more conspicuous than in the words for its parts.

Take the names for Sera's primary administrative units: 'monastery' (*dgon pa*)
(syn. 'monastic-seat' *gdan sa*), 'college' (*grwa tshang*), 'regional house' (*khang
tshan*).[1] Gather these lexical items into an institutional partonymy, asking of each,
"Is *x* a part of *y*?" and an elegant Matryoshka-like whole snaps into view. Regional
houses nest into colleges, and colleges into monasteries, so that Sera's two colleges,
Sera Jey and Sera Mey, look "equivalent." And once they are subsumed as equal parts
within a single corporate body, it does not take much to imagine them enjoying a
friendly, fraternal existence.

At first I could barely see Jey and Mey. Little signage distinguishes the two, and
the colleges' perimeters are not staked out with obtrusive fences, walls, or paths. Many
regional houses of Jey and Mey, I discovered, stand side by side, as if seamlessly integrated. Nor do monks broadcast their college affiliation through dress, badge, or
comportment. No legible clothing or garish emblems of group membership. Monks
of Jey and Mey brush by each other on the road, dressed in indistinguishable ma-
roon robes. And Sera boasts just one major circumambulation route on its premises. At dusk, a brisk current of monks from both Jey and Mey eddies clockwise
around the route in a scuffling whirl of casual talk and murmured mantras, set to
time by the click of prayer beads counted off with thumb and forefinger.

As weeks pass and more Jey and Mey structures come into relief, I begin to feel
an odd sense of redundancy about this veritable town, peopled by some 4,500 monks.
It is not just that each of the monastery's two colleges has its own semiautonomous
administrative apparatus, its own 'abbot' (*mkhan po*), 'disciplinarian' (*dge skos*), 'finan-
cial officer' (*phyag mdzod*), and so forth. Nor is it just that each boasts its own central assembly hall, debating courtyard, fleet of regional houses, and secular schoolhouse. For nearly every imaginable category of building in this townscape—library,
bookstore, phone station, publishing center, restaurant, general store—there is (at
least) one allocated for Jey and another for Mey. The buildings in Sera's townscape
are divisible by two, with little if no remainder.

And this integrated but divided townscape comes with unambiguous loyalties
of patronage and consumption. I had chosen Mey and felt the consequences at once.
On my first visit to Mey, I decided to explore the libraries of both colleges and shared
these plans casually with a senior Mey monk. His response was dampening. Sera
Mey's library is 'better' (*yag ga*). It would be a 'sin' (*sdig pa*) to go to the Jey library.
Goods ought to be purchased from one's own general store, calls placed at one's own
phone center, food eaten at one's own restaurants, and so on, so that there is little
question of where the best *momo* (steamed meat dumplings, a traditional delicacy

and a weakness of mine) is found, though I once posed the question to Pasang,[2] ten years of age and new to Mey, who responded without hesitation: 'Norling restaurant.' I had heard Norling was a Mey restaurant and pressed: 'So Jey college has no good *momo*?' Pasang stiffened, nonplussed by my stupidity. Jermey, an adolescent monk standing nearby, responded for him: "There's no need to go to Jey restaurants. There are [already] Mey restaurants.'[3]

. . .

I find Pasang vrooming a black matchbox car along the surface of the flat concrete roof of his two-story regional house. It's quiet up there, and the brick balustrade makes a great highway. He got the car free from a bag of Milky Bar chocolates but had been saving for a real purchase. Would I like to see the new set of wheels he's thinking of buying? he asks, a question he rattles off with the velocity and matter-of-factness of someone with a serious avocation. He adds that he's just finished storing up 105 rupees. Sure, I say weakly, worrying what my participation will mean. I am whisked away to a cramped Sera Jey-owned-and-operated general store the size of a large shed, located meters from his regional house. Gesturing his way through a thicket of items behind the counter, Pasang picks out a foot-long battery-operated "Tour Autobus" whose price tag is 105 rupees. Inside sits a driver with a blue body and beige head. In the passenger seat sits a woman, smaller, stuck with the job of waving to passersby. The two Jey monks who man the store spring into action, volunteering a demonstration, a test drive, and this scene unfolds far too fluently to have been the first. One monk plants a few massive D batteries inside a bay and flips a switch. The Tour Autobus, a Bump and Go, jounces to life and hurtles blindly forward, careening into walls as it issues a grating, metallic rendition of "It's a Small World."

Small, that's how Sera felt. No trace of collegiate allegiance and antagonism here, I thought. For monks like Pasang in the early stages of socialization, the commitment to patronize one's college may not be fixed and categorical, but for well-socialized monks the townscape of Sera Monastery—with its dual administrative apparatus, its parallel buildings, its collegiate loyalties—is divided. A line between Jey and Mey is drawn, and monks should not cross it. Pasang never told me whether he ended up buying the bus, but one day I began to hear its bleating song blocks away. As the batteries wore, the tune warped and slowed till, finally, I never heard it again.

## REMEMBERING DIVISION:
### SERA JEY AND MEY IN INDIA

Intercollegiate polarization is nothing new. For the Geluk monastic seats of Tibet, "a monk's loyalties were primarily rooted in his college" (Goldstein 1998:20). And rooted deep, it would seem, as often illustrated by the 1947 Sera Jey uprising against the Tibetan central government. Mey had aligned itself with the Tibetan government in a dispute over the regency of the fourteenth Dalai Lama and did not come to the defense of its neighbors, nor was it targeted by government troops. When Jey's walls were shelled the Mey college remained unmoved. Though collegiate loyalties have not been tested in so dramatic a fashion in exile, Mey was swept up in controversy surrounding the propitiation of the deity Dorje Shugden, held by the Dalai Lama to be a hazardous practice. The Dalai Lama began to oppose the practice in the 1970s, and events came to a head in February 1997 with the murder of Shugden critic and longtime confidant of the Dalai Lama, Geshe Lobsang Gyatso, the seventy-year-old founder and principal of the Institute of Buddhist Dialectics in Dharamsala. He was discovered in a pool of blood near his two slain monk-assistants, each stabbed more than a dozen times. Indian police and those at Dharamsala believed the murderers to be Shugden devotees. Sera Mey's large Pomra regional house had a number of monks who refused to abandon the deity, and tensions persisted with Dharamsala, which in turn exacerbated tensions between Jey and Mey.[4]

While binding past to present is not what I intend here, intercollegiate polarization has been and remains a vital institutionalized feature of the Geluk monastic seats in South India. The importance of these divisions is suggested by comments about their loss and restoration in exile that surface in oral narratives about the critical Buxa decade before the Geluk monastic seats were constructed in South India.[5] Buxa Duar is situated in the district of Jalpaiguri, in Northwest Bengal, near the Bhutanese border. It had been one of the main arteries and old trade routes into Bhutan and was the site of an ex-British fort and prison. Taken by the British during the Anglo-Bhutanese Duar war of 1864–65, the fort housed political dissidents during India's independence movement, including several who participated in the Civil Disobedience Movement of 1930. After the Quit India movement of 1942, Buxa ceased to function as a prison and served instead as British barracks, till independence. Barbed wire still haunted the camp's perimeter when the Tibetans arrived, and the irony of inhabiting a former prison, especially one that had housed freedom fighters, was not lost on the new occupants. It was one of the first things veterans would tell me about Buxa. Much about Buxa made its refuge feel like incarceration. Located on a ridge encircled by three densely wooded hills, the camp suffered from stifling heat and pounding monsoon rains. A lone road stretched from Langapara, the nearest town, and wound its way to the remote site. As a news correspondent observed in 1968, "Immediately below the camp a signboard says ironically, 'To Lama Ashram and Police Office'" (Central Tibetan Administration 1968:2). An Indian commandant manned a station at the entrance. Permits slowed entry and departure. It was hard for visitors to get in, and for residents to get out.

Buxa initially served as a transit camp for Tibetan refugees arriving in India via Bhutan in 1959. In September 1959 a weeklong meeting among representatives of the major sects of Tibetan Buddhism was held in Kalimpong in West Bengal. There they worked out the details of a plan to transfer to Buxa some of the monks who had made it into exile. Fifteen hundred were to be accommodated at Buxa, three hundred of whom were allocated for Sera's two monastic colleges, Jey and Mey.[6] Having recognized that Buxa would be trying—the heat alone was proof of that— a couple hundred Buxa monks who had belonged to Tibet's Upper and Lower Tantric colleges, many of whom were senior members, were relocated to the cooler slopes of Dalhousie in 1959. It was still a privilege to stay at Buxa. Entry was not automatic. A rudimentary screening process ("What level of study did you reach? What texts did you read? Were you disciplined?") filtered out all but the minority of monks who had actually studied philosophy in Tibet; those who made the list escaped road construction work. Buxa was meant especially for monks whose studies had been interrupted by exile; most were rather young, and there was a relatively small number of lamas and senior scholars, enough to tutor and provide instruction. Buxa became "Buxa Lama Ashram" and would serve as a temporary settlement in which the shoots of Tibetan Buddhism would take root. This monastic community would then be transplanted back to Tibet when independence was won.

Or so the plan went. The hardships of the Buxa decade occupy a special place in the memory of senior Geluk monks. Their recollections circle around recurrent themes: heat, ghosts, suicide, abject poverty, the scourge of tuberculosis, the acute mental anguish of not knowing when, or if, one would return to Tibet. A series of jagged images—like "frozen slides," as Veena Das (2000:61) observed in an essay on memories of the trauma and violence of India's partition—obtrude from these oral narratives: razors that ended the lives of a few; a beam from which a monk was found hanged; the icy body of a local South Asian teenager who worked at Buxa, discovered facedown in a bathing area, having drowned mysteriously, as mysteriously as the stones that clattered off rooftops but could never be found and had no human source; an absurd, motley assortment of donated clothes; sandals fashioned from tire rubber purchased for a rupee and a quarter (a shipment of nine hundred pairs of shoes arrived finally in January 1961); barbed wire and whispers of past torture; long, aimless walks in the hills that could free you for a while from the cramped quarters in which TB spread so virulently. "*Beggars*, that's what we were reduced to," one said, condensing his train of memories into a single, resonant figure. As the current principal of the Institute for Buddhist Dialectics in Dharamsala recounted—he, too, is a veteran of Buxa,—they were despondent at first, and that drained the life from study and debate. As they struggled to bring routine to their lives, monastic life in Tibet came to a sudden, violent halt.

All of this made Buxa doubly important. Without it Tibet's religious patrimony, at least that of the Geluk sect, would be lost. Expectedly, the topography of difference within and between the Geluk monasteries was all but flattened in the early years at Buxa. Intercollegiate distinctions and allegiances once fortified by separate buildings and halls and courtyards were indistinct as monks shared the fate of displacement and inhabited a landscape not scripted to remind them of their differences.

Sera's Jey and Mey colleges sought to reinscribe their differences in small ways almost immediately. Sera monks resided in several structures. Those of higher relative status—Geshes and reincarnate lamas—tended to live separately in bamboo dwellings that were constructed from materials from the neighboring forest. (That these were less than commodious was brought home to me by a senior monk, who drolly dubbed them chicken coops.) Several of the larger regional houses, like Sera Jey's Triu house, reconstituted themselves in separate bamboo dwellings. A large concentration of Sera's monks initially settled in a single structure, one of Buxa's old, long, rectangular buildings. It was a gloomy, dispiriting place. According to some oral accounts, most of Sera's monks—104 in all—roomed together here initially, 52 of whom were from Mey, 52 from Jey. The thick stone walls had narrow windows that sliced daylight into thin, frail shafts. Only later were these enlarged to let more light in. The building's interior had been left bare and hollow, though in some cases monks fashioned room dividers from bamboo and fabric. A door in the building's center conveniently gave the space bilateral symmetry, carving it into two equal halves, for Jey and for Mey.

At each building's end were bathrooms that were demolished and renovated into makeshift altar areas on which offering bowls and each college's respective texts could be placed. Texts were scarce at first and had to be painstakingly reinscribed on whatever materials could be found, including labels peeled from powdered milk tins donated by international aid agencies. Early in their stay at Buxa, monks of all the Geluk monastic seats would frequently debate together in one area; only later were they able to establish separate debating courtyards as had existed in Tibet. Though the colleges had to share the same courtyard—Sera Jey with Mey, Drepung Loseling with Gomang, Ganden Shartse with Jangtse—they broke up into subgroups based on their college ties when they debated; at other times, they debated together, affording a degree of contact between the colleges that had occurred less frequently in Tibet. Other practices continued to presuppose the colleges' autonomy and distinctiveness, however. The daily tea assembly (*mang ja*), for instance, was convened by each college and led by each college's chant leader (*dbu mdzad*). If the boundaries between the units of 'colleges', 'regional houses', and perhaps even the monastic seats themselves, seemed at first indistinct, owing to the hardships faced at Buxa and the lack of a built environment that could reinscribe old distinctions, they would eventually be reinscribed, and quite durably so.

Sera's move from Buxa to Bylakuppe in the early 1970s was no less disruptive. In terms of intercollegiate distinctions, the move southward was a step backward, for once again Sera's monks faced a new and relatively inhospitable environment, this time in the wooded environs of southern India. Collegiate and subcollegiate distinctions were again flattened as monks lived and labored under cover of tents while land was cleared. Though not without resources to the same degree as they were at Buxa, they were still struck down by illness and faced the daunting tasks of clearing untamed forest, preparing agricultural fields, and laying the foundation for a durable monastic community. The collegiate distinctions were not wholly neutralized, of course, nor were the important regional house (*khang tshan*) divisions. Of the relative salience of the regional house distinctions upon first arrival in the south, for instance, one monk remarked: 'It was not as if [the regional houses] were non-existent' (*med pa 'dra ma red*). If asked, one would easily identify with one regional house, but the lack of a proper built environment hindered their visibility. The Jey and Mey monastic colleges and their subcollegiate regional houses came into sharp relief only in the 1980s, when new refugees from Tibet began to arrive, and when a wave of construction brought new, durable structures to the monastic settlement. As fitful as the monastic divisions had been from the Buxa period to the 1980s, their status since has been relatively stable.

## PRINCIPLES OF DIVISION

On what does this corporate division into two colleges rest? In response to this question, my interlocutors from Sera typically cited doctrinal differences enshrined in the textbooks of Jey's and Mey's respective curricula. Both trace descent to Tsongkhapa, the founder of the Geluk sect, but they uphold and teach monastic 'textbooks' (*yig cha*) composed by different authors, contemporaries of one another in the mid-fifteenth and early sixteenth centuries.[7] Jey uses the textbooks of Jetsun Chökyi Gyaltsen (1469–1546);[8] Mey, those of Khedrup Denpa Dargye (1493–1568).[9] Adherence to different textbooks is no small matter, since intellectual life at places like Sera very much revolves around these works. The textbook literature consists of Tibetan commentaries on Indian commentaries, yet these "sub-sub commentaries" are, as Jeffrey Hopkins (1999:12) notes, "elevated to a status of primary concern and adherence" in the curriculum (though not exclusive concern; Dreyfus 2003). The textbook literature is part of a circuit of intellection that includes memorization, oral commentary, and twice-daily public debate. While most monks tell me it is fine to poke at imperfections in a rival college's textbook, there is no question about how one ought to orient oneself toward one's own textbook: one should accept its claims.

During my first trip to Sera Mey, I befriended a twelve-year-old monk, Chögyel, who had recently started training in debate under a tutor. His tutor was my tutor, so Chögyel and I would occasionally spar, if only briefly and clumsily on my part, just enough so that I could learn more about the practice. At a certain point he quotes an authoritative line from the textbook, ending with 'because it is said' (*zhes gsungs pa'i phyir*). I reject the quote. Chögyel is aghast. 'You *must* accept this' (*khas lan dgos red*), he snaps.

For Chögyel—being young and new—allegiance is rulelike not normlike, so I put the question in Chögyel's stark, categorical terms to Tenzin, the personal assistant

TABLE 1 'Textbooks' (*yig cha*) of the Geluk monastic seats of India

| 'Monastic university' (dgon pa) | 'Monastic college' (grwa tshang) | 'Textbook' author (yig cha) |
|---|---|---|
| Sera | Sera Jey (*byes*) | rje btsun chos kyi rgyal mtshan (1469–1546) |
| | Sera Mey (*smad*) | mkhas grub bstan pa dar rgyas (1493–1568) |
| Ganden | Ganden Jangtse (*byang rtse*) | rje btsun chos kyi rgyal mtshan (1469–1546) |
| | Ganden Shartse (*shar rtse*) | paṇ chen bsod rnams grags pa (1478–1554) |
| Drepung | Drepung Gomang (*sgo mang*) | 'jam dbyangs bzhad pa (1648–1722) |
| | Drepung Loseling (*blo gsal gling*) | paṇ chen bsod rnams grags pa (1478–1554) |

of a more senior Geshe from the same regional house (this Geshe is both a relative of Chögyel's tutor and has Chögyel under his care): 'Must one absolutely accept [Sera Mey's textbook]?' (*yin cig min cig khas len dgos red pe*). Yes, but rejecting Sera Jey's textbook is fine, he says, as if that would reassure me. Moving up the ladder, I turn to the senior Geshe whom this assistant serves. If a Mey monk fails to cite and defend his textbook's distinctive claims in such a debate, it would be a source of 'shame' (*ngo tsha*), he says bluntly. Allegiance to one's college's textbook may be firmly prescribed, but what exactly the textbook says is not always clear, hence some wiggle room is available, and there are maverick monks who brave public opinion and even delight in being contrarian.[10] Other variables that modulate degree of expected allegiance include debate type (public, formal 'defenses', *dam bca'*, tend to require "more" allegiance to textbook than the twice-daily one-on-one debates with a partner, *rtsod zla;* Dreyfus 2003) and topic of study (e.g., topics that appear later in the curriculum, like Middle Way philosophy, center less around textbook literature; Dreyfus 2003:471 n. 65). Still, it is difficult to overstate the normative commitment to the textbook literature and the place of this commitment in the socialization of monks.

This commitment to different monastic textbooks is not unique to Sera. It is the case for each of the three major Geluk monastic seats replicated in South India—Sera, Drepung, and Ganden. Each contains two colleges, and each of the two colleges uses different textbooks. This guarantees perpetual doctrinal friction within each monastic seat.

While doctrinal friction exists intramonastically, alliances exist with colleges of *other* monasteries, forming two larger-scale intercollegiate groupings that knowledgeable monks would spell out for me. Both the Jey college of Sera located in Bylakuppe and the Jangtse college of Ganden located in Mundgod adhere to Jetsun Chokyi Gyaltsan's textbooks (table 1). Shartse college of Ganden and Loseling of Drepung adhere to Panchen Sonam Drakpa's (1478–1554) textbooks.[11] For the remaining two colleges, which do not share textbooks (viz. Sera's Mey college and Drepung's Gomang college), monks stipulate that these colleges maintain close relationships

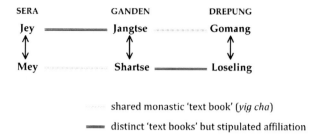

FIGURE 1. Opposition within and between the Geluk monastic seats in India

with other colleges: specifically, Sera Mey is said to be linked to Ganden Shartse and Drepung Loseling, while Drepung Gomang is said to be linked to Sera Jey and Ganden Jangtse. (This linkage is often characterized using either the term *mthun phyogs* or the more colloquial *nye logs,* 'near', 'close'. One might compare this to the prescribed forms of interclan alliance and antagonism in small-scale societies, familiar in the ethnographic record; the college textbook is akin to a totem for the corporate college.) Reciprocal privileges and responsibilities are upheld between the two sets of partner or affiliate colleges. When the Geluk exams (*dge lugs rgyugs 'phrod*)—partly standardized exams in which Geluk monks from different monasteries in India can participate, and on whose basis they can compete for the highest rank of Geshe, *Hlarampa* (*lha ram pa*)—were held at Sera Monastery in 2000, for instance, monks from Ganden and Drepung stayed on Sera's premises for the duration of this multiday event. Monks from Ganden's Shartse college and from Drepung's Loseling college were housed at Sera Mey, for these are Mey's two partner colleges. During a visit to another monastic seat, one ought to reside, I was told, in an affiliated college.

In sum, through their adherence to different monastic textbooks, and through their stipulated alliances, the six major Geluk colleges are neatly divisible by two (fig. 1).[12] Doctrinal fractiousness between the colleges that make up each of the three major Geluk monasteries is hence institutionally ensured. While the Geluk sect often treats its authoritative literature as if it possessed a seamless interpropositional and intertextual coherence, it chronically undermines this ideal.

### Sanctioned Doctrinal Contests: Jey-Mey Rigchen Debates

As traced out earlier, the monastic townscape appears elegantly dipolar, with Jey and Mey colleges at either end. Add to this the manner in which these colleges stick to their respective monastic textbooks—some of whose assertions are at odds—and difference becomes opposition. Though there is the constant potential for ruptures along the fault line of doctrine, it is especially in the context of certain annual, scheduled debates between Jey and Mey that such doctrinal differences may be aired. The scheduled encounters between the two colleges are the annual Rigchen debates, which convene in Sera's general assembly hall (*lha spyi*). Over the course of two days, two representatives from each college face off in one of the most anticipated series of debates in the monastic calendar.

The Rigchen debates contrast with the annual Rigchung debates (see chapter 2) in two primary respects. First, the Rigchen is more statusful, for it is reserved for those who have completed the study of 'Middle Way' (*dbu ma*) philosophy; the Rigchung, in contrast, is reserved for those who have completed the preceding course of study, entitled the 'Perfection of Wisdom' (*phar phyin*). The Rigchen is also an intercollegiate debate held between Jey and Mey, while the Rigchung is strictly intracollegiate.

In the Sera of pre-1959 Tibet, the number of Rigchen candidates had been higher, for the Rigchen had been larger affairs, explained one of Sera Mey's former abbots. There were thirty-two candidates from Jey and thirty-two from Mey who would participate annually in Tibet. Two monks would face off against each other twice a day, with one morning session and one evening session. At Buxa, monks from Sera Mey did manage to briefly revive the Rigchung debates, though they did so for only one year and had only eight candidates, as opposed to the sixteen candidates who now annually participate at Sera in Bylakuppe. They did not succeed in reinstituting the Rigchen debates at Buxa, and not even at Bylakuppe till the 1980s.

With only four candidates per year, Sera's current Rigchen debates may seem to have suffered a sharp diminution of value relative to the Sera of pre-1959 Tibet, as a former abbot suggested when he called the practice's revival a symbolic gesture a commemorative act (*dran gzo*). Symbolic it may be, but for participants at least its status has not diminished; if anything, its prestige has increased as a consequence of the smaller pool of candidates allowed to participate annually. The attention lavished upon the Rigchen debates is also considerable. Prior to this two-day event, the two candidates from Mey sat as defendants in a large public debate held in Mey's own debating courtyard. The monks of Mey gathered there, with the defendant's classmates serving as challengers. Mey's abbot emeritus paid a visit to this preparatory, pre-Rigchen debate and at a certain point decided to prod the candidate himself, delighting the crowd.

### *The Unsanctioned World of Monastic Soccer*

Doctrinal contests are not the only scheduled engagements that can reinscribe collegiate distinctions. There's also soccer, which sometimes breaks along college lines. As Khyentse Norbu's film *The Cup* (1999) ably dramatizes, soccer is firmly proscribed at the major Tibetan Buddhist monasteries of South India. Sera is no exception, but this has done little to dampen enthusiasm for the sport. At Sera I saw a wealth of games and sporting activities—badminton, mock kung fu, and table tennis—and even tried my hand at a few. These activities are often supposed to be restricted to certain age groups and limited to specific time periods, to recess periods at the schoolhouse, to Tuesdays (which are designated as days off for Sera Mey), and to the vacation period of the monastic year known as *dga' dbyings.*

Soccer, however, is categorically prohibited—testimony to the fever the sport ignites. So concerned is Sera with curbing the sport's contagion that, as the disciplinarian's assistant from Sera Mey explained, one isn't even permitted to watch live soccer being played in the neighboring town of Kushalnagar. If apprehended, monks must first offer prostrations in the assembly hall shared by the two colleges of Sera, Jey and Mey. On the second offense they must prostrate before their own teachers. On the third they face expulsion.

Clandestine soccer matches convene frequently at Sera, at times weekly. The frequency of the matches keeps pace with international matches, most notably the World Cup. In 1998 the World Cup was under way, and Sera was abuzz with news and updates. (It was rumored that the final between France and Brazil drew scores of monks, who, at five rupees a head, pressed themselves into a hall in a neighboring Tibetan refugee camp to watch the televised match in the early hours of the morning.) Besides closely following the tournament on radio and television, monks took part in matches, including between Jey and Mey, with greater frequency.

. . .

6 July. It is the Dalai Lama's birthday and a holiday for Sera's monks. In the afternoon, Trinley, a young monk I know and with whom I jogged a couple times in the early morning, lumbers through the door, disheveled, limping conspicuously, as if to bait me into asking him what happened. I take the bait. With a mischievous smile he mutely points out two tears in his yellow monastic vest. A sign of some kind of struggle, I suppose, but he wants me to guess. I ask for more clues. He begins scurrying about the room, imitating dribbles, turns, feints. Finally, the confession: he had been playing soccer—a match between Jey and Mey. The stakes? Pepsi and cookies for the winners to be paid for by the losers.

Monks like Trinley steal away into clearings in the woods or even into neighboring towns, sometimes for elaborate multiday tournaments. The stakes can be high. In one, each monk had to ante forty rupees. After the final, I catch up with Trinley and ask him how his team did. Exhausted, he tells me only that the winning team took in over a thousand rupees; a pregnant pause, then he flashes a string of sweat-wilted ten-rupee notes slung around his belt, beaming when he announces that it was *his* team that won.

Stealing away isn't always easy. With Fevicol—a "synthetic resin adhesive," the plastic jar reads, but that's a charitable term for what is really just gloppy white paste—applied to their faces, players block sunburn, a symptom of the sport and incriminating evidence. And arranging a match on a hot afternoon requires supplies and careful planning and execution. Sometimes you need a lot of water. Trinley tells me of the time they hauled a forty-liter container of water on the back of a bicycle to the match site, an hour from the monastery. Food is smuggled out of the mess hall in plastic bags tucked under arms and beneath robes.[13]

Real soccer, ball and all, is played only periodically, with stealth and care, but surrogates of the sport surface daily. For the ball, there are socks stuffed with paper, Hacky Sacks (*thebs le*), even coconuts—though they hurt your feet, one monk remarked soberly. In one large assembly, I watch two young monks strike up a little soccer match using offering bread—consecrated bread, which shouldn't be played with at all, and certainly not in assembly. The monk on one side of the aisle uses his index and middle finger to form an inverted V on the floor: the goal. Across the aisle his conspirator squeezes a wad of dough into the size and shape and density of a marble: the ball. I watch him take shots on the goal by firing the ball with thumb and index finger.

One afternoon, Pasang arrives with a large sheet of white paper whose edges have been carefully folded upward. It is a soccer stadium with players represented by tiny upward-facing flaps, each of which is meticulously numbered and arranged on the pitch in offensive and defensive formation. He delicately sets his paper stadium on the floor. Chögyel, who up until that point had been in repose on a nearby seat, eyes glazed over the pages of a religious text, perks up as if voltage is applied to his spine. He plunks himself down cross-legged on the floor next to Pasang, who then produces a compact little wad of paper—the ball. Using plastic straws pulled from the back of two Frooti mango juice cartons, they blow the ball back and forth in an all-out huffing-puffing lung-bursting effort to drive it through the opponent's goal, represented by a hole Pasang had carefully torn in each side of his stadium. Chögyel introduces a clock, marking off periods with clicks of his tongue. "Goal!" "Red card!" "Heading!" And when the ball sticks on the paper flap, "Holding!" Penned in the center of this paper stadium are the acronyms "S.T.S." and "S.J.S": "Sera Thosam Ling School" (Mey's schoolhouse) and "Sera Jey School." A fictive contest between Jey and Mey. Colleges no more, Jey and Mey assume the guise of teams locked in a decidedly this-worldly contest, governed by an unforgiving zero-sum logic officially banned from debate.

· · ·

When asked to evaluate performance in debate, most monks demur. Indisposed to judge, they avoid vulgar terms like 'winning' (*thob pa*) and 'losing' (*shor ba*), terms habitually used for sports like soccer. Verbal evaluations of performance in the philosophical curriculum are not uncommon. It is just that they take the form of parsimonious ready-mades like "He is 'good [in] scripture'" (*dpe cha yag po*) or 'intelligent' (*rig pa yag po*); tellingly, positive evaluations outnumber the negative, for if one has nothing good to say . . .

Over a lunch I ask Geshe-la about a monk named Dawa who served as lead challenger in a debate at our regional house the evening before. Is he a good debater? Geshe-la says nothing. He sticks up his thumb and says: "He's not like *this*." "And he's not like *that*," raising his pinky. Then he raises his ring finger, a gesture I translate for clarification, though with a little more charity than Geshe-la insinuated: "So you're saying he's not 'the best' (*yag shos*) and not the 'worst' (*sdug shos*)?" No verbal response, just a faint, affirmative nod.

If monks seem loath to evaluate and rank, this is especially true when it comes to themselves and when the evaluations are positive, and public. During my first visit to Sera Mey I taught English from time to time to a handful of monks in a makeshift classroom. The monks I taught had just participated in a debate the prior evening. In a feeble attempt to enliven the lesson with humor, and partly just out of curiosity, I decided to ask about last night's defendant, who was a visitor from another regional house. "*Last night,*" I say, pausing to let them process the English, "*did* he . . . de*bate* well?" It had looked to me like they were tearing the guy apart, so I expected a resounding no. Instead, it is Dawa, the lead challenger from last night, who speaks up, with others echoing him. Yes, that defendant did well. And when I turn the tables on Dawa and ask about his own performance, his response becomes predictable: "*No . . . I did not . . . de*bate well." He repeats this several times.

There are exceptions. Without prompting, a former debate tutor of mine complains that a debater 'doesn't understand anything' (*khyon nas go gi mi 'dug*) and dismisses another as just 'so-so' (*a 'u tsi 'dug*). After a debate at our regional house, I ask Jermey how it went. (This was a debate in which the whole regional house had hosted a debater from another regional house, who served as defendant.) 'It went well *for us*' (*nga tsho la yag po byung*). Circumspect, but not terribly subtle. Though rare, I do hear monks on occasion use the verb 'lose' (*shor ba*) to evaluate debate performance. It is even less common to hear monks, as individuals, crow about their success. Infrequent though this language is, it invokes a zero-sum framework, inviting an analogy between debate and sport, perhaps even Sera's premier, albeit forbidden, sport, soccer. Though the discomfort that surrounds talk of winning and losing in debate does lend support to Cabezón's (1994:85) general observation that "in Tibetan formal disputations there is rarely any talk of victory or defeat," debate spills into adjacent domains that are overtly competitive. The boundary between debate and nondebate—and sport in particular—is, expectedly, far more porous than official discourses let on, and debate-based behavior is, like all conventionalized behavior, subject to second-order parodies and tropes that blur the practice's edges.

One Tuesday evening, Tuesdays being the weekly day off at Sera Mey, I step into Trinley's room and find it jammed with monks. There is Jermey, the disciplinarian's assistant, absorbed with Chögyel in the game called corram. Reminiscent of billiards but without cues, it is played on a flat wooden board with four corner pockets, its surface so well chalked that the plastic poker chips used can sail from end to end with a flick of the finger. At a certain point, Chögyel, who at the time was in the throes of the early stages of the debating curriculum, scores, and on scoring bellows a taunt drawn from the debate register: *oh tsha* ('Shame [on you]!'). He even adds the taunt's kinesic accompaniment, a loud, open-palmed hand-clap uncharitably aimed at Jermey's face.

And then there is the analogy between emblematic debate gestures and mock kung fu. Over breakfast one morning, Chögyel and Dondrup have one of their little scraps, which never get serious as far as I can tell. Then Dondrup raises the ante by head-butting Chögyel in the chest. He's *crazy*, Chögyel turns and says to me in Tibetan, ending the bout. Minutes later, Dondrup stands and breaks into a series of mock debate gestures that look like the kung fu moves he has just finished showing off. He caps his performance with a feat of virtuosity: removing his prayer beads, 108 beads in all, he begins whipping it over his shoulder with one hand and catching it under his armpit with the other, in one fluid motion: prayer beads weaponized as nunchuks.

## DOCTRINAL ATTACHMENT: THE CARE OF TEXTS

Sera Monastery's dual administrative structure and its dipolar townscape divide the monastic community into two autonomous and parallel colleges. Other practices—some scheduled and sanctioned (e.g., annual Rigchen debates), some not (e.g., clandestine soccer matches between Jey and Mey)—turn these comparable entities into rivals (even if the evaluative framework operative in each domain is not strictly the same: soccer is zero-sum; debate, at least officially, is not). But the most widely reported criterion for the division of the monastery into the two colleges, and the most oft-cited basis for their antagonism, is doctrinal. The curricula of Jey and Mey colleges rest on different monastic textbooks, and the scheduled Rigchen debates that occur annually between the colleges serve as public venues in which doctrinal differences can be aired. Ensured, even scheduled, is perpetual tension, and dissension, between the colleges.[14] All this dissensus, both corporate and doctrinal, makes attachments to curricular texts all the more intense and consequential. Each college's distinctiveness rests on doctrinal foundations that are threatened by a neighbor who stands by a different textbook.

Within each college, monks exhibit tremendous care toward their textbook literature as well as toward the canon of authoritative Buddhist literature. In the commentarial literature of the Geluk sect, and in the debating courtyard, monks act as if each and every proposition expressed in the received corpus of authoritative Buddhist books fits together with the rest or at least ought to. This commitment to tradition's interpropositional and intertextual coherence is best appreciated in concert with the countless acts of deference that monks perform daily toward their books. The delicacy with which monks at Sera Mey handle their text-artifacts— be they the primary Buddhist scriptures or the vast wealth of Indian and Tibetan commentaries—is difficult to miss. Reminders of the texts' status are ever present and seldom subtle. If the books are of the long, traditional, unbound sort, they are swathed in auspiciously colored cloth when not in use. In one assembly hall, the Buddhist canon and the collected works of Tsongkhapa are set at the farthest reaches of the room and on the highest ledges. Farthest from the exit and from the floor and safeguarded from dust in neat glass cabinets, these books tower above an altar on which iconographic embodiments of Buddhas, bodhisattvas, lineage masters, and protectors are arrayed. In terms of the vertical axis, no other class of cultural artifact enjoys such rarefied heights.

The sins that come from their mistreatment are equally steep. In terms of bodily hexis, once off their shelves, books of such caliber are never to be handled lightly. One's feet should never pass over, point at, or touch them; their pages are not to be marred with ink, nor should their corners be bent; they are never to be set upon bare ground, sat upon, or buried in a heap of mundane things. When taken from or returned to their shelves, they are typically touched to the crown of one's head— a deference display of considerable gravity in a monk's kinesic repertoire. Once, during a session with my philosophy tutor, I shifted my knotted legs out of a cross-legged posture but allowed one foot to pass over the religious text from which we had been reading, a text I had set down in front of me. As my foot cast a shadow over its pages, the pitch register of his voice spiked. 'Scripture!' (*dpe cha*), he cried out several times in rapid succession, wincing as if I had pricked his skin. '[This] is Buddha's word, right?' (*sangs rgyas kyi gsungs red pa*).

The care extended to the content of Sera's prized text-artifacts is just as striking. Their content is transmitted to monks by way of memorization practices and periodic tests that occur at all stages of Sera Mey's curriculum. The sheer volume of doctrinal material that monks commit to memory is impressive. Long before monks set foot in the debating courtyard at Sera Mey, they begin committing to memory prayers drawn from two sizable volumes. For two sessions daily—usually from six to eight in the morning, and from six to eight in the evening—young monks attend 'scripture class' (*dpe cha 'dzin grwa*), where they memorize and recite prayers (this class is a precursor to what is later called *dpe khrid*, described below, a kind of scripture class where texts are not just memorized but given an interpretation by the teacher). The cycle of the day begins and ends with memorization. Inside a cramped room, monks as young as six sit cross-legged in tightly packed rows, feverishly rocking and swaying as they belt out memorized lines. To this mass of material their instructors pile on new words each day. Thirty or forty for the brightest students, one instructor explains. Pasang's book has check marks made delicately in pencil next to the prayers he has completed; the rest await memorization. One's store of memorized material is then recited aloud again in the evening. Formal memorization exams occur biannually at Sera Mey, and senior members of the college administer and monitor them; they are exams of no small importance.

With the foundational prayers down, monks turn to longer and far more demanding philosophical treatises whose content is left opaque till their studies formally commence. Memorization precedes analysis, a normative sequence often said to reflect a religio-developmental sequence comprised of three stages: 'hearing, thinking, meditating' (*thos bsam bsgom gsum*). Primary texts (e.g., Maitreya's *Clear Ornament of Realization*)[15] are memorized in full, though monks typically train only for serial access to their content; these works (or portions thereof) can be recited in linear order but not accessed randomly. For random access to these texts—a highly sought-after skill—monks must master the dense, hierarchical 'outline' (*sa bcad*) that each textbook possesses. The text fragment's location can be pinpointed and recalled with the help of the hierarchically organized chapter, section, subsection, and division titles. A monk with sufficient prowess can use this outline like a polar-coordinate system to locate any piece in the text-artifact.

With the outline, monks can both cite and swiftly recognize citations—prized skills in debate, where lapses of memory can be perilous for both challenger and defendant. At the outset of the debate analyzed in chapter 2, for example, the challenger feeds the defendant three syllables selected from the chapter of a monastic textbook. The defendant must quickly recognize the syllables, locate them in the book, reconstruct the clauses from which they were torn, and then spell out the citation's provenance, using the book's outline. The debate proper begins only after the three syllables have been specified, and only after the citation's provenance has been meticulously established. As the debate itself unfolds, citation continues to figure prominently. Citations range from the invocation of a diffuse and impersonal "tradition" through use of the quotative clitic *–s* to quotations surgically extracted from authoritative books, where author name and book title are denoted, and where the left and right boundaries of the quoted segment are unambiguously marked (through the ablative *las* on the left, to show where it's 'from'; the quotative *zhes* on the right to mark the quote's edge; and the honorific verb of speaking *gsungs*).

In addition to the care cultivated toward books, the stress on memorization practices and tests, and the vital role citation plays in debate, there is a certain generalized hermeneutics that applies to the entire corpus of authoritative Buddhist works, specifically, to the universe of propositions these works contain. Inherited doctrine, especially doctrine attributed to the historical Buddha and to revered lineage masters like Tsongkhapa, the founder of the Geluk sect, is often treated as if it were flawless in its interpropositional consistency. When confronted with diverse and competing philosophical assertions, Geluk monks work indefatigably to reconcile all signs of contradiction—as if to display the genius of an omniscient Buddha who could pragmatically adjust his message to fit the needs of his diverse disciples. This ability to tailor discourse to its occasion and to the diverse capacities of the audience is sometimes typified as an expression of the enlightened attribute termed 'skill in means' (*thabs mkhas*). As a hermeneutic, it is expansive, for there is no effort to sort texts into the pure and the apocryphal and to purge the latter (see Lopez 1988; Cabezón 1994). All authoritative text-artifacts and their propositional content should be accommodated, though additional distinctions may be added to resolve any apparent inconsistencies, of course. Hopkins notes how this official commitment to doctrinal cohesion is conveyed when a teacher makes remarks such as this to his students: "It is amazing how there is not the slightest internal contradiction in all of the works of the Foremost Precious One [Tsongkhapa]!" (2002:5). (Yet "shortly thereafter," continues Hopkins, the teacher confronts the student "with an apparent inconsistency as if the student were the origin of the original proposition that there was no inconsistency." The irony Hopkins identifies is the crux of the matter. In a manner reminiscent of debate, the teacher Hopkins describes initiates a chiastic, counterdirectional turn, sundering interpropositional coherence and obliging the student to restore it. Much like a defendant in debate, as we shall later see, the student must uphold the textual ideology, creating doctrinal consistency in the midst of dissension.)

For monks engaged in the philosophical curriculum, each day brings 'scripture class' (*dpe khrid*). Indoors, in the pacific ambience of their teacher's quarters (*not* the din of the courtyard, note)[16] monks sit cross-legged and absorb the daily lesson. These classes tend to last an hour or two and may be peppered with questions from the instructor, questions designed to be carried into the debating courtyard. The courtyard is understood to be the prime site for philosophical learning. In scripture class there may be a few brief bouts of debate-style interaction, with the teacher playing the role of challenger, but the whole tenor of these lessons is quite unlike the twice-daily debating sessions. In class most religious instructors guide pupils through passages of text, reading aloud and offering delicate exegesis. As for the many "doubts" that arise from reflection on these passages—doubts should arise, they come from serious intellectual engagement—these are to be fielded and resolved in the courtyard, not indoors. Indoors, monks for the most part remain still and attentive, taking in received doctrine as if dutiful 'vessels' (*snod,* a classical figure for ideal discipleship). This mode of learning articulates with mnemonic practices, where scripture is learned whole. Monks are baited with assurances of a secure, stable, monolithic body of knowledge to which they are heirs and without which their college would be rootless.

And so, bodily hexis in which monks habitually pay deference to authoritative text-artifacts; daily mnemonic practices through which monks incorporate, take in, textual form and content; periodic exams where efforts at textual incorporation are inspected and graded; copious citation of text in debate; scripture classes where the propositional content of texts is picked apart through exegesis; an official hermeneutics that ascribes interpropositional coherence to a universe of propositions encoded in authoritative books—all these practices, while by no means of a piece, help inspire a diffuse feeling about authoritative text and textuality. A congeries of semiotic practices shapes sentiments about text, forming what we can caption loosely as a kind of textual ideology. Whatever else they do, these practices conspire to imbue authoritative Buddhist doctrine with an aura of inviolable "integrity" and "wholeness."

By design the monastery threatens this textual ideology. Curricular texts that support each college are threatened by virtue of being placed "next to" similar-but-competing texts that support a similar-but-competing neighboring college (a college that is its rival in respects other than just doctrine, to boot). This means that should the textbook literature begin to buckle during a debate, it can threaten the integrity of the whole college. This explains why a defendant's poor performance in a public defense (*dam bca'*) is not just bad for him as an individual whose career very much depends on his capacity to debate well. It may also offend the college. It risks being shameful in the maximal sense of the word. "These scholars know," reflects Dreyfus (2003:319), "that any doubt they express publicly about the orthodoxy of their school or even of their . . . [college's] . . . manuals will be taken as attacking the overall value of these institutions and their legitimacy."

## DEBATE, A TRAGEDY IN TWO ACTS

It is the textual ideology and the institutionalized threat to it posed by the division into two colleges that together set up debate's effectiveness as a "rite of institution," as Pierre Bourdieu might put it, a rite that in broadest terms tends to "consecrate and legitimate an *arbitrary boundary,* by fostering a misrecognition of the arbitrary nature of the limit and encouraging a recognition of it as legitimate" (Bourdieu 1991:118; cf. Bourdieu 1996:102–15). In Bourdieu's study of elite schools and the reproduction of state nobility in France, rites of institution—examination, training, isolation, selection—help distinguish and naturalize differences among groups. Debate, too, may help distinguish monks from their lay peers and set off the subcategory of elite monk who does well in philosophy and ends up pursuing a Geshe degree from the kind of monk who does not do well on the debating courtyard and ends up shuttled into monastic labor and service, but my concern here is with what debate does for the college, and in turn for the monastic university. Debate is placed at the nexus of fierce centripetal and centrifugal forces, those that would bind the monastic college to its curricular texts, others that would sunder it, in turn compromising the integrity of Sera Monastery itself. Debate aspires to mediate these tensions.

Debate features two primary speech-event roles: "challenger" and "defendant." In simple terms, the challenger, who stands and paces while the defendant sits cross-legged in front of him, tries to induce inconsistencies in the defendant's speech and authoritative Buddhist doctrine. The challenger does this relentlessly, regardless of his personal views on philosophical matters and irrespective of any likes or dislikes he may harbor for the defendant. The defendant, by contrast, is expected to be committed to what he says and have a consistent set of views, and his task is to repair the challenger's damage. He restores consistency and is judged competent in debate to the extent that he succeeds in this. Monks take turns inhabiting these roles in daily courtyard debate. They learn to play both parts.

As for debate's plot, at first all is placid. The defendant is assumed to be knowledgeable, and the challenger does little to disturb this. Through a series of seemingly innocuous questions, the challenger elicits what is known and shared between them, thereby establishing consensus on what doctrinal tradition says. Challenger and defendant thus recount and put on public record what both hold dear: the college's literature and its warren of definitions and divisions—material that is scrupulously memorized and toward which deference is owed.

Just when challenger and defendant seem solidary, and consensus has been established, just when the textual ideology is brought into plain sight, elevated, held high for collective praise and obeisance, the ritual plot takes a tragic turn. Tragic, in the sense of "peripety," the chiastic, counterdirectional emplotment that Aristotle felt was an ingredient of tragedy. With peripety, a plot's positive trajectory, the sense that all is well and will be well, is violently halted, then thrown into reverse, and shot into the opposite direction with equal if not greater force. The challenger starts to turn against doctrine and against the defendant, sundering the coherence he helped dialogically construct. Merciless and indefatigable, the challenger ferrets out inconsistencies in the defendant's discussion of doctrine, threatening doctrine's integrity and holding the defendant responsible for any harm done to it. Violently foregrounded here is the hallowed textual ideology itself. As the defendant struggles to mend text, he is met not with support or sympathy but taunts, piercing open-palmed claps, and menacing facial gestures that issue from challengers (plural, because public debates start with one challenger but become many-versus-one affairs) who pace back and forth, retreating and advancing, as if to erode the very ground on which the defendant sits.

Debates end abruptly. Dissensus replaces consensus, and consensus is never restored for the rest of the debate. There is no attempt to seek common ground or forge synthesis or strike a compromise. To sunder consensus is not to expose the incoherence of inherited doctrine. It is to expose the incompetence of the defendant's grasp of it—his inability to find or forge coherence amid the welter of philosophical claims.

How does the defendant handle this reversal of fortune? His demeanor throughout is, or should be, one of majestic poise and unflappability in the face of the challengers' provocations. (As described in detail in chapter 2, these effects are created through various semiotic resources and methods, including speech rate "decelerations" and an ostentatiously nonresponsive uptake when provoked.) This "stability" is no random demeanor. It has everything to do with debate's role as a rite of institution, for the defendant exemplifies in demeanor what he tries to do in terms of text, as if to present himself as doctrinal tradition ought to be. If successful, the defendant appears as a cross-modal figure of and for doctrinal tradition's "stability," or, more dynamically, its "re-unification." This figure is forged in the crucible of an agonistic dialogue, where doctrinal integrity is threatened so that it can be saved. And since the texts about which monks wrangle are typically the college textbook literature that the monastic college claims as its foundation, this stability spreads by default to the college, too.

## MIMETIC SYMPATHY THROUGH
## INTERACTION RITUAL

Debate permits—rather, it requires—the challenger to introduce dissenting views, but these views are not his, nor those of anyone in particular, and as such they do not risk disturbing the college as much as the views articulated by the defendant, who is assumed to be committed to what he says and who defends the textual ideology. The whole practice appears designed to permit but contain threats to doctrinal stability. This paradox is a familiar one. Max Gluckman's (1954, 1963) classic notion of "rituals of rebellion" suggested that expressions of societal tension within the ritual proscenium mitigate the risk that "real" outrage will erupt outside it, ironically preserving societal cohesion. The literature on ritual since has looked more critically at a host of issues, including the issue of the logics and dynamics that characterize the relation between ritual and social structure, event and context.

About this relation, it is instructive to ask: What primes monks to jump scale, as it were, to ascend from the defendant's stability to doctrinal stability to the stability of the monastic college? What forges affinities across these seemingly nested domains so that what transpires in debate can touch the whole college? "To get hold of something by means of its likeness," to quote Michael Taussig (1993:21) again, is a gloss for the old, mimetic, and instrumental sense of the word "sympathy" that I wish to recover, because this sense draws attention to the way agents can try to induce sympathy from a spectator through the craft of mimicry. As anthropological work on mimesis has often shown, ritual is a frequent site for mimetic performance—no surprise, since one key way in which ritual works is by tacitly modeling what it tries to do. And any ritual can model more than one thing. While debate may model the authoritative stability of the college, it also has the potential to model qualities of liberal subjecthood.

If interaction rituals like Buddhist debate are to materialize the liberal subject, and draw the affective sympathies of spectators, participants must rely on the craft of liberal mimicry and emulate this subject in some respect or capacity. This is no mean feat, because likenesses cannot be fashioned from the gossamer of a few resonant words like "rights" and "freedom." The semblance must be textured and multimodal—made of vocal and nonvocal dimensions—and in this case it must also occur within a ritual matrix that remains essentially Buddhist in character. And, more importantly, you cannot accomplish this merely through editing the ritual text. No amount of alteration to the ritual itself—its textual architecture, roles, register, stages, standards of appropriateness—can secure what the practice looks like, because this resemblance depends on habits of construal formed "outside" the event's perimeter. To appreciate the labor needed to transfigure debate into something new, a topic I address later, we must first interrogate our assumption that ritual—including interaction ritual—is naturally modular and neatly circumscribed, a spatio-temporally bounded event situated "in" some larger surround. Resemblances may be exhibited in ritual events, but they are not formed, or reformed, there.

In the Durkheimian imagination, the steps that explained ritual's effectiveness were remarkably few, because one leapt straight from ritual to "the social." In *Primitive Classification,* for instance, Émile Durkheim and Marcel Mauss (1963:11) famously argued that the "classification of things reproduces . . . [the] . . . classification of men." They found cultural classifications that seemed to resemble a group's structure, and assumed this meant that that structure was primary. Durkheim and Mauss have been faulted on a number of grounds, and the critiques of functionalism are too familiar to be repeated here. As Rodney Needham recognized long ago, there is no reason to assume a one-to-one correspondence between social morphology and cultural classification, and in stating that the "classification of non-social things 'reproduces' the classification of people," the term "reproduces" "immediately assumes that which is to be proved by the subsequent argument, viz. the primacy of society in classification" (Durkheim and Mauss 1963:xix, xiv). Nor did it help that Durkheim neglected the formal properties of signs, so that we are never quite sure what motivates ritual's social effectiveness (why have *these* particular signs been chosen for the ritual and not others?) (Silverstein 1981b; Parmentier 1997).

The Durkheimian tradition also never appreciated how precarious social mimicry is, how much labor is involved in creating and stabilizing what ritual seems to exhibit. Consider what it takes to "get" that in Catholic churches from Trent to the Second Vatican Council the architectural division between nave and sanctuary—a division projected by the sanctuary's height and by a communion rail that stretches across its width—reinforced the divide between clergy and laity (Lukken and Searle 1993:63–64); that New York's Guggenheim Museum's "continuous floor surface consisting of a wide, corkscrewing ramp rising through seven stories on a cantilever principle" conveys "the quiet of an unbroken wave," as its architect Frank Lloyd Wright suggested (Forsee 1959:156); that Zeus stands "exactly in the same relation that an absolute monarch does to the aristocracy of which he is the head," as Herbert Spencer observed in the nineteenth century (cited in Evans-Pritchard

1965); that Hindu mantras framed fore and aft with the seed syllable oṃ (oṃ . . . [body of mantra] . . . oṃ) model the purification of life's two great impurities, birth and death (Yelle 2003:24–25).

None of these is self-evident. Not everyone registers the same likenesses, and those that do may feel differently about what they see. This alone exposes the cheat of that old but still alluring functionalist trope of "reproduction," a trope that would have us jump from event to context, ritual to the social, as if no labor or mediating materials were involved. Rather than be taken in by ritual's scalar magic—the way it seems to telescope large scale into small scale—or reject all this as illusory, we need to explain what motivates and stabilizes the mimetic tie, and for whom and under what conditions it is felt at all. Close readings of transcribed ritual texts are indispensable, as the next chapter shows, but debate's mimetic power—its capacity to "do" things by modeling them within its own spatio-temporal horizon—cannot be read directly off such signs and their formal arrangement, nor will invocations of "the social" suffice as an explanation. Notice the tiresome seesaw between event and context, ritual and the social, micro and macro, as if there were nothing in between. Observe how both reflexes continue to presume the modularity of interaction ritual rather than study its placement. I have moved elliptically around the debating courtyard partly for this reason, drawing close briefly for now so that we can sense how debate depends on other practices at Sera. By disaggregating the assemblage of discursive practices that make up Sera's landscape—by prying apart mnemonic practices from rites of examination from the deferential handling of books, and the rest—it becomes easy to appreciate just how distributed and heterogeneous the conditions and materials and practices that afford debate's effectiveness are.

This is not to deny that debate looks bounded, and is. As ritual is so often at pains to distinguish itself from its surround by suspending or flouting norms of "ordinary" speech and behavior, so Buddhist debate sports its own lexical register (a repertoire of technical terms and expressions) and has its monks behave in ways that would look boorish and violent off the courtyard. In debate, as with ritual generally, cross-modal arrays of signs, vocal and nonvocal, also tend to cling together in hypertrophic fashion, forming a tight and seemingly seamless fabric of coexpressivity that gives the whole event an aura of formidable autonomy, a "semblance of formal plenitude-in-itself" (Silverstein 2004:626). It looks so tightly integrated that there is no question that the event is distinct from its surround, a world apart (how else can you get away with behavior that would otherwise look violent?). Not to mention the ways in which debate is perimeterized spatially and bound temporally, through strictures that limit it to designated places (a debating courtyard), through calendars and schedules that set it metrically to time (twice-daily two-hour-long debate sessions that occur from nine to eleven in the morning and seven to nine in the evening).

Debate's effectiveness as a rite of institution at Sera depends on it first being perimeterized and "placed" in relation to a congeries of other discursive practices that helps shape what debate does. Debate's plot—its biphasic progression from consensus to dissensus—does appear to recapitulate at a lower scalar order tensions that exist in its surround. When monks argue, they foreground and even heighten these tensions while containing them dramaturgically within debate's ritual prosce-nium. By design, debate has its participants strain toward "stability" and "reunifica-tion" in a context of doctrinal division and dissension. So is this just a familiar ex-ample of the way ritual mimics something beyond its perimeter in a bid to affect it? Is this just another neat case of fractally recursive "reproduction," where one set of distinctions is reproduced at a higher or lower scalar order (Irvine and Gal 2000), like the rippling out of tiered concentric circles from a pebble tossed into a pond?

Consider just a few of the more glaring imperfections that make debate a poor picture of its surround; or better, consider some of the surplus materials in the sur-round that can alter a monk's sense of what debate does as a rite of institution. Monks from each college cultivate attachment toward their college's textbook literature, es-pecially during the foundational years of their philosophical training, but they do *share* some literature with their neighbors, such as works by the sect's founder, Tsongkhapa. The care of books and the hermeneutics that views these works as co-hesive do not just apply to college-based textbooks. This suggests that debate does not always and everywhere help reproduce the distinction between Jey and Mey. Or consider the fact that the challenger-defendant role-relation is not perfectly ho-mologous with the Jey-Mey relationship (i.e., challenger : defendant :: Jey : Mey); this, because the colleges are *symmetrical* (they are structured similarly and share the same rights and obligations), and challenger and defendant are *asymmetrical* (or rather, they are symmetrical in the way mirror-image opposites are similar to each other). Or note how the threat posed by a neighboring college's doctrine waxes and wanes in intensity. It is periodic, not constant. It has a calendrical metricality to it, spiking in intensity especially during events like the scheduled intercollegiate Rigchen debates.

Elements like these are not "exceptions" to an otherwise tight fit between ritual and its surround, but reminders that we need to distinguish the impossibly clean and neat resemblances people can see in interaction rituals from the ragged, un-even assemblages of practices and materials that motivate these impressions and make a "place" for interaction as a predictable rite of institution.[17] The mimetic work of ritual offers participants pictures that are not unlike what Bruno Latour (2005: 187–90) calls "panoramas"—"staged totalities." He draws this metaphor from spe-cial rooms invented in the nineteenth century that "see *everything*"—as the ety-mology suggests—"but . . . also see *nothing* since they *show* an image painted (or projected) on the tiny wall of a room fully *closed* to the outside" (187). Panoramas are weak, Latour reminds us, not just because if one stares at them long enough one can glimpse the proscenium on which they are produced and the semiotic labor that affords their impossible views. ("Most of the time, it's the excess of coherence that gives the illusion away"; 188.) Connectionwise, they are precarious, for despite the sweeping vistas and God's-eye views, their scale is not a function of the expansive views they offer and the imperious confidence they project, but only that of the sum of the connections that permit them to continue to exist.

In surveying the intricate assemblage in which debate has been placed in Sera, it may seem that I have pulled the whole monastic fabric taut, but such a synchronic and synoptic view, which envisions these practices as operating in concert and at a single point in time, would exaggerate the degree of coordination, inviting a totalizing, deprocessualized reading that is not what I intend here. Many other things at Sera affect what monks can see in debate, like things said about the practice when monks undergo socialization into it, tacit norms adhered to and violated in the debating courtyard, representations of debate encountered in the books monks read and in things said about the practice. I have simply traced out some of the more salient, institutionalized design features at Sera that aspire to fix debate's place as a rite of institution. It is debate's emplacement that helps people see certain things in debate and not others, which means that debate cannot be studied as some isolated ritual event whose significance lies within its perimeter. If we were to neglect the assemblage in which debate has been placed, the ritual drama would be lost. Without observing the care and delicacy with which monks treat authoritative text, we would be numb to the challenger's violence as he attacks these texts, and we would miss the glory that comes from defending doctrine. We would not feel the gravity of collegiate belonging that makes the defendant's claims about the college's curricular texts such a high-stakes affair, that brings his words into earshot of a whole community, a community he may offend, or delight and make proud, even though he is really just sitting cross-legged on a cushion for an hour or so before a clutch of monks in a little corner of the monastery.

Is all of this orderliness just a reflection of something else? A second and more familiar temptation would be to foundationalize this reconstruction of Sera's orderliness, to bolster the assemblage from below with some sturdy underlying doctrine, ideology, culture, or master trope. Imperfect though Sera's orderliness may be, perhaps it is best explained as the output of some durable, underlying, group-relative cognitive code or schemata. Perhaps it is inscribed in the body, in embodied habits that are difficult to shake. Perhaps we are witnessing the sub rosa machinations of ideology, doxa, power, discourse. I do not mean to suggest that these abstractions lack utility, but it would do little justice to Sera's complexity to invoke these at the expense of tracing out features of its discursive landscape (and it does too often come at this expense, as Latour appreciates well); and explanationwise, such abstractions would do precious little, except maybe feed a nostalgia for the halcyon days when disciplines had irreducible objects of knowledge (e.g., language for linguistics, religion for religious studies, the social for sociology, etc.). Those wary of such abstractions may prefer a lighter, less committal "aesthetic," so let us play along, for argument's sake, and give this aesthetic a name. At Sera perhaps what we have from this viewpoint is an "adversative poetic," whose primary metric is, of course, two—a time-honored way to figurate "opposition." Perhaps what we are witnessing is a way of producing moral persons at Sera. One figurates stability—of persons and institutions—through repeated forms of dyadic interactional violence: challenger against defendant, college against college, alliance group of colleges against alliance group, and so on. And as the pattern repeats, each tends to appear more natural, like two mirrors that face each other, from which there is no escape.

Such exercises of consolidation and captioning have their place, so long as we do not conflate achieved coherence with the achievement of coherence (Bourdieu 1977), and so long as we do not forget that it is not entirely clear what is happening on Sera's premises. How many times did I hear, from various quarters, that Sera was prone to repeat the historical failings of its namesake from Tibet? Why, for instance, as one Mey monk complained, do Sera's two colleges in India continue to vie separately for international resources rather than pursue funding jointly? Is the divisiveness cultivated between colleges, both corporate and doctrinal, not a dangerous analogue of a pernicious, centuries-old "sectarianism" that the Dalai Lama has been asking Tibetans to transcend, a sectarianism that could rend the refugee community at a time when it must unite? And doesn't all this allegiance to college and textbook run counter to the aim of ensuring an autonomous, rational-critical engagement with Buddhist doctrine, such that Sera risks sliding back into priestcraft and an outmoded Geluk "scholasticism"? To explore these longer-lasting, slower-motion diasporic disputes over what debate—and monastic education more generally—looks like, modern or retrograde, liberal or illiberal, we first need to appreciate the quick text of this discursive practice, without which debate would not look like anything.

# Debate as a Rite of Institution

Tsongkhapa (1357–1419), founder of what would crystallize into the Geluk sect, is reported to have had repeated visionary encounters with Mañjuśrī, a deity who embodies Buddha's insight into the nature of reality and who, on a more mundane plane, is associated with intelligence, learning, and skill in speech and composition. So close was Tsongkhapa to Mañjuśrī that he could quiz him on thorny matters of doctrine. Mañjuśrī had become his tutor, and Tsongkhapa, in turn, came to be deferred to by the faithful as Mañjuśrī incarnate. Sightings are reported in the hagiographical literature, like the tale of a lama who saw Tsongkhapa melt into Mañjuśrī before his eyes during a tantric initiation (Thurman 1981), and Geluk literature is replete with praise that speaks as if Tsongkhapa and Mañjuśrī were one, a kinship that some take to exemplify the Geluk sect's valorization of reason and confidence in intellectual pursuits, especially debate.

Mañjuśrī, like Tsongkhapa, is invoked frequently at Sera in India. In scroll paintings and statues, he materializes iconographically in forms that range from wrathful to pacific. At one end of the spectrum is Vajrabhairava (*rdo rje 'jigs byed*), with a vast array of weapon-bearing arms and blazing head of an enraged buffalo. At the other sits Mañjuśrī's peaceful manifestation: cross-legged, sword in one hand and copy of the *Perfection of Wisdom* in the other, and wearing a cool, sage countenance. In tantric meditative rites trained on him, monks invoke his agency and review his spectacular attributes, and at the outset of every debate the challenger utters his "seed syllable," *dhīḥ* (Yelle 2003) and recalls his prowess. *Dhīḥ* is a syllable I hear a lot. Outside my window at night young monks belt out his peaceful form's seven-syllable mantra, which ends with *dhīḥ*. When they reach this final seed syllable, the mantra's nucleus, they begin a kind of cantillation with tremolo, repeating *dhīḥ* as

rapidly as they can, for as long as they can, on a single breath, till they slow, sput-
ter, stop, inhale sharply, then begin again. His mantra boosts memory and improves
fluency in speech, I am told, hence its utility for the young and the unsocialized.
Those schooled in the philosophical literature on path structure ("path" structure
being a normative scheme of a Buddhist's stepwise development toward enlightenment) will tell you that the meditative equipoise in which one directly perceives
emptiness involves no conceptual appearances whatsoever, and the mind appears
fused with its object "like fresh water poured into fresh water" (Gyatso and Hopkins 1985:20). Add to such descriptions the tenet that a Buddha's consciousness is
nonconceptual, and you may suspect that the Geluk sect finds conceptuality im-
potent when it comes to the realization of the ultimate. But the Geluk sect main-
tains that conceptuality and analysis are integral to the path forged by Śākyamuni
Buddha, that it is through disciplined intellection that one learns to recognize the
nature of self and the phenomenal world. This "commitment to reason," summarizes Jeffrey Hopkins (2002:20), "and its harmony—albeit in a preparatory way—
with the most profound religious experiences of compassion, wisdom, deity yoga,
and manifestation of the fundamental innate mind of clear light" is, officially at least,
the reason the Geluk order leans heavily on debate-based philosophical inquiry as
a propaedeutic discipline.

Buddhist debate evolved into a prestigious form of learning and language socialization at the major monasteries of the Geluk sect, a sect that emerged as a hegemonic force over much of central Tibet beginning in the mid–seventeenth century.
The inception of Indian Buddhist logic and dialectics in Tibet is typically traced to
the activities of Sangpu Monastery,[1] founded south of Lhasa in the eleventh century, some three centuries before Tsongkhapa's birth.[2] At Sangpu, Ngok Lotsawa
(1059–1109)[3] composed commentaries on Indian Buddhist logic and epistemology (tshad ma; pramāṇa) and helped spread this tradition in Tibet. In this he was
aided especially by Sangpu's fifth abbot, Chapa Chökyi Senge (1109–1169),[4] who
helped vault Sangpu into scholastic prominence. A half millennium before, in the
sixth century, Indian Buddhism experienced its own epistemological turn in which
formal logical means were developed to adjudicate among propositions and establish doctrinal validity (Arnold 2005). In this logico-epistemological tradition, the
writings of Dignāga and Dharmakīrti (sixth and seventh centuries, respectively)
were critical and assumed considerable importance in Tibet as well. In Tibet, though,
there were serious reservations about the place of formal reasoning in Buddhism.
Was formal reasoning, as Atiśa (982–1054) suggested, an intellectualist practice that
was useful for debating non-Buddhists in India but less relevant in Tibet where such
contests didn't exist (Dreyfus 1997a:21)? Was formal reasoning a soteriological art,
or was it more a "secular" practice (or at least not specifically Buddhist) akin, say,
to medicine? Some textual evidence suggests that there were Tibetans during the
twelfth to thirteenth century, for instance, who did not think debate-based inquiry

was organic to Buddhism, and Tsongkhapa's own writings suggest that well into the fourteenth century it was a minority opinion to argue that formal reasoning was soteriological, that it could advance progress on the path to liberation (Jackson 1994). Tsongkhapa was famous for suggesting that formal reasoning could be used even in the analysis of the ultimate.

Tsongkhapa and his disciples founded three monasteries around Lhasa in his lifetime, institutions that came to be known as the "Three Monastic Seats" (*gdan sa gsum*): Ganden, Drepung, and Sera, the last being founded in 1419 by Tsongkhapa's close disciple Sakya Yeshe. The influence of the monastic seats grew considerably after the Geluk sect emerged victorious from its conflict with the Kagyud sect, which had tried to curtail the spread of Geluk influence. With the aid of an army led by Gushri Khan, his Mongol supporter, the Fifth Dalai Lama (1617–82) deposed the Kagyud's patron in 1642, ascended to power, and unified the country. The Geluk state formed, with Lhasa as its capital, and the Fifth Dalai Lama then instituted social and economic reforms that facilitated monasticism's expansion. Land was granted, subsidies provided, and monastic enrollment quotas enforced (if quotas were not met, monasteries were entitled to conscript monks from local communities). The Fifth Dalai Lama's reforms allowed monasticism in Tibet to become, in Melvyn Goldstein's (1989:21) words, not "an otherworldly domain of a minute elite but a mass phenomenon."

With state power consolidated to an unprecedented degree, the three monastic seats came to form the hub of an expansive Geluk field. Smaller, satellite monasteries were distributed across a vast region, reaching Ladakh, parts of Nepal, and Mongolia. The monastic seats of central Tibet became statusful, transregional institutions to which Geluk monks from smaller, provincial monasteries might aspire to come (though only a modest percentage of monks studied philosophy at the monastic seats). As Georges Dreyfus (2003:125–26) notes, the smaller Geluk monasteries were once "scholastic centers in their own right, but they were gradually drawn into the orbit of the three seats and lost their scholarly relevance." (Despite its earlier prominence, Sangpu Monastery itself was reduced to a mere branch of Drepung Monastery in Lhasa.) This consolidation of the Geluk monastic field was at least partly enabled through the standardization of monastic textbooks in the sixteenth and seventeenth centuries, as some have suggested. By replacing local textbooks with those of the three monastic seats, a measure of doctrinal common ground was assured. The replacement of local Geluk textbooks bolstered the status of the three monastic seats in central Tibet, making them premier centers for dialectical training and thereby centralizing and nucleating the field.

For the Geluk monastic seats around Lhasa, and hence for the vast Geluk network of monasteries, debate-based study evolved into the main intellectual pursuit. Though the history of debate's promotion within the Geluk curricula has yet to be written, Dreyfus (2005:293) directs attention to a roughly two-century-long period, from the mid-fifteenth to the mid-seventeenth century, that suggests one major correlation: as debate ascended, the Geluk commentarial industry began to flag and wane. After about 1700, observes Cabezón (1994:84), "Tibetan monastic debate (*rtsod pa*) came to replace commentary as the prevalent form of scholastic exegesis." Dreyfus (2003) notes that the turn away from composition at the Geluk monastic seats in central Tibet at times bordered on suspicion of writing *tout court,* and as elder Geluk monks I met confirmed, there were unlettered Geluk scholars in Tibet who could debate brilliantly but not pen their own names.

## WHAT KIND OF ARGUMENTATION IS THIS?

Studies of Buddhist debate by Tibetologists and Buddhist studies scholars have remained overwhelmingly textualist. Some explain debate by appeal to the philosophical primers monks use when they start the debate-based curriculum. Others examine debate as it appears in and is explicitly theorized by logico-epistemological treatises.[5] While undeniably important, such work is no substitute for an account of debate as a discursive practice. In this scholarship, the speech genre named *rtsod pa* in Tibetan goes by many names, including "dialectics" (Liberman 1992), "debate-logic" (Tillemans 1989), and, perhaps most frequently, "debate" (Perdue 1992). I use "debate," but at least three senses should be divested from this word. First, "debate" suggests a method abstractable from its content and applicable to any topic, yet the debate genre has not been wrested from its Buddhist moorings. It has not been applied to extradoctrinal subject matter (unlike, for example, the extension and promotion of the so-called Socratic method in US law school pedagogy in the nineteenth century; Mertz 2007a); it remains an organic part of the Geluk philosophical curriculum, and of the curricula of other Buddhist sects, as well as the Bön order.[6] Second, "debate" suggests a relatively infrequent event, yet at places like Sera it occurs twice daily for around two hours per session—to say nothing of numerous formal debates or 'defenses' (*dam bca';* see below) that punctuate the monastic calendar. Third, the term implies a contest between individuals who are accorded equal discursive rights and obligations, as in televised debates in US electoral politics. Liberal-democratic principles of "civil" argumentation—like symmetrical rights of participation, rights presupposed in many familiar genres of argumentation—seem irrelevant here. The default participation framework of Tibetan debate is asymmetrical.

A deeper obstacle to understanding this practice is the way we typically approach the study of argumentation. With his charge that formal logic has "lost touch with its application," and with his turn toward "logical *practice*," Stephen Toulmin (1958:9) helped inspire what has been a burgeoning industry of interdisciplinary work on argumentation. At first blush, Toulmin's turn to argumentation may seem congenial to research on argumentation in linguistic anthropology and allied fields,

especially if we consider anthropological interest in the varied "'wranglings' of disputing talk" (Brenneis 1988:221), from presidential debates and children's disputes
to courtroom arguments and labor-management deliberations. Yet the distance between these approaches to argumentation is considerable and needs to be bridged
to understand Buddhist debate. The linguistic anthropological literature has not had
the same preoccupation with normative argumentation (e.g., to promote "critical
thinking" or caution against "fallacies"; Hansen and Pinto 1995; Walton 1995); it
has tended to motivate its claims from transcripts of actual discourse, not from intuitions about or ex post facto reconstructions of argumentation; and it has been
open to a wider range of things argumentation can do (e.g., "sociability" in Jewish
argument; Schiffrin 1984)—to name only a few of the more immediate differences.

The disparity between the literatures is perhaps most acute when we consider
the privilege that the argumentation literature continues to accord to logic's hallowed unit, the proposition, whose canonical linguistic carrier is the declarative
sentence, and whose accompanying view of language is, as Alessandro Duranti
(1997:163) succinctly puts it, "an instrument for informing or describing the
world." When we turn to the anthropological literature on argumentative talk, the
concern with propositionality all but vanishes. Though "taking alternative positions
on the same issue" (Goodwin 1990:156) is sometimes deemed criterial to a "dispute," it is not "ethno"-logic that is of primary concern for these authors. That is, it
is neither the group-relative standards of a well-formed propositional argument that
are sought nor the procedures used to craft one, though such standards and procedures are often noted in passing. Instead, qualities of the interaction command
attention: "oppositional moves" (Goodwin 1990:141); "tropic aggression" (Agha
1996); "unruly" interaction (Haviland 1997).

To understand Buddhist debate we must bridge these approaches to argumentation, and debate, in a sense, forces us to do this through its conspicuous the-
atricality. The bridge I throw down here is admittedly narrow, for it consists of
what may seem to be a rather minor facet of argumentation—demeanor, or more
technically, "demeanor indexicality" (cf. Goffman 1967b). I demonstrate how displays of demeanor in debate are fashioned out of diverse semiotic resources and
parallel the operations monks concurrently perform on the denotational content
of their discourse, what they are wrangling about. This narrow bridge—demeanor
indexicality—has far-reaching, scale-jumping implications, though, because in Tibetan Buddhist debate, denotational textuality and demeanor indexicality conspire
to produce this interaction ritual's core mimetic effects.

## TEXTUALITY AND DEMEANOR

In his reflections on the contemporary study of argumentation, David Fleming
(1996:16) notes that "in the 20th century, the traditional definition of argument as

one or more propositions in support of a further proposition has been called into question." Argumentation theorists turn increasingly to how people interact, to the pragmatic and interactional matrix within which propositional content is expressed and evaluated. Propositions and the utterances that convey them are often recast in pragmatic terms as "assertive speech acts" (e.g., Grootendorst and Van Eemeren 2004:63 ff.), which are viewed, in turn, as building blocks of more complex events of argumentation. To account for the behavioral regularities of such speech events, argumentation theorists then try to figure out the procedural presuppositions, "rules," or schemata that serve as principles for construing and conducting argumentation.

Despite their attempts to "situate" (Fleming 1996:16) arguments in real-time events of interaction, propositional content, and speaker-based stances toward such content (e.g., epistemic modalization), still enjoy pride of place. R. Grootendorst and F. H. van Eemeren, for instance, have developed an influential "pragma-dialectical" theory of argumentation wherein argumentation is defined as "a verbal, social, and rational activity aimed at convincing a reasonable critic of the acceptability of a standpoint by putting forward a constellation of propositions justifying or refuting the proposition expressed in the standpoint" (Grootendorst and Van Eemeren 2004:1). Here, as elsewhere, speakers purportedly express propositions to justify or refute other propositions.

Insofar as arguments are held to consist of at least two propositions ("premise" and "conclusion"), or alternatively of "claims" and "support" whose utterances express propositional content (Fleming 1996:13),[7] they are *textual* achievements, in the expansive sense of involving the "quality of coherence or connectivity" of signs (Hanks 1989:96). Yet they are textual objects of a specific kind, for their cohesiveness in the traditional view is evaluated strictly in terms of the way states of affairs are represented, what Michael Silverstein (1997:267) refers to broadly as "denotational textuality." If this kind of textuality alone were privileged, and debate were studied as some species of "ethno"-logic, to be compared and contrasted with familiar forms of Western logic, attention would be focused too narrowly on denotational textuality, as if discourse were reducible to "syllogistic or inferentially coherent propositional organization of conceptual 'information'" (Silverstein 1997: 267), and as if language in general were reducible to reference and modalized predication. In examining the debate genre, my primary intent is not to extract the ethnological standards by which monks evaluate the denotational content of their discourse as "rational" (e.g., standards of coherence and logical entailment, codified in "rules of inference" or other publicly circulating maxims); nor is it to catalogue exhaustively the operations that monks perform on discourse to induce such evaluations. These concerns, while valuable, would leave unexplained the most visually arresting facet of the debate genre: the way monks look when they practice it. As anyone who sets foot in a Tibetan debating courtyard will attest, the noise is so deafening, the gestures so raucous, that to narrow one's eyes and let in only a sober propositional argument would be to miss what stops observers in their tracks. It would also lead one to miss how debate serves as a rite of institution.

Debate features two primary roles: challenger and defendant.[8] Though procedures can vary slightly from monastery to monastery, only one monk typically inhabits the defendant role for the duration of a debate. And while only one monk initially serves as challenger, in formal, public debates any number of cochallengers from the audience will typically join him. In daily courtyard debate, monks spend most of their time sparring with a partner in a mode of debate called *rtsod zla;* they pair off and take turns inhabiting the roles of challenger and defendant. In formal, public debates termed *dam bca'* ('defense'), which are many and varied, ranging from class debates that convene weekly to annual debates like the Rigchung and Rigchen, the challenger and defendant roles last for the entire debate session. (Makeshift *damcha* can spontaneously arise in the courtyard as well, but these lack the intricate seating arrangement and built environment characteristic of formal defenses.) Behaviorally, challengers stamp their feet, hurl taunts, and deliver loud claps as they argue. The seated defendant, who enjoys a certain gravitas and is assumed to be knowledge-able, responds with a demeanor of poise and unflappability. Why the provocations and the defendant's effort to remain unflappable? Challengers may not simply be try-ing to persuade their opponents, as if their forms of self-presentation could be re-duced to means-ends rhetorical strategies (note how such attempts to explain the effectiveness of sign behavior would neglect to explain why forms of self-presenta-tion look the way they do); nor may defendants simply be trying to uphold a philo-sophical position. In addition, both may be indicating contextual facts about them-selves—what Goffman (1967b) long ago analyzed in terms of "demeanor." That is, they may be publicly marking themselves as *kinds* of people endowed with cultur-ally valorized characterological attributes. To the extent that such signs regularly in-dicate or "index" contextual facts about the speaker, they can be termed "speaker-focal indexicals," or to preserve some of Goffman's original terminology, "demeanor indexicals." The type of demeanor indexicality explored here concerns forms of so-cial personae and personae-attributes linked specifically to speech-event roles.[9]

In Buddhist debate, demeanor indexicality and denotational textuality are in-dissolubly associated. After an initial phase of consensus building, challengers start to rend the interpropositional coherence of authoritative Buddhist doctrine while inciting the defendant with claps, taunts, and other provocations. The seated de-fendant, in response, struggles to preserve a textual ideology of interpropositional coherence while maintaining a demeanor of majestic poise and unflappability. As we shall see, the defendant unifies doctrinal tradition on the plane of denotational textuality and simultaneously enacts tradition's successful unification by way of his demeanor of unflappability. If the defendant is convincing, he mimics how tradi-tion ought to be: stable, coherent, whole.

## PRIMING MONKS FOR THE COURTYARD

Prescriptive treatises that spell out debate's "rules" or catalogue strategies for argumentation are nowhere to be found at Sera. Unlike books like the Roman rhetorician Quintilian's works on the art of oratory, or books on etiquette or pedagogy, there are no debate "manuals" used at Sera that describe with comparable explicitness how to comport oneself in the debating courtyard. Nor can an understanding of debate be reconstructed solely from remarks culled and gleaned from interviews, from what monks say about what they do; commentary on debate elicited from monks neither exhausts nor even accurately represents the operations that can be discovered in actual debates through transcription and close analysis.

Debate-based studies begin with a slim volume called the *Collected Topics* (*bsdus grwa*), which, in a narrow sense, is a class of primer made up of roughly eighteen topics. In its broader sense it is a metonym for "beginning dialectics" (Onoda 1992:38) or introductory "lessons" (Tillemans 1989:266). It is during this initial phase of study, which may last between one and three years, that young monks develop fluency in the debate genre, and once that is achieved, proceed to the study of 'Awareness and Knowledge' (*blo rig*), 'Signs and Reasoning' (*rtags rigs*), and, finally, to the 'Five Great Texts' (*gzhung chen bka' pod lnga*) themselves, which make up the heart of the curriculum. As primers in the Geluk philosophical curriculum and vehicles through which monks acquire fluency in debate, they are of no small importance. These primers contain their first written examples of debate and serve as templates for daily courtyard debates.

There is a telling detail about the internal chapter structure of Mey's *Collected Topics* primer, authored by Geshe Yeshe Wangchuk.[10] The first thirteen lessons account for about 90 percent of this volume's content, and nearly all of the chapters share a tripartite organization. This tripartite structure recurs and is a principle of organization found in the monastic textbook literature read later in the curriculum.[11] In compact form the sequence goes as follows: 'Refute, assert, dispel' (*'gag bzhag spong gsum*). Unfurled, the three name a sequence: '*Refute* other systems, *assert* one's own system, *dispel* objections'.[12] In the primer monks at Mey use (and in those used elsewhere), these sequences constitute the three primary sections of each chapter. (Only two of the thirteen lessons in this primer lack final "dispelling objects" phases, but they still have the first two section types). The first and last phases ("refutation" and "dispelling objections," respectively) are alike in one obvious sense: they both consist of debates, albeit in a much terser format than what you find in the courtyard. Lesson 2, 'shapes and colors' (*dbyibs dang kha dog*), begins like this:

> *gnyis pa gzugs 'chad pa la / dgag bzhag spong gsum las / dang po la / kha cig na re / gzugs yin na / dbyibs kyi gzugs yin pas khyab zer na / sngo ser dkar dmar bzhi po chos can / der thal / de'i phyir/ der thal / kha dog yin pa'i phyir.* (dbang phyug 1997:11–12)

> With respect to the second [lesson], the explanation of forms, [there are] three [sections]: Refute [other systems], assert [one's own system], [and] dispel objections. With respect to the first [section]: If someone says, "Whatever is a form is necessarily the form of a shape," [one responds], "It [absurdly] follows that the four [colors] blue, yellow, white and red, are [shapes], because of [being forms]. That follows, because of [the four] being colors.

The reader is thrust into debates about a topic that has not yet been presented. He finds himself in a virtual courtyard swarming with debaters, their positions introduced with the formula 'If someone says . . . ' (*kha cig na re*). Only after this initial flurry of debate subsides does the author reveal his own positions (*rang lugs*) for the reader. Readers do not learn what the author's positions are, and hence what their own position should be, till after a bout of debate in which other positions (*gzhan lugs*) are refuted. This does not mean that one must study the primer linearly. My tutor at Mey would begin with the middle section on definitions and divisions, then flip back to the debates at the beginning; still, this does not erase the impression that the textbook's architecture leaves on readers through each chapter's internal organization. In most of the lessons, the middle, nondebate section is brief relative to the debates staged before and after it. On balance the lessons lean heavily toward debate.[13] In terms of each chapter's narrative arc, the claims of the textbook author to which allegiance is at least prescriptively owed are thus surrounded by contentiousness, and the contentiousness is thick. Even after the author unveils his own position, he does not shelter his 'definitions' (*mtshan nyid*) and 'divisions' (*dbye ba*) from criticism. In the final "dispelling objections" section, he invites dissent. The dissent is orchestrated, naturally, but it is nonetheless a polyphonic environment, a din of voices of unnamed critics who outnumber the author's own voice. The author does neatly dispose of the criticism he invites, yet the atmosphere of contention is never really dispelled. It infects the entire book. One is left with the impression that doctrinal propositions are inherently precarious and cannot be just memorized and recited, even if the curriculum often encourages this, and even if it often treats and speaks of inherited doctrine as if it were flawless in its coherence.

Viewed as text-artifacts, like palimpsests that contain traces of their natural history (Silverstein and Urban 1996), works like the *Collected Topics* primers can be inspected for how they reflect and refract facts about the historical context of their original inscription (where unnamed, hypothetical defendants are thinly veiled references to actual opponents or sects). But viewed in terms of its stipulative functions, its capacity to supply monks with tacit principles for interpreting what kind of interactional practice debate is, the tripartite chapter structure would seem, at the very least, to issue a caution to novices in the early stages of socialization into debate: mere recapitulation of settled truths is never enough. Defensibility is needed, by means of sound argument.

## TEXTUAL IDEOLOGY:
## CHALLENGERS AND DEFENDANTS

There is a certain textual ideology projected through the reciprocal, mutually re-inforcing effects of a number of discursive practices at Sera, and this ideology in-vites one to view the canon of authoritative books as if they were inherently co-herent. In broadest terms, challengers try to render incoherent the defendant's claims about inherited doctrine by exposing two primary types of denotational-textual con-sistency: consistency with respect to the denotational content of authoritative books reportable in debate, and to claims made by the defendant himself over his turns of talk. Challengers problematize relentlessly while the defendant upholds the textual ideology. One monk put it frankly: 'There are many texts that don't agree, right?' 'Likewise,' he continued, 'within texts, there are many things that don't agree, right?'[14] The defendant, he concluded, needs to show that 'the meaning is the same,'[15] and he does this by resolving signs of interpropositional inconsistency.

Expectations of epistemic commitment differ by speech-event role. By default, epistemic commitment is not expected of challengers, who must counter the de-fendant indefatigably and at any expense, even if it means advancing a baldly coun-terfactual claim. A philosophy tutor of mine once recounted with amusement and admiration how a rhetorically gifted challenger once coaxed a defendant into de-claring that carrots were sentient, a proposition no Gelukpa would accept. One monk reduced this to a rule of thumb: if a defendant says something *is* so, the chal-lenger should counter that it *isn't*, and vice versa. (A verb phrase sometimes used to describe this kind of relentless problematization is *gnod byed gtang ba,* which may be glossed as 'to attack' or 'to assail.') Monks who inhabit the challenger role bedevil the defendant, and must. They should not succumb to favoritism or dis-crimination. Friendships are to be suspended, and status ignored. No heed is to be paid to the defendant's identity whatsoever. In certain cases—cases where one's own teacher sits as defendant—most monks confessed that they tended to be more cir-cumspect, less likely to deliver the most cutting taunts. Certainly they would re-frain from the more outrageous stunts, like trying to grab the stubble on the de-fendant's scalp while uttering the *'khor gsum* taunt (see below). Some recommended using honorific forms liberally when reincarnate lamas sit as defendants. (I looked at this systematically in a handful of debates and noticed not only a tendency for challengers to use honorific forms for such high-status defendants but also that the onset of taunts occurred later when the defendant was a reincarnate lama rather than an ordinary monk.) Still, the vast majority stated that challengers are obliged to be—to use a much maligned word—objective. Challengers should perform op-erations on the defendant's discourse regardless of who the defendant is and what challengers themselves really think about the matter, and I should add that in non-debate contexts monks involved in the curriculum can be quite firm and forthcoming with their opinions on a range of philosophical issues. In contrast to the challenger, the defendant is obliged to evaluate the propositions thrust at him and have a thesis, and from him epistemic commitment is indeed expected.[16] It is the defendant's knowledgeability that is on trial. It is where he stands that counts.

## REDUCTIO AD ABSURDUM: WHAT CHALLENGERS DO

To induce inconsistency, challengers perform operations on the defendant's discourse, including an oft-reported mode of argumentation termed 'consequences' (*thal 'gyur*) that monks first learn in their primers.[17] "Formally," summarizes Dreyfus (2003:47), "consequences are set apart from arguments by their use of the format 'it follows . . . because' (*thal phyir*) instead of 'it is . . . because'." Some have compared consequences to enthymemes, syllogisms with an unstated premise held by the addressee but not (necessarily) the speaker. Consequences show up robustly in Tibetan texts from the fifteenth century onward (Hugon 2008), and, philosophically, consequences (*thal 'gyur*) are associated with the Middle Way Consequentialist School (*dbu ma thal 'gyur ba, prāsaṅgika-mādhyamika*), which Tibetan exegetes across sects have generally taken to be the pinnacle of Buddhist "schools." The scare quotes should remind us that these so-called schools must be appreciated as "hermeneutical devices intended to bring order to a wide variety of individual texts and ideas" (Dreyfus and McClintock 2003:1–2); this association between school and mode of reasoning should not be treated as a historical link, since consequences were evident in India, but the division of Middle Way philosophy into 'Consequentialists' (*thal 'gyur ba, prāsaṅgika*) and 'Autonomists' (*rang rgyud pa, svātantrika-mādhyamika*) is a Tibetan innovation.

Consequentialists assert that when a defendant is intellectually primed, a consequence can trigger in the opponent "a consciousness that infers the implied opposite meaning" (Hopkins 1996a:445). Of the sample debates found in the primers, one of the most elementary is the well-known "colors" debate initiated by a hypothetical opponent: "If someone says, 'Whatever is a color is necessarily red, [the challenger responds],' it [absurdly] follows that the subject, the color of a white religious conch, is red because of being a color" (Perdue 1992:222–23). Though transparently absurd, this debate is a vehicle through which monks begin socialization into the genre. Consequences can be schematically represented as follows:

1. [ . . . *a* . . . ]ₙₚ *chos can*          [the topic,] *a*
          TOP

2. [ . . . *b* . . . ]ₙₚ *yin par thal*    [it] follows that [it] is *b*
          be-NZR.ACC follows

3. [ . . . *c* . . . ]ₙₚ *yin pa'i phyir*    because of being *c*
          be-NZR.GEN because

As Tom Tillemans (1989) observes, *chos can* is a register-specific topicalizer. It marks the end of the topicalized segment (typically a noun phrase) and the right edge of an intonation unit. Faced with a consequence, the defendant responds by evaluating it, and he evaluates it by using one of a handful of canonical response types. If the challenger ends his turn on an 'it follows that'-clause (*thal*), the defendant responds either affirmatively, with '[I] accept [that]' (*'dod*), or negatively, with 'why?' (*ci'i phyir*). If he concludes with a 'because'-clause (*phyir*), the defendant has two choices other than acceptance (*'dod*). He may respond with 'the reason [is] not established' (*rtags ma grub*) or 'there is no pervasion' (*khyab pa ma byung*).[18] Other, less frequent responses do exist, but these are primary.

As for the example of the opponent who asserts, absurdly, that all colors are necessarily red, it is telling that the challenger does not try to establish the antithesis, that *not* all colors are red. In an act of transposition, he instead hypothetically inhabits the defendant's ground. This is no gesture of sympathy or compromise but a bid to demonstrate just how unreasonable the defendant's premise is: reductio ad absurdum.

When challengers utter consequences, they perform a visually arresting kinesic sequence that culminates in an explosive open-palmed hand-clap:

> When the Challenger first puts his question to the sitting Defender, his right hand is held above the shoulder at the level of his head and the left hand is stretched forward with the palm turned upward . . . . At the end of his statement the Challenger punctuates by loudly clapping together his hands and simultaneously stomping his left foot. Then he immediately draws back his right hand with the palm held upward and at the same time holds forth his left hand with the palm turned downward. (Perdue 1992:29)

Elements of the challenger's clap sequence are routinely glossed through explicit metadiscourses (discourses about discourse) that stipulate what each gesture "means." The sound waves (*sgra*) that ripple out when you stamp your left foot and clap your hands are the resonating sounds of dharma being spread; the foot stomp is the trouncing of "pride" or the closing off of bad future rebirths for fellow sentient beings; the right hand raised above the head is Mañjuśrī's sword that slices through ignorance. Many glosses exist, and while these emblematic gestures are all typified as benevolent, the martial idiom—the fact that these signs look awfully similar to a physical strike—is difficult to pass over and may suggest why these gestures should be glossed at all with such fastidious care. You probably would not need to explain them if there weren't the risk of misconstrual. Noninitiates are prone to misconstrue the challenger's clap sequence as vulgar ("literal," nonmetaphoric) aggression, as the monks I interviewed frequently noted. Asked to recount their first impressions of debate, my interlocutors often laughed, then confessed that they were shocked at first. "It looked sort of strange," one admitted. "I sort of thought to myself, 'Why are they fighting?'"[19] Another said that debate initially "looked strange"[20]

FIGURE 2. Clap sequence (Sera Mey, 2000)

and that "if [you] talk to outside[rs], [they'd say] a fight has broken out, right?"[21] He added that his father disliked debate because it looked too combative, and discouraged his son from practicing it. But what his father failed to see, he continued, is that it "isn't real anger" that is expressed in debate,[22] as evidenced by the fact that after a debate ends, no residual hostility is said to exist. One can go and sip a soda with an opponent in the local canteen. Warnings about taking debate's martial idiom literally were conveyed to me with some urgency when I first visited Sera Mey. I was cautioned about the 'bad words' (*tshig nyen*) I might hear in the debating courtyard, like 'idiot' (*lkugs pa*) and 'donkey' (*bong gu*). Technically, such words are not permitted but slip out (*shor ba*) anyway, one monk explained. Doctrinally, consequences catalyze learning in defendants, but the kinesic accompaniments iconically figure this method as a kind of violence (fig. 2).

To return to the color debate, a hypothetical opponent absurdly claims that if something is a color it is necessarily red. To induce incoherence, the challenger need only propose a color that isn't red, and assert that it (absurdly) must be red if the defendant's premise were upheld. While straightforward, a number of recurrent problematical topics exist—for instance, nonexistent phenomena like 'rabbit horns' (*ri bong rwa*)—which complicate philosophical matters considerably and serve as excellent fodder for debate. Before challengers introduce such topics, they elicit claims from the defendant, then typically restate them. Challengers create a public record of the defendant's claims, preparing the ground for the charge of inconsistency. Restatements are not always innocent, for skillful debaters can alter the defendant's discourse during uptake to make it vulnerable to the charge of inconsistency. Challengers may, for instance, make denotationally explicit what was only presupposed in the defendant's discourse. Or they may transpose a claim from colloquial Tibetan into the less-forgiving consequence format. Such transpositions are hazardous for the defendant, for they turn tentative lines into indelible claims, which partly explains why defendants frequently break register, shifting *into* rather than out of colloquial Tibetan, when they feel cornered. As Dreyfus (2003:45) notes, debate permits "the use of lawful tricks such as play of words, dissimulation of conclusions, addition of useless propositions to mask the real topic, or use of false premises." The operations surveyed above have a specific distribution in debate, though. The event begins not with aggressive problematization but with consensus building,[23] and a measure of deference, as we can see by turning to an actual debate.

## DEBATE AT SERA MEY: A CLOSE READING

In July 2000, Sera Mey monastic college began preparing for its annual Rigchung series of debates slated for August. Rigchung debates are intracollegiate and reserved for monks finishing the roughly six-year philosophical course of study known as the 'Perfection of Wisdom' (*phar phyin*).[24] Unlike twice-daily courtyard debates, these 'defenses' (*dam bca'*) enjoy a proud place in the monastic calendar, and obtaining candidacy is no easy feat. Eligibility is based primarily on exam scores, though exceptions are frequently made for monks who enjoy reincarnate lama status. Mey permits only sixteen candidates annually. Weeks before the Rigchung commences, the candidates make rounds through the college's regional houses (*khang mtshan*), where they serve as defendants.[25] It can be harrowing to pass from regional house to regional house and be subjected to criticism in each, but it conditions you well for the big event, some say.

Posted on the wall near the door of our regional house's small assembly hall are two pages listing the Rigchung's eight topics; below those pages is a neat, white computer-printed sheet. The sheet features a table whose cells contain the names of the challengers scheduled to face the visiting defendants in verbal combat. Almost all the challengers hail from our regional house, though a couple come from one of Mey's smaller regional houses, because that house is too small to host a debate on its own. Each evening of debate is split into two debates, each roughly forty-five minutes in length, the first of which I consider here. For each of the two forty-five-minute debate sessions, two local monks are listed and will serve as lead challengers. One starts the debate in a one-on-one fashion, in front of everyone; the other joins after a spell, and then the event becomes open, in principle, to everyone in the hall, though the junior members seated in the back would never get up to do anything

other than fetch and serve tea to participants, since they have not yet begun studying the material covered in these debates. To participate, all you have to do is get
up from your cushion, step outside to fetch the sandals you left by the door, and
then shuffle back in to join the fray.

This evening I had set up my video recorder and tripod well in advance and
waited inside for the guest defendant to be ushered in. This defendant hailed from
an area in eastern Tibet and had come to Sera a decade ago, I later learned. He had
sold cattle in Tibet as an adolescent—a fact that some monks found amusing—but
at age twenty-one decided to become a monk and, like so many others I met, braved
the treacherous overland trek from Tibet into Nepal by foot.

The evening's topic was 'refuge' (*skyabs 'gro*), the foundational commitment that
Buddhists cultivate toward the 'Three Jewels' (*dkon mchog gsum*)—that is, the Buddha, his teachings, and his religious community. This was the defendant's topic,
the topic on which he would need to debate before the whole of Sera Mey in August. In distinguishing the'distinctive refuge' (*skyabs 'gro khyad par can*) of a Buddhist from the 'ordinary refuge' (*skyabs 'gro phal pa*) of a non-Buddhist, monks
often ask: Is distinctive refuge to be posited in terms of an individual's commitment to certain *objects* of refuge (viz. the Buddha, his teachings, or his community), or do subjective factors matter? Early in this debate, for instance, the challenger asks the defendant whether distinctive refuge should be posited by way of
objective or subjective criteria. Are the "objects of refuge" *themselves* distinctive,
he asks, and are they criterial for distinctive refuge? The objects of refuge are criterial, the defendant responds, but slips in a caveat. He adds that it is not 'merely'
(*tsam)* the objects of refuge that are criterial. He is wary of saying that the objects
of refuge alone are criterial because, to put it crudely, appearances can be deceiv-
ing. Case in point: a Buddha who chooses to appear as a non-Buddhist deity. This
is a problematic topic raised repeatedly in this debate. If one tries to posit "distinctive" refuge solely on the basis of the objects of refuge, then it would absurdly
follow that non-Buddhists who take refuge in a non-Buddhist deity would be Buddhists. The defendant, of course, anticipates this criticism and makes space for subjective factors. He argues that it is on the basis of a cognitive state, 'discriminat-
ing awareness' (*'du shes*), that distinctive refuge should be posited, not the objects
of refuge alone. But again, the defendant adds the caveat that distinctive refuge
isn't 'merely' (*tsam*) based on subjective criteria either, for if one were to hold that
position—that only subjective criteria mattered—one would lose sight of the Buddha, his teachings, and his community. Without some reference to the objects of
refuge, distinctive refuge would make little sense. The defendant, in brief, tries to
steer clear of objectivist and subjectivist extremes. In fact, the topic of Buddha man-
ifesting in a non-Buddhist form preys upon a weakness in a claim to which the
defendant committed himself early in the debate. The defendant accepted the position that refuge in any of the Three Jewels, the objects of refuge, is necessarily

the distinctive refuge of a Buddhist. This claim says nothing—nothing explicit at least—about the relevance of subjective factors and thus begins to buckle and sway under the weight of this topic.

### The Seat of Knowledgeability

Indoor debates unfold, scenographically, in well-scripted built environments. Like other assembly halls at Sera, this prayer hall has parallel rows of crimson cushions set on a smooth, cool, carpetless floor. At the hall's rear is an elevated thronelike seat reserved for the defendant, offering a time-honored iconism: relative seat height figurates relative status. Behind this "throne" is an altar area on which statues and images "of" Buddhas, bodhisattvas, lineage masters, and protector deities are arrayed. The genitive *of* begs qualification, since these are not symbols that stand for their objects by means of a conventional rule. They are not treated as mere mnemonic triggers for exegetically learned meanings, as are glosses that equate Mañjuśrī's 'sword' with Buddha's 'wisdom'. A practice of glossing symbols in this manner does exist (in tantric Buddhist meditation, for example, where one mentally reviews the symbolism of one's own body visualized as a deity), but this practice coexists, often uneasily, with an orientation toward signs based upon sympathetic ties (in Peircean semiotic terms, indexical-iconicity). These signs manifest what they resemble by means of their resemblance. Mañjuśrī, in whatever material medium he should appear—clay or bronze or painted cloth—is to be treated as Mañjuśrī incarnate. He is *there,* potentially anyway, a potentiality suggested by the way monks pay deference to these figures: at the feet of these figures sits a ledge on which offerings are arranged with punctilious care. White offering scarves are draped around the necks of statues and over scroll paintings, as if high-status humans. Tea, when distributed to monks in the room, is offered to these agents first, before any human gets a taste. They are treated as if they were alive,[26] which means that the defendant has the presence of "tradition" quite literally behind his back. His front-to-back bodily orientation parallels the figures on the altar behind him (fig. 3). He appears contiguous with tradition, though he juts out from this exalted assembly as if he were tradition's envoy—and in a sense he is.

That the defendant's seat in this indoor debate is redolent of "knowledgeability" is also suggested by two institutional practices at Sera Mey. First, it is a policy that debate participants with reincarnate lama status get assigned the defendant role, not the challenger role.[27] Second, eligibility to participate in the annual Rigchung debates is based in large part on one's numerical rank, which, in turn, is determined on the basis of formal examinations. The Rigchung debates are made up of eight separate debates, each of which addresses a distinct topic within the Perfection of Wisdom course of study. For each of the eight topics, and thus for each debate, a challenger-defendant (C–D) pairing is required, yielding sixteen participants annually. Revealingly, in cases where two ordinary monks (i.e., not reincarnate lamas)

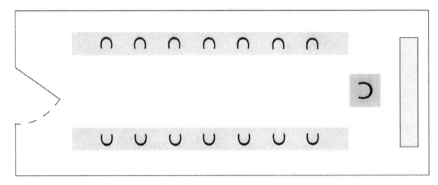

FIGURE 3. Seating configuration for the debate

debate each other, the monk with the higher examination rank is assigned the role of defendant, while the lower-ranking member serves as challenger. These policies correlate *relative rank* (as reckoned in terms of exam scores, and reincarnate versus nonreincarnate religious status) and C–D *role inhabitance* in debate. The defendant position, in other words, is positioned as more statusful than that of challenger.

Another way in which the defendant role, at least in *damcha* (*dam bca'*) debate, is presupposed as the position of knowledgeability can be found in the behavior of senior monks. I commonly observed, and heard many others describe in interviews, how more senior and statusful monks (e.g., those who have already obtained their Geshe degree, and especially elder teachers and abbots), are less apt to stand and adopt the demeanor of a challenger when they wish to argue with a defendant. When such statusful monks *do* participate, they tend to remain seated, and in place of a blistering clap, they tend to snap their fingers. Claps, if they occur, are weak. They lack the physical and acoustic intensity characteristic of the challenger's canonical clap. The senior and more statusful monks pull back from the prescribed demeanor of the challenger in at least two respects: their retention of a seated posture, and the way they mute and curb the emblematic gestures expected from a challenger. This role distance (Goffman 1961), coupled with social facts about their status, creates a vivid correlation for their publics: high-status monks need not, and should not, comport themselves like challengers. Status appears to be figured through the conspicuous absence of exertion: no standing; no wild, labor-intensive gesticulation. Perhaps this minimal kinesic expenditure figurates minimal cognitive effort. So seasoned are they as debaters, so learned in Buddhist doctrine, that they don't need to try hard. Whatever the second-order, speaker-focal indexical effects are understood to be, at the very least it is made clear to all that acting like a challenger isn't something higher-status monks do.

The defendant's fate cannot be read off his statusful seat, though. The irony, lost on nobody, and certainly not lost on the defendant, is that his seat appears to have been prepared for a high-ranking personage. Homologous seating arrangements elsewhere suggest this. In Sera Mey's main assembly hall, for instance, altar, throne, and long rows of crimson cushions are arranged similarly, but, crucially, only the abbot or abbot emeritus[28] would dare occupy the hall's premier seat. And therein lies the rub. The monks at this regional house have reverently invited the defendant into the nucleus of their prayer hall as if he were an exalted personage, a veritable Buddha incarnate, yet he lacks the pedigree. It is this inconsistency, then, between the status of the seat and the status of occupant that sparks dramatic tension. The defendant is placed in a position where if he fails to uphold tradition he will find himself engaged in an act of profanation—sitting high up, elevated on a throne, with a pantheon of Buddhist figures watching. No coronation rite awaits him. Unlike the abbot seated in the main assembly hall, the defendant's knowledgeability is called into question as the debate unfolds, even if it is not called into question immediately.

### Debate Begins: Consensus, Wholeness

Once the defendant mounts his seat, the debate begins. It begins in a hushed and deferential manner, as the debates I observed typically did. In this debate, a lone challenger paces toward the defendant, then halts a few feet away. There he delivers a subdued clap and utters a formula used to start debates, yet with such ellipsis and reduction that what escapes his lips is only the last word, barely intelligible. Daniel Perdue explains the full expression using oral commentary:

> The Challenger begins the debate with the statement "*Dhīḥ!* The subject, in just the way [Mañjuśrī debated] (*dhīḥ ji ltar chos can*)." According to Denma Lochö Rinpochay, the meaning of this statement is: "Just as Mañjuśrī stated subjects in order to overcome the wrong views and doubts of opponents, so I with a good mind will do also." (Perdue 1992:29)

Glossing it as such, the challenger frames the debate as a reenactment of Mañjuśrī's debates with opponents of old. With Mañjuśrī invoked, the challenger then presents the defendant with a sentence fragment. In this debate, he drew the fragment from Khedrup Denpa Dhargye's (1995) *General Meaning Commentary* on Maitreya's *Clear Ornament of Realization,* a textbook used during the Perfection of Wisdom course of studies. As is customary, the fragment consists of three syllables extracted from the end of a line of the challenger's choosing. As for the line's provenance, in this case he drew it from the chapter on refuge on which the defendant will debate in August. The defendant must now identify the clauses from which the syllables were torn and cite the complete line with fidelity. If the defendant fails to identify the correct sentence from which the syllables were torn, or if he hesitates, the first taunt—a chorus of *yo phyir* (see below)—is likely to ring out across the room, though the audience typically exhibits more patience with the defendant's responses at this early stage of debate. As for the three syllables, the line in the textbook to which these belong reads:

> *dang po de med na / skyabs su 'gro 'dod kyi blo mi 'byung / phyi ma de med na skyabs yul log par* **'gyur ba'i phyir.** (mkhas-grub 1995:196–97; boldface indicates the trisyllabic sentence fragment)

> Since if [one] lacks the former, a mind desiring refuge will not arise. If [one] lacks the latter, [one] will end up turning away from the objects [of] refuge.

This line is part of a passage on how to rely on the Three Jewels. The two conditions alluded to in this line are (a) an awareness of how one suffers in cyclic existence, and (b) faith that the Three Jewels can protect one from such suffering. This is what transpires at the start of the debate (for clarity, textbook citations are underlined in the free translation column; boldface in the debate transcript designates the defendant's speech; < clap > indicates an audible open-palmed hand-clap by the challenger):

C: 1a   *[dhīḥ, ji ltar]* *°chos can°*  
       cööjɛn  
       subject  
*[dhīḥ, the] subject [just as Mañjuśrī debated it]*

1b  *°'gyur ba'i phyir zer°*  
      gyur-wɛ      cir-s  
      become-NZR.GEN because-QT  
*[the text says] "because one will come"*

D: 2  *'a*  
     ʔä  
     INT  
*ah?*

C: 3  *°'gyur ba'i phyir°*  
     gyur-wɛ      cir  
     become-NZR.GEN because  
because one will come

D: 4a  *'gyur ba'i phyir*  
     gyur-wɛ      cir  
     become-NZR.GEN because  
because one will come?

4b  *log par 'gyur ba'i phyir yin da*  
    lɔgbar           gyur-wɛ     cir     yintaa  
    turn.away-NZR.LOC/DAT become-NZR.GEN because P.FCT.DIR.ASR  
[the line] is because one will come to turn away, so take note!

C: 5  *'m*  
     ʔmˀ  
     (minimal response)  
(minimal response)

D: 6  *skyabs yul log par 'gyur ba'i phyir zer*  
    gyöbyüü    lɔgbar          gyur-wɛ     cir-s  
    refuge.object turn.away-NZR.LOC/DAT become-NZR.GEN because-QT  
[it says] "because one will come to turn away from the objects of refuge"

C: 7a °*skyabs yul log par 'gyur ba'i phyir zer*°
gyàbyüü lɔgbar gyur-wɛ cǐr-s
refuge.object turn.away-NZR.LOC/DAT become-NZR.GEN because-QT

[it says] "because one will come to turn away from the objects of refuge"

7b °*da ma yin par thal ya*°
ta mɔyimbɔ taa-ya
now NEG-be-NZR.LOC/DAT follows-NZR

now, it follows that it isn't

<< clap >>

7c *phyi ma de yog red pa*
cǐmɔ tɛ yɔɔrepaa
latter.one DET AUX.NOM.CSQ

there is the latter, right?

D: 8 '*m*=
ʔm?
(minimal response)

(minimal response)

C: 9a = *phyi ma de med na*
cǐmɔ tɛ mɛɛ̀-na
latter one DET AUX-COND

[it says] "because if the latter is lacking

9b °*skyabs yul log par 'gyur ba'i phyir zer*]°
gyàbyüü lɔgbar gyur-wɛ cǐr-s
refuge.object turn.away-NZR.LOC/DAT become-NZR.GEN because-QT

one will come to turn away from the objects of refuge"

D:10a ]*phyi ma de med na*
cǐmɔ tɛ mɛɛ̀-na
latter.one DET AUX-COND

[it says] "because if the latter is lacking,

10b *skyabs yul log par 'gyur ba'i phyir zer*
gyàbyüü lɔgbar gyur-wɛ cǐr-s
refuge.object turn.away-NZR.LOC/DAT become-NZR.GEN because-QT

[one] will come to turn away from the objects of refuge"

C: 11 *da dang po* °*ga re gzhag ga*°
ta taŋbo kare shaà-gaa
now first what posit-VLQ.INJ

now what shall you posit [as] the first?

D: 12a *dang po de med na*
taŋbo tɛ mɛɛ̀-na
first DET AUX-COND

[it says] "if the first is lacking

<< clap >>

12b *skyabs su 'gro 'dod kyi blo mi 'hyung zer*
gyàb-su dro dɔ̈ɔ̈-gi lɔ̈ mi-juŋ-s
refuge-LOC go wish-GEN mind NEG-arise-QT

the mind desiring refuge will not arise"

C: 13 *a ni*
ɔ̄ni
then

then?

D: 14a *phyi ma de med na*
cǐmɔ tɛ mɛɛ̀-na
latter.one DET AUX-COND

[it says] "because if the latter is lacking,

...

**14b**  *skyabs yul log par 'gyur ba'i phyir zer*

    gyɔbyüü      lɔgbar           gyur-wɛ      cir-s

    refuge.object turn.away-NZR.LOC/DAT become-NZR.GEN because-QT

<u>one will come to turn away from the objects of refuge"</u>

C: 15    °*skyabs yul log par 'gyur ba'i phyir zer*°

    gyɔbyüü      lɔgbar           gyur-wɛ      cir-s

    refuge.object turn.away-NZR.LOC/DAT become-NZR.GEN because-QT

[it says] <u>"because one will come to turn away from the objects of refuge"</u>

Note that the challenger and defendant reassemble the textbook's source clauses in a roughly dialogic fashion (fig. 4). The defendant offers some pieces; the challenger, others. As for the direction of their reconstructive artistry, they begin with the end, 'because of coming' (*gyur ba'i phyir*), then work backward. After reconstructing the source citation, the phase often termed 'establishing the outline' (*sa bcad sgrub*) begins. The defendant must now locate this citation within the textbook's dense, hierarchical 'outline' (*sa bcad*). He names the section that houses the line, then proceeds upward. Rung by rung, hand over hand, the defendant ascends the scaffolding of the book's outline, climbing up and out. Each laborious step is made under the challenger's prodding ('From where does that derive?' [*ga nas 'phros pa*]). Challenger and defendant thus jointly cotextualize the original discourse fragment, figuratively restoring its wholeness by locating it within the bounded and cohesive textual universe of the textbook. Toward the close of this outline phase, which lasts approximately four minutes, the challenger returns to the source citation, but this time using the consequence mode of argumentation. Problematization begins, which marks the beginning of the debate proper, a phase sometimes called the 'actual session' (*dngos gzhi*).

### Demeanor

How do challenger and defendant comport themselves at the start, during the citation phase? With regard to the defendant, let us first consider resources for signaling mood and epistemic modality, since these help motivate demeanor-indexical readings. As Asif Agha (1993) clarifies, the *yin* auxiliary contrasts with the *red* auxiliary along several dimensions: aspect, epistemic modality, and a verbal-indexical category he labels "participant role perspective." In terms of participant role perspective, *yin*, unlike *red*, indexes speech-act participants. It indexes speaker-perspective in statements and addressee-perspective in questions.[29] Through an examination of the interaction effects of the *yin* auxiliary with co-occurring topical noun phrases, Agha (1993:156) identifies distinct types of "factive 'certainty.' " Line 4b is an assertoric mood construction whose *yin* auxiliary thus indexes speaker-perspective, yet the antecedent topic (i.e., the citation from the textbook that reads "because one will come to turn away") appears noncongruent: it does not denote anything

| Speaker (Line #) | (Initial Fragment) |
|---|---|

C(1b)               *'gyur ba'i phyir*
D(4b)               *log par 'gyur ba'i phyir*
D(6d)               *skyabs yul log par 'gyur ba'i phyir*
C(7c)          *phyi ma de*
C(9a)          *phyi ma de med na skyabs yul log par 'gyur ba'i phyir*
C(11c)   *dang po*
D(12a)   *dang po de med na*
D(12b)        *skyabs su 'gro 'dod kyi blo mi 'byung*

*dang po de med na skyabs su 'gro 'dod kyi blo mi 'byung / phyi ma de med na skyabs yul log par 'gyur ba'i phyir*

(Reconstructed Line)

(Bolded text indicates parts of source clauses contributed by (C)hallenger and (D)efendant)

FIGURE 4. Dialogic reconstruction of source clauses from textbook

straightforwardly about the speaker. What meaning in context might this fractional congruence yield? The *yin* auxiliary implies some type of "personal" association between speaker and the textbook citation. Since the defendant's line is recognizable as a memorized citation, this would most likely yield a recollection-perspective epistemic stance effect (" . . . as I recall"), an effect that is common in debate.

This epistemic stance effect is relevant primarily in the construction of demeanor indexicality rather than for the way it expresses certainty about the propositional content of the utterance; that is, its interactional, rather than strictly denotational, values are foregrounded in debate. The defendant appears to foreground *his* recollection of the book, an effect he combines, revealingly, with the directive-assertive mood marker *da* (/taa/) (Agha 1993:240–42). The defendant projects a demeanor of "knowledgeability," an attribute expected of those who occupy the most exalted seat in the room. And this demeanor is also reinforced in at least two other ways. When the challenger repeats the defendant's words in line 7a, he lowers his voice. In 10a–b, the defendant repeats what the challenger says, yet no parallel drop in volume occurs. In contrast, the defendant's utterance overlaps with the challenger's. The defendant, in short, seems eager to demonstrate his knowledgeability.

As for the challenger, consider again his first utterance, which was marked by considerable ellipsis and reduction. The challenger also bowed slightly, delivered a mild clap (not a full clap sequence), and smiled (fig. 5). When these verbal and nonverbal behaviors are viewed together, it makes it seem like he draws back from the expected demeanor of a challenger—a kind of cross-modal role distance. The challenger also makes no effort to overturn the defendant's claims to knowledgeability or to stake claims about his own competence. While the defendant uses directive-assertive mood marking (line 4b), the challenger responds with a minimal response (line 5). Further, the challenger uses a confirmation-seeking question in line 7c. Had he chosen another type of interrogative construction (a WH question or a YN question) he could have demanded a more propositionally contentful response.[30] Little attention is called to his role as challenger, even less to his own competence.

FIGURE 5. Commencement of the debate

### Unsettling the Defendant

Though the challenger tolerates the defendant's self-positioning as knowledgeable, something else is stirring in this interaction, something that augurs an altogether different future for the defendant. At line 7b, and immediately after the segment transcribed above, the challenger utters: '[It] follows that [it] isn't' (*ma yin par thal*). This expression is a harbinger of criticism to come, for it indicates that problematization is imminent.[31] The challenger then asks the defendant to "establish the outline." In response, the defendant names the superordinate section and proceeds "up" the textbook's outline. As the defendant does this, the challenger begins to alter the way he restates the defendant's claims. Earlier, the challenger had often framed his restatements with the quotative clitic -*s* (e.g., lines 7a and 15) and uttered them with decreased loudness. The quotative clitic marks the end of the represented speech segment, indicating that the prior segment is not authored by the speaker. (No distinction analogous to "direct," "indirect," or "quasi-direct" reports is directly inferable from -s usage alone.) Since the quoted segment is independently recognizable as a textbook citation, the value of the author variable is likely inferable as the text-artifact itself, though, importantly, monks claim to access doctrinal tradition through the very means of the text-artifact. We might gloss such lines more fully as '[As the text/tradition says,] . . . '

In lines 7a and 15 above, the challenger repeats the defendant's lines with word-for-word fidelity, but with lower relative loudness and with quotative clitic framing. In these ways, the challenger seems to ratify the defendant's claims. As the debate unfolds, however, the challenger begins using the matrix clause verb *byas* (/cɛɛ̀/) rather than the quotative clitic -s when restating the defendant's discourse. In colloquial Tibetan, *byas* is the perfective form of the agentive verb 'to do' (*byed* (/ceè/). As Goldstein (Goldstein, Shelling, and Surkhang 2001:733) notes, *byas* is also sometimes used as a verb of speaking, a use evident in debate as well. Consider the following lines:

**D: 38** *skyabs gsum spyi yi rnam gzhag bshad pa zer*    [the text says] **'Explanation of**
gyə̄bsum  jī-yi  nāmshaà  shēèba-s    **the General Presentation of**
three.refuges general-GEN presentation explanation-QT  **the Three Refuges'**

**C: 39** °*skyabs gsum spyi yi rnam gzhag bshad pa byas*°  [you] say 'Explanation of the
gyə̄bsum  jī-yi  nāmshaà  shēèba  cɛ̀è  General Presentation of the
three.refuges general-GEN presentation explanation say  Three Refuges'

In line 38 the defendant frames his utterance with the quotative clitic. In response, the challenger lowers his voice, repeats the defendant's utterance, yet substitutes -s with *byas*. The matrix clause verb here spotlights the defendant's act of reporting: this is what the *defendant* claims tradition says. Not all subsequent restatements are framed with *byas*, but the challenger uses *byas* frequently as the citation phase of the debate draws to a close. He increasingly positions the defendant as someone who makes personal claims, which may—or crucially, may *not*—be the same as tradition's.

As the citation phase draws to a close, the challenger, who has now been joined on the floor by a second challenger, asks: 'What definition of refuge do [you] posit?'[32] The defendant hesitates, deliberates. The challenger issues the question again. Perhaps sensing danger, the defendant offers a definition but with the caveat that it is only a 'general definition of refuge' (*spyir stang skyabs 'gro mtshan nyid*). The challenger then reads the defendant's definition back to him using the *byas* framing, suggesting that this is what the *defendant* says, not necessarily what *tradition* says. The challenger then asks the defendant to confirm that there are two types of refuge, 'ordinary refuge' (*skyabs 'gro phal pa*) and 'distinctive refuge' (*skyabs 'gro khyad par can).* The distinction between 'ordinary' and 'distinctive' refuge is widely accepted and is used to distinguish Buddhist from non-Buddhist forms of refuge. The defendant readily confirms this, and the challenger, with decreased loudness, restates the defendant's claim, using *byas* framing: '°[You] say [there are] two°' (°*gnyis byas*°).

All seems to be well, they seem to be on the same page, but with the defendant's discourse on record, the challenger suddenly doubles back to the source clauses that started the debate. Using elements of the consequence mode of argumentation, he argues that the two causes of refuge—the causes stated in the textbook they had jointly reconstructed—are necessary for distinctive refuge. Once these are transposed into the consequence format, the defendant is reluctant to agree. He responds that the 'reason is not established' (*rtags ma grub*); he presumably holds that it does not necessarily follow that distinctive refuge cannot be developed without these two causes. The challenger then argues that if that were so it would follow that the textbook doesn't speak of these two causes at all—which of course is absurd, since these were the lines they jointly reconstructed at the outset of the debate! The defendant must disagree with this proposition, and does. Though the two conditions for generating refuge are indeed articulated in the textbook, the defendant qualifies the passage: "Now, [that passage] is [just] a way of explaining the term,"[33] implying that it may not be designed to withstand the acid test of reason. (He can't fault the text, of course.) The challenger, in short, tries to position the defendant as someone on the verge of a blatant contradiction. He could have elected to position the defendant more charitably by trying, for example, to ferret out his underlying 'intent' (*dgongs pa*). Geluk monks do this when handling apparent inconsistencies with high-status authors like Tsongkhapa. No such hermeneutic care is evident here.

To recount, the debate began with consensus, and with no suspicion about the defendant's knowledgeability. Through the idiom of problematization, the shift from -*s* to *byas* framing, and the attempt to induce inconsistencies in the defendant's discourse, the challenger initiates a tragic, chiastic turn, from consensus to dissensus. He starts to set the defendant against inherited doctrine, beginning with the citation that started the debate. A fatal leak of criticism begins, and this trickle becomes a torrent so fierce that little of the defendant's status is left afloat. Despite the defendant's eager claims to knowledgeability, despite his candidacy for the Rigchung, the challenger increasingly positions him as not deserving of the very seat on which he sits. For the defendant, the debate becomes decidedly "unsettling," a felicitous term that Margaret Goldbert (1985) introduced in her dissertation on this genre. It is unsettling precisely because the event began with consensus. Once consensus is created, the challenger turns on it. Neither he, nor the other challengers who join him, relents for the remainder of the debate, which ends abruptly and without restoration of consensus, when the house leader signals for the debate to end. To

TABLE 2  Canonical "taunts" in the lexical register of debate (Sera Mey, India)

| Lexical forms and expressions | Kinesic accompaniments |
|---|---|
| (a) 'o tsha<br>ɔɔ' tsā<br>'Shame [on you]' | Back of right hand slaps open left palm. |
| (b) 'khor gsum<br>kɔ̄ɔ̄ sūm<br>'Three spheres' | Right hand (palm down) performs clockwise motion above and in the direction of the seated defendant's head. |
| (c) dpe cha dang 'gal / phyag dpe dang 'gal<br>bēja taŋ gɛɛ / cāàbē taŋ gɛɛ<br>'[You] contradict text, [you] contradict scripture' | Back of right hand slaps open left palm; back of left hand slaps open right hand. |
| (d) yo phyir[a]<br>yɔɔ cir | Clap sequence is performed. |

[a] This taunt was not glossed semantically by my informants. *Phyir* appears to be derived from the final postpositional *phyir* in the consequence sequence.

sunder consensus is not to expose the incoherence of inherited doctrine. It is to expose the incompetence of the defendant's grasp of it—his inability to find (or forge) coherence amid the welter of philosophical claims.

### Taunts

The challengers' turn against the defendant is nowhere more apparent than in the use of four "taunts" that make up part of debate's lexical register (table 2). At Sera Mey monks consistently glossed the *tsha* taunt as 'Shame [on you]' (*ngo tsha*).[34] As for its stereotypical indexical properties, it indicates that the addressee (the defendant) has erred. In interviews, monks further glossed this error as 'self-contradiction'. Self-contradiction is thus said to be the criterial context for appropriate *tsha* usage. Of the remaining taunts, (b) and (c) are also addressee-focal indexicals that stereotypically indicate "incoherence," yet they are more severe indictments than *tsha*, as evidenced by remarks monks made in interviews about the differential force of these taunts,[35] and, to turn to actual usage, by the fact that these taunts occurred after tokens of *tsha* were uttered as the pitch of criticism grew. In this debate, the first token of *'khor gsum* ('three spheres') occurred only after six tokens of *tsha* had been uttered.[36] The final taunt, (d), differs from (a)–(c) in that it typically indexes the addressee's inappropriate "hesitation," rather than "incoherence." In actual debates, challengers often use this taunt after lengthy pauses or dysfluencies in the defendant's speech, framing them as indexes of his flagging memory or incompetence. In short, three of the four canonical taunts stereotypically index addressee-incoherence, which, again, demonstrates how denotational-textual coherence is of cardinal importance. No such demand for coherence, revealingly, is demanded of the challenger. The defendant alone must uphold the textual ideology of doctrinal coherence.

A few caveats. These are only the taunts specific to debate's lexical register. Others are devised extemporaneously. Not all taunts taunt either. Their stereotypical pragmatic effects—what informants say they "do," in what scenarios-of-use they are said to be deployed—must be distinguished from their effects in discursive interaction. And pragmatic effects like "aggression" are the precipitate of cross-modal arrays of semiotic tokens, not discrete words (Agha 1996).

As for the distribution of the debate-specific taunts across phases of the debate, they are noticeably absent at the outset. None are uttered for approximately the first eight minutes, yet the number of taunts per unit of time increases significantly during the final ten minutes of the forty-six-minute debate. With the exception of a brief, two-minute flurry (minutes twenty-six to twenty-eight of the debate), the density of taunts during the final ten minutes far exceeds the density of tokens found earlier.

### Spatial Implosion

As taunts increase in density, a global proxemic shift occurs, a change in the extension of what Adam Kendon (1990:211) terms the "joint transactional space," that is, "the space *between* the interactants over which they agree to maintain joint jurisdiction and control." In this debate (and in others I witnessed), there is a noticeable shift in the distance that the challengers assume vis-à-vis the defendant, which can be seen by tracking where they stand when they deliver claps.[37] In total, the standing challengers delivered 281 claps during this forty-six-minute debate. (Claps from a senior monk who remained seated were omitted, since they did not involve proxemic contrasts.) To recount, a lone challenger makes a beeline route toward the defendant at the start of the debate, halting a few feet before him. From this position of maximal propinquity, he begins to roll back, occupying positions ever farther from the defendant. As the citation phase draws to a close (after four minutes), a second challenger joins him, and they continue this retreat. As they retreat, creating more "distance" between their bodies and the defendant, they begin to question the defendant's claims. Once the first taunt rings out, the transactional space then begins to contract, and never again do challengers stand as far back as they did when they uttered their first taunt. As problematization intensifies, and taunts fly, the space separating the challengers from the defendant shrinks, the challengers' claps exploding ever closer to the defendant. Though the overall trend is that of a contraction of the transactional space, if you look closer you see a series of advances and retreats that, while partly a reflex of the way the mechanics of the clap sequence spur challengers to take a step forward, so that they must then take a step backward, can sometimes resemble the spatial tactics of an interrogator who paces about and periodically—dramatically—gets in the subject's face. In the debate's final ten minutes, when taunts rain most densely, the challengers tend to hover just a few feet from the seated defendant. In sum, as the challengers begin to problematize the defendant's claims, spatially, they tend to draw ever closer to his seat, not to stroke him with expressions of agreement and deference, but to stoke the fire of opposition—in a word, to unsettle him.

### The Defendant's Unflappability

But what of the defendant who has been invited into this exalted, yet precarious seat? How does he comport himself in the face of the challengers' provocations? Most striking is his relative inactivity. Challengers and defendants are mirror images of each other. Consider the kinesic asymmetries: contra the challenger, the defendant neither stands nor ambulates. The challenger possesses an elaborate kinesic repertoire, but no such repertoire is prescribed for the defendant. The challenger is licensed to craft and rehearse his lines of attack beforehand, and to steer topics as he sees fit. No such privileges are granted to the defendant. In terms of the relative volume of their lexical repertoires, defendants are restricted—again, prescriptively—to a small set of short canonical responses. In practice, of course, challengers and defendants frequently break register, but these standards of behavior remain, standards that seem to cast the defendant as relatively "passive." Passivity is a misnomer, though, for when confronted with the challengers' provocations, the defendant appears ostentatiously *non*reactive.

Many semiotic resources were mobilized to help project this demeanor. Consider prosodic evidence first, namely "decelerations" of speech rate initiated by the defendant. Susanne Uhmann (1992), whose approach to speech rate fluctuation I follow here, distinguishes two parameters: the density of phonemic syllables per unit of time and accented syllables per unit of time ("accented" not in the sense of lexical stress but in the sense of perceived prosodic prominences based on parameters like pitch, loudness, and length). The defendant's responses, however, varied significantly only with respect to phonemic syllable/sec. density, on which I focus below. The unit of analysis is the intonation unit, whose lengths are noted parenthetically in the transcribed segments that follow. Phonemic syllable/sec. density is listed in brackets, and interunit pause lengths are noted in brackets on separate lines.

To set the stage for the first moment to be considered, I should note that the challengers had been prodding the defendant about his view on distinctive refuge. Remember that earlier they had asked him whether distinctive refuge should be posited by way of objective or subjective criteria. Distinctive refuge should not be posited on the basis of 'merely' (*tsam*) the objects of refuge, the defendant insisted, because subjective factors matter. When the challengers later return to this claim, they distort his position. They suggest that distinctive refuge should not be posited by way of its objects of refuge, and seek the defendant's evaluation of this claim; though it is superficially consistent with the defendant's original assertion, they edited out his 'merely' (*tsam*) qualification. The defendant dislikes this stark formulation and has avoided saying that the criteria for positing distinctive refuge are exclusively objective or exclusively subjective. Of special interest is the way he rejects the challenger's reasoning in the lines below. In lines 422 and 425 below, the defendant says the challenger's 'reason' (*rtags*) is 'not established' (*ma grub*):

| | |
|---|---|
| C₁: (421)=*skyabs 'gro khyad par can yin* ] *pa'i 'di yang*- (1.37) [6.57]<br>　　gyāmdro kyēèbarjen  yĭmbɛ　　tĭ　yaṇ<br>　　refuge    distinctive   be-NZR.GEN this also | also this distinctive refuge- |
| D: (422)　　　　　　　　　| *rta:::lgs ma grub zer:::* (2.08) \|1.44\|<br>　　　　　　　　　tāa　　mʌ-tup-s<br>　　　　　　　　　reason NEG-established-QT | [tradition says]<br>"the reason is not established" |
| C₁: (423)　　　　　　　　]*skyabs yul khyad par*- (1.08) [3.70]<br>　　　　　　　　gyōbyüü　　　　kyēèbar-<br>　　　　　　　　refuge.object distinct[ive]- | distinct[ive]  objects of refuge- |
| C₂: (424)　*skyabs yul khyad par can lab ya'di* (1.34) [5.97] =<br>　　gyōbyüü　　kyēèbarjen lʌp-ya　tĭ<br>　　refuge.object distinctive   say-NZR this | that which is called distinctive objects of refuge here |
| D: (425)  = *rta::gs ma grub zer:::* (1.79) \|1.68\|<br>　　dāà　　mʌ-trub-s<br>　　reason NEG-established-QT | [tradition says]<br>"the reason is not established" |

The defendant's articulation rates are lower than the challenger's immediately preceding utterances. In line 422, the defendant's articulation rate is nearly 4.5 times lower, and in line 425, it is nearly 3.5 times lower; he "decelerates" sharply. Further, both decelerations include a lengthened framing with the quotative clitic -*s*, whose effects require further comment. In the debate register, there is a strong tendency to omit the matrix clause of the represented speech segment. As mentioned above, in cases where debate participants use the quotative clitic without the matrix clause and without any clear value for the author variable, the default construal of the author variable can be glossed as "tradition." (By "tradition" here I mean a virtual [i.e., not empirically manifest], authoritative locus of knowledge that is temporally anterior to the utterance in which it is invoked.) In sum, the defendant decelerates and simultaneously displaces authorship onto the impersonal voice of tradition.

Other concurrent facts deserve mention. In his first response (line 422), the defendant overlaps with the challenger. In his second (line 425), he latches with him (i.e., his utterance is separated by no perceivable pause, operationalized as less than

1/10 of a second apart); he is right on the challenger's heels, as it were. The defendant anticipates the challanger's moves, responding before the challenger can even deliver the question—an index of his knowledgeability. Yet his responses are delivered not at a breakneck pace, but in a slow, lilting, majestic manner—an index of his poise. Through this deceleration, coupled with -s framing, the defendant presents himself as a calm courier of tradition. Through overlap and latching, he preserves a demeanor-indexical claim to knowledgeability.

Similar examples of "poise" projected (partly) through decelerations occurred elsewhere. For example, about fifteen minutes into the debate, one of the five challengers on the floor hurls the 'khor gsum invective at the defendant for the first time. Immediately thereafter, the challengers vie for the floor, creating a din of loud, overlapping utterances. The defendant, in his first response since the invective was hurled, utters the following over this din:

D: (766a)    *khyab pa:: -(1.05) [1.91]*          pervasion... there is no pervasion
             kyɔ̄bɔ
             pervasion

(766b)       *khyab pa: ma byu::ng (1.52) [2.63]*
             kyɔ̄bɔ    ma̱ cuŋ
             pervasion NEG AUX

He repeats the disyllabic *khyab pa*, with lengthening of the final vowels of each intonation unit. As before, this response is decelerated relative to the challengers' immediately prior talk. In contrast to the raucous discursive behavior of the challengers, the defendant speaks unhurriedly and with parallelism. Parallelism here reflexively foregrounds the orderliness of discourse, its formal patterning. This orderliness stands in contrast to the *disorderliness* of the competing utterances of the challengers who vie for the floor. The defendant's response seems to glide, as it were, effortlessly and majestically over the challengers' terrestrial clamor. If we recall that his response came in the wake of the 'khor gsum taunt, we can view this as an effort to deny indexical entailment, as if to say that he is *not* the incoherent person that challengers say he is by inhabiting a demeanor that is the very inverse of the challengers' discursive haste and disorder!

Nor are these isolated cases. With regard to the defendant's canonical responses across the debate, he tended to decelerate while responding. The canonical responses, again, range from one to four syllables. Of the defendant's fifty-nine responses (which include cases where the quotative clitic was added, e.g., '[Tradition] says "accept"' [/döö-s/], or verbs of speaking, e.g., '[I] say "accept"' [/döö lɔb/]), only three were articulated at a slightly higher syllable/sec. density relative to the immediately preceding utterance of the challenger(s). The remaining fifty-six cases involved "decelerations" by the defendant, as illustrated for the canonical response '[I] accept' (*'dod*) in table 3.

TABLE 3 Speech-rate decelerations by defendant
on '[I] accept' ('*dod*) responses

| (C) Syll./sec. at $t^{n-1}$ | (D) Syll./sec. at $t^n$ | (D) Deceleration |
|---|---|---|
| 3/0.65 [4.62] | 1/0.58 [1.72] | -2.90 |
| 3/0.82 [3.66] | 1/0.62 [1.61] | -2.05 |
| 3/0.66 [4.55] | 1/0.51 [1.96] | -2.59 |
| 3/0.69 [4.35] | 1/0.46 [2.17] | -2.18 |
| 3/0.69 [4.35] | 1/0.52 [1.92] | -2.43 |
| 10/1.44 [6.94] | 1/0.79 [1.27] | -5.67 |
| 8/0.87 [9.20] | 1/0.50 [2.00] | -7.20 |
| 3/1.10 [2.73] | 1/0.60 [1.67] | -1.06 |
| 9/1.12 [8.04] | 1/0.90 [1.11] | -6.93 |
| 9/1.39 [6.48] | 1/0.60 [1.67] | -4.81 |
| 2/0.60 [3.33] | 1/0.40 [2.50] | -0.83 |
| 5/0.87 [5.75] | 1/0.56 [1.79] | -3.96 |

(Column 1 indicates the syll./sec. density for the challenger's [C] utterance; column 2 indicates the density for the subsequent response by the defendant [D]; $t$ = "time.")[38] Speech rate, in short, was among the semiotic resources used to index a culturally recognizable demeanor of "poise."

It is not that the defendant never became rankled or returned fire. Though he appeared poised throughout, he did sometimes fail to maintain this demeanor. Late in the debate, he indicts a challenger for being nonsensical: 'There isn't the slightest bit of sense in [what you are] saying now!'[39] He also accuses challengers of indiscriminately shouting the taunt, *tsha* (e.g., 'How is that *tsha* [a real] *tsha*?'[40]). He even charges the challenger with trying to deceive him and counters: 'I am not going to be tricked!'[41] In many sequences, it is not the defendant's oppositionality that is striking, but his recovery of poise. Again late in the debate, for instance, the defendant seems to challenge the challenger, yet gazes away immediately thereafter. In another moment in this exchange, he gazes away, then begins rocking in his seat. Here he imposes a kinesically based metrical structure on his own behavior, a figure of "balance" whose orderliness is counterposed to his "unsettled" behavior in previous turns.

That the expected demeanor of a defendant is unflappability is also evident in the challengers' response behavior. Thirty-one minutes into the debate, a new challenger rises to face the defendant, and the defendant's stridency reaches new heights in this exchange. The defendant shouts his canonical responses six times consecutively. The second time he shouts his response, a smile appears on one challenger's face. Moments later, the defendant delivers his third response. Smiles, now contagious, surface on the faces of two other monks. When the defendant bellows his fourth response, laughter erupts in the room and is reignited when the defendant shouts a fifth and sixth response. As implicit evaluations of the defendant's speech, such response behavior suggests that the defendant has, to everyone's amusement, breached etiquette: defendants should not reciprocate when provoked.

Debate's theatrics and the place it gives to demeanor and comportment force us to look beyond denotational textuality in argumentation. In this interaction ritual, denotational textuality and demeanor indexicality conspire to figurate the sense of stability and coherence that doctrinal tradition is officially supposed to possess. In first presupposing, then sundering and restoring doctrinal coherence, monks work to unify doctrinal tradition, and it is to the defendant in particular that this onerous task of ritual unification falls. He carries out this labor not only by means of the propositional content of his utterances (at the plane of denotational textuality) but also through his default demeanor of poise (at the plane of demeanor indexicality). Moreover, his demeanor, and the operations he performs on the plane of denotational textuality, parallel each other, yielding a vivid, multiplex figure of and for tradition's successful unification.

The relationship between demeanor indexicality and denotational textuality here is not strictly additive or unidirectional. In his analysis of a Clinton-Dole presidential debate, Agha (1996:470) observes how semiotic effects produced by distinct functional principles and projected concurrently can "illuminate each other during usage" and "are *reciprocally reflexive* when considered in relation to each other." The "parallel" between denotational textuality and demeanor indexicality in Buddhist debate is the result of concurrently projected effects that appear reciprocally reflexive in this sense.[42] The sheer density of mutually illuminating effects in Buddhist debate—many of which occur across semiotic channels—should come as no surprise to those familiar with ritual, where such "excessive formalism" or "hyperstructure" (Parmentier 1994) has been shown to be central to ritual's ideological effectiveness (Silverstein 2004), its capacity to (re)produce cultural norms and values, as the Durkheimian tradition would have it.

Debate, Sera's foremost educational rite of institution, is a site of mimetic sympathy where a seemingly small, spatially and temporally bounded ritual of face-to-face interaction becomes a crucible in which the college's own integrity is to be tested, challenged, and, hopefully, defended. Debate's multiplex orderliness, typical of ritual, is a key to the practice's scale-jumping effectiveness. If debate were reduced to a series of logical operations, deprived of its phases, demeanor, and dramaturgy, what could it possibly model beyond itself? Little of its mimetic import would remain, for the phases of the event, especially the challengers' chiastic movement from consensus to dissensus, wholeness to fragmentation, advance the ritual plot: they create the conditions for the unification of tradition and add dramatic tension to boot. If the defendant isn't careful, the monastic college will remain in pieces, and with it, his reputation.

In trying to explain how events of argumentation can participate in projects like liberal-democratic consensus formation, most privilege what interactants wrangle about and how they agree and disagree on what is right and true. Most brush aside seemingly secondary details like the phases of argument and the forms of demeanor participants adopt, even though this is often the stuff from which signs of the liberal subject are made, or at least made recognizable.

### HOW TO ACT OUT CRITICAL RATIONALITY: A CODA ON HABERMAS'S LIBERAL MIMICRY

There is an instructive irony on this issue in the opening pages of Jürgen Habermas's classic *Theory of Communicative Action*. It is an irony worth revisiting, because Habermas unknowingly stumbled upon the role of mimetic sympathy in argumentation and liberal subject formation. In those opening pages Habermas drew on Lévi-Strauss's (1968) classic structuralist claims about the integrative power of myth. "Analogical thought," summarized Habermas (1984:46), "weaves all appearances into a single network of correspondence." Citing Lévi-Strauss, Habermas spoke of myth's alleged "gigantic mirror-effect, where the reciprocal image of man and the world is reflected ad infinitum, perpetually decomposing and recomposing in the prism of nature-culture relations" (46). "To be sure," wrote Habermas in a telling line, "the confusion of nature and culture by no means signifies only a conceptual blending of the objective and social worlds, but also a—by our lights—deficient differentiation between *language and world*" (49; emphasis in original). Not long after Habermas relegated sympathy—in the sense of likenesses that supposedly confuse word and world—to premodern semiosis, just as E. B. Tylor and countless others did before him, a curious thing happened: Habermas unwittingly used mimetic sympathy to rescue one of modernity's most beleaguered notions, rationality itself. What he provided was really a script that describes how to act out an autonomous, critical rationality in face-to-face interaction.

This was high-stakes drama, though, for the charges leveled against rationality were serious. Rationality, remember, had been charged as being parochial, not universal and singular as the Enlightenment legacy had led us to believe. It was an artifact of historically contingent cultural regimes, of language games, of "styles of reasoning" (Hacking 1984)—charges that raised the specter of cultural incommensurability and a corrosive relativism (Tambiah 1995). Just as unsettling was the indictment that rationality as a discourse had often been a handmaiden of power (e.g., by reproducing androcentric biases, by strengthening colonialism's hold on its less- or irrational subjects). And then there was always Max Weber's sobering assessment of the trajectory of the modern West, whose commitment to purposive, means/ends rationality in society was supposedly marching us toward disenchantment and confinement in the proverbial "iron cage." Frankfurt school theorists like Horkheimer and Adorno, similarly, saw the ills of modern, capitalist society as largely the result of the predominance of "instrumental reason" (Horkheimer and Adorno 1994; Horkheimer 1974). It was into this fray of critical reflection on modernity that Habermas stepped.

Habermas stepped forward to defend modernity and its homage to rationality and did so, like many others in the late 1960s and 1970s, after taking a kind of linguistic turn. He drew partly on emerging work in argumentation theory, such as that by Toulmin. Recast in "post-metaphysical" form, rationality, he suggested, should be viewed processually as something born out of dialogic interaction between people. How does argumentation work? Habermas found his answer by straining to see beneath empirical surfaces rather than by studying what people actually do. He suggested that a handful of universal pragmatic presuppositions that make up what he dubbed the "ideal speech situation" underlie all forms of argument. This set of regulative ideals is supposedly hardwired into us as a species-level competence. It was partly through this construct that Habermas could envision the project of modernity continuing despite its detractors; after some rehabilitation, rationality could continue on its emancipatory career.[43]

The ideal speech situation was never meant as a set of inviolable "rules" for argumentation but rather as an "inevitable fiction" (Habermas 2001:102) with a strictly orthogonal relationship to observable discourse. Habermas's investment in this fiction is revealing, though, for he wrote that "the counterfactual conditions of the ideal speech situation can be conceived of as necessary conditions of an emancipated form of life," and admitted that what he had done in laying out these presuppositions was to "recast in linguistic terms what we have traditionally sought to capture in the ideas of truth, freedom, and justice" (99).

Symmetry was the cardinal principle here—the "general symmetry conditions that every competent speaker must presuppose are sufficiently satisfied insofar as he intends to enter into argumentation at all" (Habermas 1984:25)—though we were never really told why. There was said to be, for instance, symmetry of role inhabitance. Habermas (25) spoke of a "cooperative division of labor between proponents and opponents," where interactants presume that there should be equal access to participant roles (so that, for example, no one shall remain disproportionately the "hearer" while others enjoy the "speaker" role). If acted out in face-to-face interaction, this symmetry would surely find its clearest expression in "dialogic" modes of discursive interaction, that is, the symmetric alternation of participant-role inhabitance, where speakers and hearers swap roles across turns of talk. This poetic structure makes turns and speakers seem "equivalent." Habermas also felt that we carry around the presumption that everyone ought to have access to the same repertoire of speech acts and have the same opportunities to draw on them (2001:98–99), which ensures that interactants cannot, through privileges of socialization or status, perform acts through language use that are not equally performable by others.

Still, why *symmetry*? On this, Habermas remained stone silent, but it scarcely takes a semiotician to imagine how a poetics of symmetry could help model the "equality" of interactants and trace out a picture of a disinterested argument in which no individual's rights are trammeled. The result—a rational consensus secured not by coercion but by the "unforced force of the better argument" (Habermas 2001:98)—appears conveniently traced out from the start, albeit in embryonic, pictorial form. The instructions for materializing the liberal subject consist of a script for acting out what this subject looks like. This means that one can argue face-to-face, participate in large-scale processes of liberal-democratic consensus formation, and exhibit a universal human propensity for communicative rationality. Quite a few leaps of scale, and leaps that would have been impossible without likenesses as a conduit. This movement from small scale to large scale is made possible through affinities—mimetic sympathies—that span enormous, impossible distances.

Less charitably, we could charge Habermas with having transduced liberal-democratic principles like individual autonomy and freedom into a dialogical poetics of symmetry, where we are invited to act out the very ideals he wishes to impart, like a rite of sympathetic magic—just the kind of word-world confusion that he relegated to premodern semiosis! This would be a humorless critique, though, since this is no semiotic sleight of hand per se. It is precisely what needs to be explained. How is it that you can discover transcendent liberal values in fleeting and mercurial stretches of discursive interaction, and what is it exactly about the shape and design of these stretches of interaction that invites participants and observers to jump scale? What debate does depends partly on what it is felt to look like.

While palpable qualities of argumentation permit one to see such likenesses, it is not as if these qualities themselves permit participants to leap from "small" scale to "large" scale. Debate's scale-jumping mimicry—the way the defendant's "stability" seems to stabilize the doctrinal tradition and the college—cannot be explained strictly by scrutinizing the qualities in the event's perimeter—as if debate's potency could be revealed purely through a close analysis of its formal properties, as if this potency were lurking somewhere in the properties of a ritual text. Interaction rituals, however much they are set off spatially and temporally, are but parts of highly distributed assemblages. An older symbolic anthropology might have invited us to glimpse the sociocultural surround through the aperture of a ritual's signs, as if rituals were windows onto rather than pieces of the surround. The surround does not stop at Sera either. Buddhist debate may be designed to serve as a rite of institution within the confines of Sera, but this does not exhaust what it looks like and does for Tibetans in India. Buddhist debate has also been swept up in a project of liberal mimicry in exile, where the practice is said to exhibit the liberal faculty of autonomous, critical rationality. And this reanalysis of debate, inspired especially by the Dalai Lama, as we shall see, is not all that different from the way Habermas invited us to leap from patterns of symmetry in discursive interaction to hallowed liberal ideals like rights, freedom, and autonomy.

# 3

## Debate as a Diasporic Pedagogy

For a half century the Dalai Lama has exhorted Tibetan refugees to hold fast to their religious patrimony and never waver in political resolve. For the exile community, "change" has been an unsettling word, especially in the domain of religion. Asked whether debate has changed in exile, the monks I spoke with often seemed uncomfortable, as if I had just scratched at the patina and questioned the authenticity of a whole way of life. Debate has remained 'the same' (*gcig pa*), most responded—save for the admission of certain minor 'stylistic' (*lab stangs*) mutations often attributed to life in India, like the way Hindi words are said to creep into the Tibetan lexicon or the way cuisine and clothing adapt to new climes. Among the elder Geshes, all change is for the worse. They recount, with a mixture of pride and nostalgia, the rigors of pre-1959 philosophical training, in comparison with which all training in India pales. (A senior Hlarampa Geshe at India's Namgyal Monastery: 'Before, in Tibet, debate was extremely strong' [*sngon ma bod la rtsod pa shugs chen po yog red*], and if one compares debate now to debate then, one has to conclude that the practice 'is nearly lost' [*shor sa red*].) Narrowing big, unsettling questions about change into smaller ones about specific reforms and their inception met with more welcoming responses. I could learn of the innumerable minor breaks from the past in Geluk monasteries, like the adoption of pen-and-paper exams, new credentialization procedures, novel modes of financing and monastic labor, and new topics of study, like English and science, offered in the monasteries' secular schoolhouses. The list seemed endless.

Feats of large-scale replication cannot be expected to preserve the detail of their originary forms, and rarely is this even the intent. But the new Sera, Drepung, and Ganden monasteries of South India presumably bear sufficient resemblance to their

central Tibetan prototypes, and the original monastic seats in Tibet have presumably become so disfigured that many find it reasonable to conclude that Sera,
Drepung, and Ganden have been "reestablished," "relocated," "reinstituted," or "reconstituted" in India. Terms like these have become a reflex in English-language
publications, and my Tibetan interlocutors in India also engaged in no special gym-
nastics when they referred to (India's) Sera. They could have appended toponyms
to disambiguate the two ("India's Sera"; "Tibet's Sera"), but unless the topic demanded it, India's "Sera" was "Sera": diasporic verisimilitude.

Descriptors like "reestablished" are not innocent. We cannot ask about the changing meaning of debate—this chapter's objective—without first interrogating these
terms, for they conscript one into an historicization of Geluk monasticism that is
freighted with commitments, the most obvious of which is that replication is treated
as accomplished and unproblematic fact, not something that even needs explanation (Urban 1994, 1996). Descriptors like "reestablish" also suggest a linear plot-
line of three acts: in the beginning was establishment; then came rupture, which
stemmed from China's violent efforts to dismantle Tibet's monastic system after
abandoning its gradualist policy of liberalization in the 1950s; then the exiled Geluk
sect willfully brought its monasteries back into existence "again" in the early 1970s,
as the re- prefix would have it.

Which is to say that no real, deep changes have occurred. Differences disappear
in the acid binary of continuity–discontinuity. What is more, descriptors like
"reestablish" and "reconstitute" harmonize with exile Tibetan discourses that stress
the lack of religious freedom in Tibet; they would have us forget that there are multiple, concurrent avatars of the "same" institution, each of which may be cited (on different grounds) as the real thing. Exile Tibetan nationalist discourses have tended
to downplay the continued existence and even revival of religious education in Tibet,
and monks I spoke with at India's Sera overwhelmingly agreed with this assessment. Many braved harrowing journeys to India by foot and cited the lack of religious educational opportunity in Tibet as part of their rationale for leaving; Tibet's
Sera seemed dead and gone. To be sure, opportunities for the Geluk sect's debate-
based philosophical study in Tibet are negligible compared to those of their namesakes on the subcontinent. It was only in the 1980s that the Geluk monastic seats
in Tibet experienced a "revival" of sorts;[1] this was the same decade when the ranks
of India's monastic seats began to swell with 'new arrivals' (gsar 'byor) from Tibet.
The real Sera—real, by the criterion of educational opportunity—is not the Sera
founded in the early fifteenth century on the outskirts of Lhasa. So there are two
parallel monastic worlds: one reduced and atrophied but physically extant in central Tibet, the other expanding and bristling with learning in South India. As refracted through terms like "reestablishment," only India's Sera is real—"active" ed-
ucationally, that is—which means that diasporic Tibetans (alone?) are entrusted with
Tibet's religious patrimony. Neglected by these terms, in sum, is the continued ex-

istence of the three Geluk monastic seats in central Tibet and their ideological positioning vis-à-vis their namesakes in India.

## IS DEBATE ILLIBERAL?

What has become of the Geluk sect's premier intellectual practice in India? A rationale for reforming or curtailing debate is easy to conceive, because it looks illiberal, even un-Buddhist. One has to strain to see any parity between challenger and defendant, who are "equal" only in the way opposites are, exhibiting mirror-image symmetry. (In this respect "debate" itself is a misnomer; as noted earlier, the term typically suggests a zero-sum contest in which participants enjoy equal discursive rights and responsibilities.) Of the many asymmetries between these two speech-event roles, the most glaring is that of the challenger's brash behavior and the defendant's pacific unflappability. How could these displays be of a piece with influential representations of Tibetan Buddhism as a religion whose essence is non-violence and "universal compassion"? How could these presuppose the defendant's autonomy, a key attribute of the liberal subject? Where are his "rights," when the Buddha taught that there is no self?

And debate looks just as illiberal for its deference to doctrine and the conservative way of canalizing information flow. (Recall, for instance, the textual ideology that ascribes coherence to authoritative Buddhist texts and faults defendants—not the texts they uphold—when coherence isn't found.) Add to this textual conservatism the fact that debate is monastic and that Tibetan Buddhist monasticism has long been associated in the West with Catholicism, and it becomes easy to imagine debate as some analogue of medieval Christian *disputatio*. At best, Buddhist debate would look vestigial, certainly not a practice that ought to thrive in exile. At worst, this analogy could replay critiques leveled at medieval Scholastics by seventeenth-century empiricists like Bacon and Locke and Renaissance humanists like Petrarch. In fact, for some unsympathetic interpreters of Geluk debate, this has already happened. (I befriended a US professor of English literature who visited Sera Mey and admitted knowing little of Tibetan Buddhism. A brief lecture on Geluk doctrine was enough to confirm his fears, though. To him the Geluk sect seemed a stodgy Asian version of Roman Catholicism, stuck in some pre-Reformation Scholasticism. Perhaps to free me, he recommended that I read Erasmus's sixteenth-century anti-Scholastic work, *The Praise of Folly*! By translating 'debate' [*rtsod pa*] as "monachal disputation" in an early anthropological essay on this practice, Sierksma [1964] helped invite analogies like this, and a few Buddhist studies scholars appear to have done the same with respect to the Geluk sect. And there is a long precedent for glossing *rtsod pa* and related terms as 'disputation': e.g., Schlagintweit 1863; Waddell 1895.)

"Hierarchical" relations among monks *have* troubled reform-minded Tibetans (as evidenced by the Institute of Buddhist Dialectics' egalitarian policies, for instance). Violence between monks—even when ritualized—*has* worried some Tibetans (as suggested by discomfort toward corporal punishment, as we shall soon see). Obedience toward received doctrine *has* disturbed Tibetans who admire the scientific method and want to distinguish their religion from religions like Christianity, which they say demand only uncritical, blind faith. While there are Tibetans and non-Tibetans alike for whom debate looks inappropriate, even backward, the Geluk sect in India has not seemed too troubled by its association with it, for no institutional measures have been taken within the sect to redesign the practice or refashion the more "uncivil" elements of the debaters' demeanor. And even if features of this practice were judged illiberal, these features could always be brushed aside as "inessential."

In spite of such scrutiny, debate persists. Not only has it been replicated widely in India without serious restylings, but its social domain has expanded. It has been adopted by several Geluk nunneries, by Geluk tantric colleges, and even by a number of non-Geluk monasteries that never had it before or never considered the practice to be that important. It would be an exaggeration to suggest that this genre has taken off, because it still has a restricted social distribution. Nevertheless, the categories of people and institutions that practice it have expanded.

I argue that this expansion should be understood in relation to the Dalai Lama's reflexive activities, which I access through a consideration of his influential public addresses to Tibetans in India (1959–2000).[2] I suggest that the debate-based philosophical curriculum has been reframed (by some, not all) as a modern diasporic pedagogy—a means by which Tibetans can cultivate an autonomous, critical rationality, the exercise of which confers a certain "stability" upon diasporic subjects. In the Dalai Lama's addresses, Buddhism is said to be a religion of reason that eschews blind faith and embraces critical thinking (including a quasi-Popperian embrace of the principle of falsifiability, where Buddhists can and should reject any aspect of Buddhist doctrine proved false). The subject sketched out by such discourses is autonomous, not dependent on any spiritual teacher or text, and endowed with the faculty of reason. Buddhism is further frequently likened to or at least treated as compatible with modern Western science and counterposed to monotheistic religions like Christianity and Hinduism. Whatever functions these discourses might serve outside India, for Tibetan refugees *in* India they are frequently linked to diasporic and nationalist concerns and projects. A diasporic pedagogy, debate becomes a method for refugees to steel themselves against pluralism in exile and hold fast to their identity and religious patrimony for an eventual return to their homeland.

These discourses about Buddhism are not new but part of a formation often captioned as "Buddhist modernism" or "modern Buddhism." In a series of incisive essays, Donald Lopez (1998, 2002, 2008) has argued that Tibetan Buddhism has been fashioned into a modern world religion in a manner analogous to late nineteenth-century "Buddhist modernism" in Sri Lanka and Southeast Asia. "Buddhist modernism" was Heinz Bechert's (Bechert and Gombrich 1984) coinage—his attempt to capture a certain family resemblance between developments in the Buddhism of East and Southeast Asia that emerged under conditions of colonialism and Christian missionization. This resemblance included Buddhism's elevation to the status of a "world religion," where it could take its rightful place next to religions like Christianity, Hinduism, and Islam. It also vaulted above the rest, for at least in its "early," pristine form, Buddhism was declared a religion of "reason." Rather than demand uncritical acceptance of doctrine, the historical Buddha allowed his votaries to think critically. Buddhism could thus be positioned as an heir of the Enlightenment legacy, a part of modernity rather than an obstacle to it. In outlook and sensibility, Buddhism could be seen as compatible with modern science. It was even possible to conclude that Buddhism is not really a religion at all; a hybrid form, it could confound the familiar Victorian cultural-evolutionist schema in which "magic," "religion," and "science" constituted unilineal steps toward European modernity.

Tibet's religion did not fare well in this account, however. Only "early" Buddhism enjoyed this privileged status, as a religion locked in the Sanskrit and Pali texts that European and American philologists had recently disinterred and over which they claimed jurisdiction; they were its self-appointed curators (cf. Lopez 1995). Behind early Buddhism stood its deprecated predecessor, "Brahmanism." In front of early Buddhism was its degenerate successor, "Lamaism," the religion of Tibet, whose texts, noted Lopez, remained largely unread. As refracted through a certain Protestantized historicism (see Gombrich and Obeyesekere 1988), Buddhism was thus said to have devolved from a "rational, agnostic faith to a degenerate religion rife with ritual and superstition" (Lopez 1998:17). Akin to Papism, "Lamaism, with its devious and corrupt priests and vapid sacerdotalism, is condemned as the most degenerate form of Buddhism (if it be a form of Buddhism at all)" (17).

Much has changed since the late nineteenth century, naturally, but Lopez directs attention to continuities in doctrine striking enough to permit him to speak broadly of a "modern Buddhism": "Modern Buddhism rejects many of the ritual and magical elements of previous forms of Buddhism, it stresses equality over hierarchy, the universal over the local, and often exalts the individual above the community" (Lopez 2002:ix). (Lopez suggests that this cluster of tenets has a genealogy that stretches back to a pivotal 1873 Christian-Buddhist debate in colonial Ceylon. This debate appeared in print as *Buddhism and Christianity Face to Face,* a book that inspired Henry Steel Olcott and Madame Blavatsky, founders of the Theosophical Society, whose influence on Buddhism in the West would be considerable; see Lopez 2002:vii–xiii. An emerging "scientific study of Buddhism" in the nineteenth-century academy also contributed to this modern, Protestantized Buddhism. French Victorian scholar Eugène Burnouf's influential *Introduction à l'histoire du Bouddhisme indien* [1844] humanized and historicized the Buddha, figuring the Buddha of India as an anticlerical, antimetaphysical moral philosopher and social reformer, a figure taken up famously by Burnouf's student Friedrich Max Müller; see Lopez 2008; Burnouf, Buffetrille, and Lopez 2010.) Since 1959 the present Dalai Lama has emerged as the chief spokesman of modern Buddhism. His assertion, for instance, that Buddhism is a religion of reason resembles earlier discourses on Buddhism forged with the help of Victorian scholarship and has received renewed support from certain forms of academic Buddhist scholarship. The Dalai Lama has also insisted that Buddhism is compatible with modern empirical science, a move which is also of nineteenth-century vintage. To be sure, the Dalai Lama's commitment to reason also bears the markings of Geluk scholasticism and the prominent place it has accorded the centuries-old Indo-Tibetan logico-epistemological traditions, which stem especially from Indian luminaries Dignaga and Dharmakīrti, to say nothing of the caustic rhetorical and political functions that discourses of reason have also served in the Geluk sect's historical struggles with other sects, principally the more "meditative" Nyingma and Kagyu.

Neither tracing the Dalai Lama's valorization of reason to an earlier Buddhist modernism that dates to 1873 nor tracing it to indigenous Tibetan or Indian discourses would suffice as an account of its performativity, what it effectuates or "does." If one were to abstract out the propositional content of the Dalai Lama's discourse and compare it to discourses of prior eras, the tenets would indeed look familiar and perhaps even derivative, the result of mere replication; but pragmatically speaking, his discourse is also an improvisational performance in a politically fraught environment. In a very broad sense, it is part of a project of establishing affinities between self and other so that affective sympathies may flow, and political support may follow. To appreciate what the Dalai Lama is trying to "do" in and by his valorization of reason (and related claims, like those concerning Buddhism's special affinity with science), one must attend to more recent discourses and historical circumstances. In the Dalai Lama's public addresses, appeals to reason and Buddhism's modern character are vociferously "double-voiced," to use Bakhtin's familiar idiom for capturing the way discourse can seem directed "toward *another's discourse,* toward *someone else's speech*" (Bakhtin [1963] 1984:185).

Toward whose speech? The Dalai Lama's appeals to reason are as much a rejoinder in a "shadow dialogue" (Crapanzano 1990:288–89; Irvine 1997) as they are a bid to persuade Tibetans assembled before him in the here-and-now speech event. Counted among the dramatis personae in the Dalai Lama's addresses to Tibetans in India are biographically individuated voices—those typified with a proper name (Agha 2005)—like Mao Zedong, who whispered the notorious line about religion being "poison" to the young Dalai Lama in 1955. There is the more generic but equally critical voice of Communist China ('Red China' *rgya dmar,* as it was sometimes named in early talks), for whom Tibet is backward, its religion rife with superstition and exploitative in nature. Whatever sympathies the Dalai Lama may have had, and still has, for Marxism, in public addresses to Tibetans in India he repeatedly countered the most caustic leftist critiques of Buddhism and of religion more generally. The Dalai Lama had already developed rhetorical means for countering such views before his flight to India. Against the charge that Tibetan religion is backward and incompatible with modernity, for instance, he could stress Buddhism's commitment to investigation and reason (see, e.g., T. Gyatso 1990:87). In exile there was a more pressing voice to address, the most pressing of all: a generalized Euro-American voice, often figured in early talks as 'outsiders' (*phyi rol pa, pha rol pa*) and in later talks as 'foreigners' (*phyi rgyal ba*). This voice has a less determinate stance on Tibet's religion—it hasn't made up its mind and can be swayed—but it, too, appears to share the Chinese Communist Party's steely confidence in reason and science. Not unlike Chinese Communist Party (CCP) voices that espouse a scientific atheism and deride Tibet's religion as prone to superstition and an instrument of societal oppression, this voice, too, holds science to be the measure of all things reasonable (though this similarity doesn't mean, of course, that the modernities are equivalent and part of a "singular" process). Within this sweeping category of 'outsiders' and 'foreigners' is a voice of special concern, 'scientists' (*tshan rig pa*). The Dalai Lama enjoins Tibetans to show scientists that Buddhism respects reason like they do and has affinities with the Enlightenment legacy, Europe's, that is.

The talks sampled below, all delivered in Tibetan, were addressed primarily to fellow Tibetan refugees in exile. When the Dalai Lama talks about the way Buddhism embraces reason and refutes those who charge that it is irrational and incompatible with modernity, two major categories of voice tend to materialize (though not necessarily in the same talk) as overhearers: (a) the CCP (and "Mao" in particular), and (b) the West (and "scientists" in particular). When the Dalai Lama tells his fellow refugees that popular religion (prostrations, mantra recitation, the lighting of butter lamps, the propitiation of protector deities) is not enough, that reliance on habit alone will make it easy to slip into an uncritical, blind faith typical of religions like Christianity, does he not therefore seem to side with the stance of both overhearers, the West *and* the CCP? In fact, the Dalai Lama's orientation toward these two voices differs. It is the West that may be swayed, and from which sympathy and support are needed *now*, in exile. Buddhism—elsewhere credited as the essence of Tibetan culture and society—is aligned "with" the West, especially through Buddhism's affinities with Enlightenment ideals and the convergence of its epistemology with that of modern empirical science; Buddhism is aligned "against" the callous, myopic scientific modernity of the CCP. The result is a triangular relationship of stance taking that augurs—and tries to create—a future in which the West comes to Tibet's aid in its struggle with China. Attention to voice and addressivity in the Dalai Lama's public discourses thus offers a window onto this high-stakes, sympathetic project of commensurating Tibetan "culture" with the West.

The voicing structure of a single talk far exceeds what I can survey here. Cited above are but a few of the more obvious, named voices so that we may begin to appreciate the addressivity at work in the Dalai Lama's talk of reason and related notions—"addressivity," in the sense of an utterance's "quality of being directed to someone," as Bakhtin (Bakhtin 1986:95) expansively put it.

To trace how these voices emerged out of socially and historically locatable discursive events—be they the Dalai Lama's meetings with Mao or his storied friendship with Heinrich Harrer (1954) or the various media (e.g., books, reel-to-reel films) to which he was exposed—and how these voices became routinized in the Dalai Lama's public addresses would require a study unto itself. In what follows, I highlight a few select moments of this history that bear on the fate of debate, specifically, on changes in this genre's movement and its reframing as a modern diasporic pedagogy. Irrespective of questions about the provenance of the Dalai Lama's claims about Buddhism—whether they owe their existence to events from colonial Ceylon or late seventeenth-century England or to older Indo-Tibetan logico-epistemological traditions or to some combination of these and other things—"reason" has strength, and it has reach. It has become indispensable for the modern Tibetan diasporic subject, not just because it can create and stabilize certain dispositions in refugees as individuals, but because it both counters discourses and courts sympathies of imagined others in productive and interested ways. Reason—and the whole suite of notions and ideals attached to it—is part of a pointedly interdiscursive diasporic pedagogy. A means of collective self-styling, this pedagogy asks exile Tibetans to remake themselves, but this project is not solely for them alone. This project of self-refashioning is also for—is in dialogue with—a host of distant voices, voices formed over many years and produced and spread by different social actors and in diverse media. These critical voices—"Mao," "Communist China," "scientists," "foreigners"—say (or at least suspect) that Tibetan culture is on the wrong side of modernity. These voices serve as rhetorical foils that define and chart out a future for the modern Tibetan diasporic subject. It is thus a kind of *characterological antithesis* that the Dalai Lama recommends, where Tibetan refugees should cultivate and exhibit precisely what others say they lack. As embodied habits—counterhabits—these new dispositions may in turn be registered by those watching and listening to them and hence serve as "rejoinders" in a large-scale and global argument about the state and future of a people. And the sense of urgency here is palpable, for this argument is designed to be overheard especially by the West, a kind of "superaddressee" (Bakhtin 1986) who looms as a virtual spectator, a tertium quid who can aid exile Tibetans in their conflict with China. Cross the threshold of equivalence, so that Buddhism's rationality seems "like" the autonomous, critical rationality of the West's Enlightenment, and perhaps attitudes will change. Perhaps the networks that connect exile Tibetans with foreign scholars, supporters, and new Buddhist converts will result in sympathy, and from sympathy should come political and economic support, so that Tibet's fortunes will one day change.

## DEBATE EXPANDS

Namgyal Monastery, the Dalai Lama's personal monastery, founded by the Second Dalai Lama (1476–1542), was "reestablished" in Mcleod Ganj, upper Dharamsala. The monastery adjoins the Dalai Lama's compound. Debate-based study was introduced in the early 1970s, and Namgyal monks now assemble in the debating courtyard twice daily, once in the afternoon for about an hour, and once in the evening for an hour and a half. In the southern Indian town of Hunsur stands the Lower Tantric College, and there, too, debate has been welcomed into the curriculum; it was not welcomed by the college's predecessor in Tibet. Nechung, a Geluk monastery that became the seat of the State Oracle in the seventeenth century, was recreated in Gangchen Kyishong, Dharamsala, and was formally inaugurated by the Dalai Lama in 1985. Debate is now found there, too. Then there is the unprecedented movement of the debate genre across gender lines. In the 1980s, Ganden Choeling Nunnery in Dharamsala adopted debate. With assistance from instructors from the neighboring Institute of Buddhist Dialectics and from certain Geluk monastic colleges of South India, the nuns began to follow parts of the curricula found in the Geluk monastic seats. Other Geluk nunneries followed suit, including the Dolma Ling Institute of Dialectics, in Sidhpur (whose name invites comparison with Dharamsala's Institute of Buddhist Dialectics); Jamyang Choeling,[3] in Dharamsala, which features twice-daily debate; and Jangchub Choeling,[4] in South India, whose instructors hail from nearby Ganden Shartse monastic college. This syndicate of Geluk nunneries has even inaugurated its own, parallel version of the Jang Kunchö (*ljang dgun chos*), an intensive, roughly monthlong period of debates on Dharmakīrti's *Commentary*,[5] a tradition that was rekindled in India in 1984.

In addition to crossing gender lines, debate has also been recently adopted by a number of non-Geluk monasteries, the Ngagyur Nyingma Institute,[6] of Namdroling Monastery in Bylakuppe, being a prime example. Located a short rickshaw ride from the sprawling Sera Monastery, it is, to use Georges Dreyfus's (1997b) terminology, a prototypical example of a "commentarial school" (*bshad grwa*). Unlike "debating schools" (*rtsod grwa*) like Sera, commentarial schools use debate sparingly. Their monks read more texts in less time and dedicate more energy to oral and written exegesis. The mere presence of debate there is considered novel.

Nor is debate confined to monks and nuns. Though it has failed to make real serious inroads in the secular educational sphere,[7] it has found a modest curricular home in the Central Institute of Higher Tibetan Studies (now the Central University of Tibet) in Sarnath, near Varanasi, whose population is overwhelmingly non-monastic.[8] In sum, even without exhaustively mapping the social distribution of debate in India, it is evident that the scope of this genre has expanded.

Why, and under whose urging? Of its many advocates, the Dalai Lama is invariably cited by Tibetans as the principal agent behind debate's dissemination. At the conclusion of an evening interclass debate at the Ngagyur Nyingma Institute in 2000, for instance, I heard an instructor credit the Dalai Lama for bringing debate to the institute. When I later asked a Geluk Lama from Sera Mey about debate's movement to places like the neighboring Ngagyur Nyingma Institute, he suggested that the Dalai Lama has, indeed, been behind debate's dissemination:

*da de nas rgya gar la slebs nas rgyal ba rin po che bka' gnang pa red pa / dgon pa sgang gar mtshan nyid blta yas tog tsam tog tsam sbyong gi 'dug ga.*

Now, after that, after having arrived in India, the Precious Conqueror [the Dalai Lama] offered advice, right? At all monasteries, [monks] are [now] learning by studying philosophy a little bit, right?

He continued:

*sku mdun gis ga dus yin na'i gnang gi yog red..bka' slob / dgon pa chung chung de tsho a ni mtshan nyid tog tsam sbyong dgos gi 'dug zer [/-s/] / mtshan nyid sbyang yas de gdan sa'i grwa pa gcig po'i las 'gan ma red zer [/-s/].*

The Exalted Presence [the Dalai Lama] is constantly offering [this] advice. [He says]: "'These small monasteries need to study a bit of philosophy. The study of philosophy is not the responsibility of the monks of the [Geluk] monastic seats alone."

He then recounted how the Lower Tantric College in nearby Hunsur introduced debate-based philosophical study—again, a development he attributed to the Dalai Lama. Also in Hunsur is a small Geluk monastery called Dzongkar Chöde,[9] and in a brief written history of its founding in India, the author credited the Dalai Lama for encouraging monks there to offer debate-centered philosophical training.

In 2000 I interviewed a renowned Geshe and former abbot of Sera Mey, who had escaped Tibet after enduring a grueling period of "reeducation" and hard labor. He remarked about Sera's premier intellectual practice:

*rtsod pa de ma byas na / dpe cha'i nang log cig bris 'dug zer [/-s/] bzhag na / a ni brtan po ma red pa / red zer nas mi gis ma red zer nas sgrub byed mang po cig btang na a ni brlag 'gro gi red pa.*

If one doesn't debate and asserts [something because] "[it] is written in a religious text," then that isn't firm, right? Having said "[it] is," if [another] person says "[it] isn't" and then presents a lot of reasons, one will be destroyed, right?

*da rtsod pa rtsod na red zer na ma red zer ma red zer na da rgyu mtshan mang po 'dris nas zhu gu der so so brtan po chags gi red pa / yin pa da ga re yin / ma yin pa de ga re yin pa / so so brtan po chags kyi red pa / de mar mi gis 'di 'dras bsgyur thub gyi ma red ba / de 'dras yog red / slob gnyer yar rgyas btang yas rtsod pa dpe yag po 'dug ga.*

Now if one debates—if one says "[it] is," and [someone else] says "[it] isn't, [it] isn't"— through questioning [each other using] many reasons, in the end, each becomes firm, right? [One asks:] "Now why is that so? Why is that not so?" Each becomes firm, right? Later, [people] can't change [you] in that way, right? That's how it is. Debate is excellent for improving one's studies, isn't it?

*de gis rgyal ba rin po ches sngon ma rtsod pa med pa'i dgon par rtsod pa btsug yog red / rgyud grwa smad la sngon ma rtsod pa yog ma red / rtsod pa btsugs yog red / rnam rgyal la sngon ma rtsod pa yog ma red . . .*

That's why the Precious Conqueror [the Dalai Lama] establishes debate at monasteries that have previously lacked it. Previously, there was no debate at the Lower Tantric College. [He] established debate [there]. Previously, there was no debate at Namgyal [Monastery] . . .

In explaining debate's utility, the abbot emeritus summons the voice of a social type, the kind of monk who fails to learn debate. If pressed, nondebaters can only mutely point to books. Dependent on textual authority, they are left defenseless and vanquished by those who brandish reasons for their views. That's why the Dalai Lama has promoted debate, the abbot suggests. Debate makes students and refugees "firm"—a trope I return to later, for this, as well as his other remarks, articulates with discourses the Dalai Lama had been producing for decades.

Attributions of responsibility must be handled with care, especially when they involve no less a personage than the Dalai Lama. To reduce these attributions to their propositional content—as if they were just descriptions of historical states of affairs to be evaluated in terms of truth or falsity—would be to miss the presence of deference indexicality. The monks cited above are not just describing the Dalai Lama's role in disseminating debate; they are also paying deference to him. In certain respects, the Dalai Lama has become a "mobile semiotic resource" (Agha 1998:179), a voice of authority to whom one can always defer. Deference is expected in this diasporic context, where Tibetans often feel that all good ideas come from the Dalai Lama and succeed because of his blessing; hence he deserves the credit.

Deference aside, I do wish to suggest that the Dalai Lama has affected the distribution of Geluk debate in India, though not in any top-down, mechanistic fashion. He has influenced its movement by urging Tibetan refugees in India to exercise reason and avoid *rmongs dad,* what we may gloss as 'blind faith'. To his audiences in India, which typically consist largely of Tibetan refugees, the Dalai Lama has from early on politicized Buddhist education, at times considering it a diasporic pedagogy. No longer can Tibetan refugees afford to rely on habit alone, like the way they rattle off mantras or learn to spin prayer wheels or light butter lamps before religious icons. Without reason and learning as scaffolding these habits remain precarious, unstable.

This means that the curricula of Tibetan Buddhist centers of learning—monasteries and nunneries, and all sects, not just the Geluk—should offer at least some measure of philosophical study. As the Dalai Lama himself has acknowledged and even harped on at times, historically, few monasteries in Tibet really taught doctrine well. In most, prayers and recitations and rituals had to suffice. Even in the renowned Geluk monastic seats of central Tibet, philosophical training was pursued by few, perhaps as few as 10 percent. More ambitious still, the Dalai Lama has tried to expand the scope of such education to all Tibetan refugees, arguing that Buddhist philosophy can no longer be for monks alone. (There is an obvious note of egalitarianism in this call and the desire to extend equal educational opportunities to all.) Though the objective of mass Buddhist education has not been realized, the former objective has been, at least to some degree. The debate-based philosophical curriculum has been adopted by a broader range of Buddhist educational institutions. It has expanded.

. . .

3 February 1960. In Bodhgaya, a pilgrimage site in the state of Bihar where the historical Buddha is said to have attained enlightenment under a pipal tree, the Dalai Lama offers commentary on Tsongkhapa's short work, *Foundation of All Good Qualities* (*yon tan gzhi gyur ma*). As is customary, when he finishes his commentary he offers 'advice' (*bka' slob*), a kind of loosely structured public discourse that ranges from religion to politics to practical matters. Of note is the way he invokes the voices of foreign 'scientists' and 'scholars' and urges his audience to clarify Buddhism for a wider world. One needs to counter ill-informed books about Tibet's religion, he says, like those that call it "Lamaism." It is in the spirit of countering claims that he calibrates Buddhism with modern science:

> *deng tshan rig mkhas pa tshos lus kyi yan lag dang / nying lag gi rtsa rgyus la brten nas mi yi bsam blo 'khor tshul gang 'tshams shes kyi yod kyang / dbang po dang ba dang / rten pa dbang shes / yid shes kyi gnas tshul dang / shi 'phos nas ji ltar 'gyur ba'i gnas tshul rnams ji bzhin shes pa dka' zhing / skye ba phyi ma zhig yod pa la ni mkhas pa 'ga' shas kyis ngos 'dzin byed kyi yod pa red / de yang grub pa'i mtha' 'jig rten bkod pa po khas len pa dang / bdag rtag gcig rang dbang can du 'dod pa sogs de dag ni tshan rig mkhas pa tsho'i rig pa dang mi mthun / rang re'i rten 'byung gi rnam gzhag 'di tshan rig mkhan tshor rgyab skyor du 'gro gi yod 'dug der brten nga tsho'i chos kyi gnas tshul rnams rigs lam tshad ma'i sgo nas go nus chen po zhig legs par shod thub na / rang re'i chos 'di lung khug 'brog 'thoms glen pa rnams kyis ma gtogs yul lung dar rgyas yod sa'i rigs gsar mkhan tsho'i spyod yul min par lta ba'i gnas tshul sel thub / rang re'i spyi tshogs 'gro*

*stangs kyi cha nas rjes lus yin pa ni nges par khas len byed 'os pa las / sbas bskungs dgos
don med / 'on kyang 'dzam gling gzhan na med pa'i chos kyi shes yon ni ngos 'os pa zhig
red.* (T. Gyatso 2000a:vol. 1, p. 4)

Today scientists know quite a bit about how to think about humans based on the veins
and ligaments of the body's limbs and parts. But it is difficult to know exactly the sense
faculties' clarity,[10] the sense consciousnesses that depend on them, the nature of the
mental consciousness, and all the changes that occur through death and rebirth. A
few [foreign] scholars recognize that future lives exist. Moreover, tenets like the acceptance of a creator God and the assertion of a permanent, autonomous soul do not
accord with scientific knowledge. This presentation of dependent-arising[11] of ours is
gaining support among scientists. So if [we] can explain the facts of our religion well,
with a deep understanding through reason and logic, then [we] can dispel report[s]
that view this religion of ours as not being the province of scientific people[12] in a developed country but just that of some confused, stupid nomads in a remote region.
From the standpoint of our social system, it is appropriate to say with certainty that
[we] were backward; there is no need to hide that. However, [our] religious learning,
which does not exist elsewhere in the world, is something of which to be proud.

Though he credits science with discoveries of things external—the body, the material environment—Buddhism's own quasi-"scientific" expertise stems from its
explorations of interiority, and in this it is peerless.

On 29 June 1960 the Dalai Lama delivers a public address in Dalhousie,[13] a
former British colonial hill station in the state of Himachal Pradesh. Among the
residents are members of the former tantric colleges and a number of prominent
reincarnate lamas and senior monks. Again the Dalai Lama invokes the voice of
scientists and reports their views toward Buddhism and religion generally. 'Scientists' (*tshan rig pa*), the Dalai Lama says, have long been convinced that religion
distorts reality. But times are changing, and Buddhism is poised to prove them
wrong. He reports that some scientists have started to see truth in Buddhism. Their
interest piqued, they now wish to understand Buddhism's 'key points' (*gnad don*)
and system of knowledge. Therefore, he concludes, we must oblige them and at the
same time show the world that Tibet's religion is not some 'Lamaism' (*bla ma'i chos*),
a canard launched by an anonymous 'few' (*'ga' zhig*).

Teaching foreigners about Buddhism will require a new pedagogy, though.
"Nowadays it is not appropriate if [you] teach exactly according to the tradition of
the *lam rim* or 'Stages of the Path'" (*deng skabs phyi mi gzhan dag la lam rim gyi
gsung rgyun ji lta ba bzhin bshad na mi 'grigs*; T. Gyatso 2000a:vol. 1, pp. 18–19).
Though a popular literature in Tibet, the first stage in the Stages of the Path involves
"reliance on the spiritual teacher"—just the kind of topic that could confirm rather
than dispel fears that this religion is "Lamaism." (Consider, for instance, Tsongkhapa's *Foundation of All Good Qualities,* which the Dalai Lama had taught a few
months before in Bodhgaya. This digest of the Stages of the Path literature makes

unapologetically illiberal demands of the disciple right from the start. The disciple ought to think of himself as "ill," and of his teacher as a doctor; he should be unflappable, his mind tough and resilient as a diamond, ever ready and willing to do whatever he is told.) Rather than begin with a topic like this, which does not assume the subject's autonomy and his capacity to think critically, the Dalai Lama recommends that students be introduced to Buddhism's commitment to reason:

> ngos kyi bsam par / dang po chos de yang dag pa yin pa'i rigs pa'i rgyu mtshan dang bcas gsal bar ngo sprod / pha rol pos chos la yid ches byung na / de nas chos nyams su len thabs lam rim bzhin brjod dgos par bsam gyi 'dug. (T. Gyatso 2000a:vol. 1, pp. 18–19)

> As I see it, first clearly introduce [others] to the logical reasons why Buddhism is correct. If outsiders come to believe in the dharma, then [I] think that it is necessary to explain the method of practicing dharma based on the Stages of the Path.

This is not just a technical, pedagogical issue, a way to aid Western comprehension of Buddhism. It also involves countering views of Tibetans and their religion before an overhearer. Later in this address, the Dalai Lama encourages his exiled people to spread the dharma widely—even globally[14]—if only to correct misconceptions about it:

> phyi rgyal la chos lugs rgya cher spel thub pa byed dgos / phyi rgyal gyi mi brgya la chos bshad na / de khongs nas gcig gnyis la don dam gyi phan pa nges par yong srid / gal te khong tshos don la yid ches kyis nyams su blangs pa ma byung yang / chos 'di rigs lam dang ldan par ngos 'dzin dgos pa zhig chags kyi red. (T. Gyatso 2000a:vol. 1, p. 19)

> We need to be able to disseminate widely [our] religious tradition abroad. If [we] explain the dharma to a hundred foreigners, it is definitely possible that one or two among them will truly benefit. Even if they don't come to practice [Buddhism] through belief in [its] meaning, they will come to recognize that this religion [of ours] is based on the path of reason.

Again, there is an acute sensitivity of voices that find Tibet's religion backward and irrational. A similar point is made in another address in Dalhousie on 1 July 1960. If students of dharma exert themselves in teaching, debate, and the rest, they will be able to show the outside world that Buddhism is 'genuinely rational' (rigs pa khungs dag dang ldan pa) (T. Gyatso 2000a:vol. 1, p. 45), and 'outsiders' (pha rol po) will come to respect Tibetans more.[15] That there may be a political boon is never far from the surface. Bringing Europeans and Americans into the fold may translate into support. As the Dalai Lama acknowledges in this address, the spread of the dharma will likely mean that foreigners will also support the exile Tibetan community's political cause.[16] Sympathetic communication, and the moral and political action it can inspire, are never far from his mind, just as the plight of his people never leaves him.

Even in this handful of early talks—delivered just a little more than a year after the Dalai Lama's harrowing escape from Lhasa, and in the midst of bloodshed in

Tibet and a refugee crisis in India—one can make out some of the cardinal tenets of a "modern Buddhism." Besides the stress on Buddhism's embrace of reason, there is the desire to flatten hierarchy. In another talk, for instance, the Dalai Lama notes that women have not been permitted to participate enough in Buddhism, and that ought to change. Still, there are small but telling differences between these early talks and later ones when one considers who this discourse is really "for." When the Dalai Lama asks Tibetans to defend Buddhism against the charge of Lamaism and prove that it is a religion of reason, he is primarily talking to the traditional carriers of religious knowledge and authority: lamas and Geshes, and 'readers' or 'scripturalists' (*dpe cha ba*) generally (the term *dpe cha ba* distinguishes the elite minority of monks who study philosophy seriously from the majority of monks who do not, and from the lay public). The scope of addressivity for these elements of Buddhist modernism appears to be rather narrow in the first years of exile. Monks who study scripture remain the bearers of Tibet's religious patrimony. They are the ones tasked with defending Buddhism against critical voices, who must learn the "essential points" of other competing religions and traditions, if only so that they may better defend their own. The Dalai Lama has not enjoined—at least not yet—all Tibetan monks and Tibetan refugees to learn something about Buddhist philosophy in order to stabilize and secure their own religio-cultural identity. Such a generalized diasporic pedagogy—a pedagogy meant for all Tibetans—is in embryonic form. There are signs of this diasporic pedagogy to come, a pedagogy that would soon recommend Buddhist learning for all categories of Tibetans so that faith may become firm.

### FAITH: POISONOUS, BLIND, OR REASONED?

In 1955 the Dalai Lama entered Mao Zedong's office for what would be their last and, for the Dalai Lama at least, most unsettling meeting. In an infamous aside, oft recounted by the Dalai Lama and cinematically reconstructed in Martin Scorsese's *Kundun,* Mao leaned forward and confided with chilling calm: "Religion is poison." "At this," writes the Dalai Lama, "I felt a violent burning sensation all over my face and I was suddenly very afraid. "So," I thought, "you are the destroyer of the *Dharma* after all." " (T. Gyatso 1990:98–99; see also Ngawang Lobsang Yishey Tenzing [1962] 1997).[17] Mao had at times conveyed respect for Buddhism during the Dalai Lama's visit to Beijing (see, for example, Goldstein 2007:516), and the Dalai Lama had expressed sympathies with Marxism and noted its affinities with Buddhism. He left Beijing with some hope for Tibet's future, but Mao's words profoundly unnerved him. For the Dalai Lama, Mao had leaked his true intent. This proved to be a haunting moment that would shadow the Dalai Lama in the years and decades ahead. He recounts the episode in a number of his public speeches, yet in these retellings he responds decisively to Mao. In a public address on 17 March 1965 in Dharamsala, the Dalai Lama recalled this fateful meeting:

*1955 lo ngos rang maʾo tse tung mthaʾ maʾi mjal ʾphrad skabs maʾo tse tung gis ʾdi ʾdra gsung gi ʾdug . . . khong gis chos zer ba de dug red / chos kyis miʾi rigs la gnod pa las phan thogs gang yang med / lhag par bod dang / sog po la chos kyi dug chen po zhig khyab yod pa red / ces gsung gi ʾdug / de khong la khag med / phyogs gcig nas maʾo tse tung gis brtag dpyad nan po zhig ma byas pa dang / gnyis nas / nang pa sangs rgyas paʾi chos kyi lta ba gting zab po zhig yod pa de ma sbyangs ma shes pa yin stabs / hob ste maʾo tse tung gi bsam bloʾi mthong snang du / chos zer ba rgyu mtshan gtan nas med pa dngos yod kyi gnas tshul dang rtsa ba nas mi mthun pa / sngar gyi mi las ka mi sgyid mkhan / bsam blo grung po yod pa zhig gis rang gi grod pa rgyong thabs dang / rang gi ʾtsho ba skyel rgyuʾi ched du grub mthaʾ brtsams.* (T. Gyatso 2000a:vol. 1, p. 232)

In 1955, during my final audience with Mao Zedong, he spoke (hon.) in this way. . . . He said (hon.): "That so-called religion is poison. Religion only harms the human race. It does nothing helpful. The great poison of religion is particularly pervasive among Tibetans and Mongolians." He is not to blame [for] that. On the one hand, Mao Zedong did not make a careful examination [of religion in general]. Secondly, he neither studied nor knew that Buddhism has a profound view. Consequently, to Mao Zedong's mind, what he called "religion" just appeared to be utterly irrational and out of touch with reality, that some clever people in the past who did not like to work composed [religious] tenets as a means to fill their own stomachs and promote their own livelihood.

Mao's contempt for religion is chalked up to 'ignorance' (*ma shes paʾi skyon yin;* T. Gyatso 2000a:vol. 1, p. 232), not true animosity. The truth is that Buddhism is rational, the Dalai Lama retorts, a decade after the memory of this encounter first set.

This fundamental commitment to reason has been a steady refrain in exile, even when the voices this commitment counters are not that of Mao but those of "scientists" or "foreigners" or some other other. In exile this commitment has also become a diacritic that distinguishes Tibet's religion from competing world religions. Christianity and Hinduism, for example, are said to discourage their followers from exercising reason:

*dkon mchog des ji gsung ltar sgrub pa kho na ma gtogs dkon mchog la rtsod gleng dang / brtag dpyad bya rgyuʾi go skabs sprad med / der brten nang pa sangs rgyas paʾi bshad tshul dang bsdur na / brtag dpyad byas mi chog pa dang / rtsod gleng mi chog pa / dkon mchog nyid kyi bkaʾ kho na la yid ches bya dgos.* (T. Gyatso 2000a:vol. 1, p. 235)

One only practices what God says. No opportunities are given for debating and investigating God. Thus if one compares [this approach] with the way Buddhists explain [things], one is not allowed to investigate or debate; one must believe only in the words of God himself.

Later in the address from March 1965, the Dalai Lama condenses these remarks into a single, resonant expression that can be glossed as 'blind faith' (*rmongs dad*) (T. Gyatso 2000a:vol. 1, p. 257). This expression appears to have a shallow history in

Tibet, but it has two primary foreign sources. First, the English expression "blind faith" was a common way for theosophists and Buddhist modernists to characterize what sets Buddhism apart from religions like Christianity. Second, a contemporary Tibetan-Chinese dictionary (Zhabs-drung 1986) glosses *rmongs dad* in Chinese as "mi xin" ('superstition'), and indeed the Tibetan *rmongs dad* was used to translate *mi xin* in Chinese Communist propaganda from the 1950s.[18] In the context in which the Dalai Lama invoked this expression, he stated that Tibetans have been long accustomed to "belief by way of about half blind faith and about half reason" (T. Gyatso 2000a:vol. 1, p. 256). No longer can Tibetans afford to rest content with blind faith. Reason is needed, especially in exile.[19] And in a brief public address on 26 June of the same year, the Dalai Lama again draws on this resonant expression:

> *rmongs dad tsam ma yin par rig pa*[20] *yang dag gi lam nas nges pa drangs te ston pa tshad mar nges pa na / des bstan pa'i dam pa'i chos kyang khungs dag yid ches kyi gnas su 'gyur thub.* (T. Gyatso 2000a:vol. 1, p. 306)

> If [you have] determined [Buddha] to be a valid teacher after having induced [this] recognition through the path of correct reasoning, not through mere blind faith, then this [recognition] can also become the basis for confidence in the trustworthiness of the sacred doctrine taught by him.

One acquires confidence in Buddha as a valid teacher not through blind faith but through investigation and knowledge, and from confidence in the teacher springs confidence in Buddha's teachings. The scope of addressivity has expanded, for while a familiar cast of voices populates his talks, voices he engages with critically, as noted above, the primary addressees are no longer just the Tibetan clergy. That the path of reason is no longer confined to the clergy is evident, for example, in a talk to teachers delivered in Dharamsala on 28 January 1964 (T. Gyatso 2000a:vol. 1, p. 67). Here, the Dalai Lama appeals to the teachers before him, asking them to integrate religious and secular instruction (the amalgam is termed *chos srid*). And religious instruction, he explains, must involve more than parroting truth claims encoded in Buddhist treatises. Learners must think, and think critically: 'In saying "the Lama and Buddha are great sources [of truth]" and so forth, without stating any reasons whatsoever, there is the danger of stabbing ourselves at some point with our own knife.'[21]

Blind faith is hazardous, because it means you let down your guard and do not cultivate the skill of answerability—a point that the Dalai Lama has repeated and elaborated in other public addresses. When pressed or challenged by those who hold competing truth claims—which presumably happens a lot in exile—how can a Tibetan refugee respond? This capacity to respond, to justify Buddhism, is indispensable for all refugees, no longer just for the few. In the same address from 1964, the Dalai Lama makes an even stronger plea for all Tibetan refugees to exercise reason by learning elementary Buddhist logic:

*chos kyi tshul la thog ma nas rigs lam*[22] *du bkri rgyu gal che ba las / de min khyod bod pa yin pas ma ṇi bgrang dgos zer ba lta bu byung na mi 'grigs / . . . / ma 'ongs par bod mi rigs ser skya pho mo dbyer med tshang mar mtshan nyid kyi rigs*[23] *pa'i rnam gzhag gi 'gro lugs slob dgos / rnam 'grel le'u bzhi'i bdag nyid can lta bu cha tshang min na yang / tshul gsum la sogs pa'i 'gro lugs rnams nges par bslab dgos.* (T. Gyatso 2000a: vol. 1, p. 69)

In terms of the dharma's method, instruction in logic from the very outset [is] vital. Otherwise, if [you] come to say things like "you need to recite *maṇi*[24] because you are Tibetan," [that is] not right. . . . In the future, all Tibetan people without distinction—monks and laymen, men and women—will need to study the approaches found in the presentations of philosophical reasoning. Even if it isn't everything, like all four chapters of [Dharmakīrti's] *Commentary on Valid Cognition,* approaches like that of the "three modes" certainly need to be taught.

It is no longer enough to inherit religious habits from one's parents, from whom one acquires the practice of reciting mantras, making prostrations, and the rest. And while the Dalai Lama admits that the massive, baroque edifice of Buddhist philosophical literature will remain impenetrable to most Tibetan men and women, elementary reasoning (e.g., the "three modes" of logical proof, which refer to the "criteria that a correct sign must satisfy"; Perdue 1992:38 ff.; see Rogers and Phur-bu-lcog 2009) ought to be studied by all. Since monks learn logic through Buddhist debate—the two are inseparable in the monastic curriculum—this motivates the dissemination of Buddhist argumentation even if debate is not singled out.

Blind faith and its antidote, reason, have persisted in the discourses of the Dalai Lama.[25] If we page forward to an address given in Bodhgaya on 5 February 1987, for example, in a decade in which thousands of new refugees started streaming into India from Tibet, we see blind faith reinvoked to similar effect. In addressing the new refugees who have ventured to India, the Dalai Lama concedes that 'nowadays in Tibet the Chinese give [you] a freedom of religion'[26] (T. Gyatso 2000a:vol. 2, p. 327) but swiftly qualifies this. 'It is not right,' he adds, 'if you are tricked into being content with mere things like learning prostrations.'[27] True religious education must mean more than mechanical, "external" routines like prostrations. If you fail to get a real religious education, he cautions, you will be drawn willy-nilly down the path toward blind faith:

*nang pa sangs rgyas pa'i chos bsreg gtub 'pher ba yag po 'di rmongs dad ma yin kyang slob sbyong yag po byed rgyu ma byung ba'i rkyen gyis chos dad de rim bzhin rmongs dad la 'gyur rgyu'i nyen kha zhig mthong gi 'dug.* (T. Gyatso 2000a:vol. 2, pp. 327–28)

The burning, cutting, and rubbing well of the Buddha's dharma [as if it were gold being tested for authenticity] is not blind faith. But since there are not opportunities to study well [in Tibet], [I] think there is the danger that [your] religious faith will gradually become blind faith.

In suggesting that there are inadequate resources for studying Buddhism in Tibet, the Dalai Lama questions the degree to which China has eased restrictions on religious education in Tibet; he also tacitly promotes India's educational institutions, notably the Geluk monastic seats in South India, which began to expand in the 1980s, the decade in which he delivered this talk. Indeed, in this talk he appeals to Tibetans to join the Tibetan monasteries of southern India.

In sum, the price of not studying Buddhism well is high, because blind faith means cultural loss. Tibetans must be careful to avoid the fate of ethnic Buddhist groups like the Mon of Myanmar and the Tamang of Nepal (e.g., T. Gyatso 2000b:vol. 1, p. 59), both of whom are said to have only faith and ritual left. All real knowledge of Buddhism has left them. Popular religion thus comes under scrutiny: prostrations, mantra recitation, refuge prayers, the lighting of butter lamps at altars. All are recast as rote learning, as mere religio-cultural habits inherited in the family.

The exercise of reason, in contrast, confers upon refugees a certain stability of mind and self, figured at times in the Dalai Lama's public addresses through the trope of 'firm'-ness (*brtan po*). 'Firm'-ness belongs to a family of related terms and tropes like 'tough'-ness (*mkhregs po*) and words and expressions denoting 'stability', 'continuity', and 'immutability'. All are used to describe valued characterological attributes of the ideal diasporic subject. 'Firm'-ness typifies a self that resists the pressures of assimilation and conversion, that never loses sight of the fact that one is Tibetan and that one's religious patrimony is Buddhism.[28] Tokens of the trope appear in the Dalai Lama's public discourses as early as 1960, and while it is predicated of a range of abstract nouns, such as "resolve," "loyalty," "mind," "courage," and "confidence," firm 'faith' (*dad pa*) in Buddhism is of special importance. On 15 March 1987, the Dalai Lama explains what can stabilize faith:

> *gong du lab pa nang bzhin nang pa sangs rgyas pa'i chos tshul ji 'dra yod pa de dag shes pa byed rgyu gal chen po red / de shes pa'i thog nas bcom ldan 'das la dad pa byas na de rgyu mtshan mthong ba'i dad pa red / rgyu mtshan mthong ba'i thog nas dad pa skyes pa'i dad pa de dad pa brtan po yod / 'di byung na rkyen phra mo zhig gi[29] dad pa 'gyur sla po de 'dra yong gi ma red/ rgyu mtshan mthong ba'i sgo nas nges pa brtan po rnyed pa'i dad pa dbang rnon chos kyi rjes 'brang gi dad pa med par dbang rdul dad pa'i rjes 'brang gi blun dad lta bu yin na de rkyen phra mos 'gyur sla po yong rgyu red / . . . / slob sbyong byed rgyu de nges par du gal chen po red.* (T. Gyatso 2000a:vol. 2, pp. 367–68)

As [I] said before, it is vital to learn what Buddhism['s] approach is like. If one has faith in the Blessed One [Buddha] by way of that knowledge, that is reasoned faith. The faith that comes from reasoned faith is faith that is firm. If this happens, then [your] faith will not be changed easily by a minor circumstance. If [you] lack the faith that religious adherents with sharp faculties have, faith which has found firm certainty

through understanding reasons, [and your faith instead] is like the foolish faith of adherents with dull faculties, then that [faith] will change easily by a slight cause. . . .
Studying is absolutely vital.

It is the exercise of reason that makes faith "firm," so that external conditions and
events cannot shake one's core beliefs. For this study is mandatory. (The Dalai Lama
invokes a technical distinction between two categories of Buddhist disciples, those
of 'dull faculties' [*dbang rtul*] and those of 'sharp faculties' [*dbang rnon*], whose capacities differ and require different teachings. Buddha is said to have used skill in
means, teaching different things to different audiences, depending upon their abil-
ities and spiritual maturation.) The consequences of such study are not narrowly
curricular but partake of nationalist, diasporic concerns with cultural preservation.
At an assembly hall at a Tibetan school on 25 March 1999 the Dalai Lama explains:

> *chos byed dang mi byed so so'i 'dod pa red / gal te chos byas pa yin na / sangs rgyas kyi*
> *chos kyi gnas lugs shes pa byed dgos / de ltar byung na shes nas dad pa thob pa yin pas*
> */ dad pa de spus dag po yong rgyu red / de ltar min par pha mes kyi goms gshis 'jags pa*
> *lta bus sangs rgyas dang chos dang dge 'dun bcas la skyabs su chi zhes brjod pa yin na /*
> *de ni tshig tsam gyi skyabs 'gro yin pas dad pa brtan po med la / de tsam gyi nus pa yang*
> *med / spyir btang chos lugs tshang ma'i nang dad pa gal chen po yin pa bshad yod kyang*
> */ sangs rgyas kyi chos nang rgyu mtshan mthong nas dad pa thob pa zhig dgos zhes bshad*
> *pa de ni nang pa'i chos kyi khyad chos yin.* (T. Gyatso 2000b:vol. 2, pp. 532–33)

> Whether one practices dharma or not is one's own choice. If one practices dharma,
> one needs to comprehend the nature of Buddhism. If one does, then, by acquiring
> faith through knowledge, that faith will become first-rate. Otherwise, if, by virtue of
> habits from one's ancestors, one recites, "[I] go for refuge to the Buddha, [his] teach-
> ings, and [his] community," this is a refuge of mere words; [one's] faith, consequently,
> is not firm and to that extent [it] also lacks potency. In general, faith is said to be very
> important in all religious traditions. Yet, in Buddhism, it is said that "one needs the
> attainment of reasoned faith." This is a distinguishing feature of Buddhism.

Faith that consists merely of habits sedimented in the family lacks 'firm'-ness
(*brtan po*) and 'potency' (*nus pa*). This turn toward the family as a site for cultural
preservation comes out with even more vividness in an address at Hunsur in South
India on 7 October 1999. There the Dalai Lama reiterates the claim that Buddhism
is unique for its commitment to reason. As he does so often, he begins by stating
that the religions of the world have benefited millions in the past and continue to
do so in the present. They deserve respect. Still, one should recognize the 'distinguishing characteristics of different religions' (T. Gyatso 2000a:vol. 3, p. 648).[30] And
it is at this juncture that the Dalai Lama declares Buddhism's commitment to reason to be unique among religions:

> *rgyu mtshan shes nas thob pa'i dad pa de brtan po yong gi red / rgyu mtshan ma shes*
> *na blun po chu sna gar 'khrid chags nyen yod / pha ma tshos do snang byas te nang pa'i*

*chos kyi gnad 'gag shes thub pa byung na bla ma dang / dge bshes gcig la bsten ma dgos*
*par phru gu tshor khyim tshang nang du pha mas sangs rgyas kyi chos kyi go brda sprod*
*thub pa yong gi red / de 'dra byung ba yin na / mi rabs nas mi rabs la sangs rgyas kyi*
*chos la dad pa brtan po gnas thub pa'i phan thogs tan tan yong gi red.* (T. Gyatso
2000a:vol. 3, pp. 648–49)

Faith acquired through understanding the reasons [behind Buddhist doctrine] will
be firm. If one doesn't understand the reasons, there is the danger of becoming foolish [and] easily swayed. Parents, if, having taken heed, [you] become capable of understanding the key points of Buddhism, [you] will be able to transmit Buddhism,
[your] patrimony, to the children in [your] household without relying on a Lama or
Geshe. If that happens, there will definitely be the [additional] benefit in which firm
faith in Buddhism will be able to live on from generation to generation.

Tibetan parents should transmit reasoned faith to their offspring, ensuring inter-
generational continuity. Reason is tied to diasporic preservation, and this project
is not just for the clergy, as it was at the beginning of exile in India. The scope of
addressivity has been expanded to include all Tibetan refugees. The Dalai Lama has
entrusted all categories of Tibetans with the task of religious instruction and
preservation.

## THE CUTTING EDGE OF MAÑJUŚRĪ'S SWORD

Debate, in a word, has spread, and this expansion, or "rescaling,"[31] iconically
models the inclusion of ever more categories of people. As a practice that involves
the exercise of reason, debate ensures that reason's reach is extended. The natural
autonomy of subjects is recognized in ever more categories of refugee. Though all
this is fractionally of liberal, Enlightenment provenance, debate's dissemination
and the metadiscourses that have accompanied it are also informed by historically
specific diasporic concerns: the nationalistic bid to court sympathy and shore up
international support for rights and freedoms in Tibet and, as an adjunct to this,
the attempt to counter voices that spread negative stereotypes about Tibetans, like
the views that Tibetans are "backward" and "superstitious," that their religion is
"Lamaism."

While discourses of reason were evident in the Dalai Lama's addresses from the
start—and even arguably before his flight to India—and while these discourses have
always been interdiscursive, a way to counter negative stereotypes about Tibet's
people, culture, and religion, they did not constitute a diasporic pedagogy all at once.
In the first few years of exile it was not a generalized pedagogy, but by the mid-
1960s the Dalai Lama began to recommend philosophical study for all categories
of Tibetan refugee, and at least some suggestions were made about what such study

might look like.[32] In the 5 February 1987 talk in Bodhgaya, cited above, the Dalai Lama says that one can study philosophy in all the sects of Tibetan Buddhism, even though the Geluk and Sakya are stronger in this respect, and even though the Geluk sect 'in particular has become the strongest' (*yang sgos dge lugs pa drag shos chags yod;* T. Gyatso 2000a:vol. 2, p. 322). In the same talk he praises the flourishing Geluk monastic seats of South India and tells his audience that all categories of Tibetans— even rural, provincial folk (*yul mi*)—should take an interest in studying their religion and should frequent their local monastery.

Without reasoned faith at their core, Buddhist practices risk becoming hollow and brittle and are hence easily shattered by a secularizing modernity and by non-Buddhist religious traditions whose truth claims differ. In pressing Tibetan refugees to cultivate a reasoned faith in Buddhism, the Dalai Lama sounds a preservationist note: in the face of a corrosive pluralism, reason can help refugees preserve Tibetan Buddhism, a religion that he has elsewhere objectified as Tibetan culture's "essence." To be sure, reason has been a cherished faculty for the Geluk sect (and for other Buddhist sects) for centuries. It has been central to its soteriology, where liberation is sometimes figured as an act of "cutting" through deceptive appearances, an act executed, at least initially, by a well-honed intellect. Mañjuśrī exhibits well this agonistic figuration of Buddhist liberation. In his peaceful manifestation, he brandishes a sword that slices through ignorance's veil. But reason burns with new significance in exile. It has been recast by the Dalai Lama as an indispensable faculty of the modern Tibetan diasporic subject. Debate becomes a diasporic pedagogy and should spread.

A similar logic of expansion can be sensed in the 'ecumenical' (*ris med*) framing of debate-centered activities and institutions in the 1970s and 1980s. This 'ecumenical' framing is a complex one, with roots especially in Tibet's nineteenth-century 'ecumenical' movement, but a few basic observations can be made. From the start, the Institute of Buddhist Dialectics had insisted upon its 'ecumenical' orientation. While this label was partly motivated by its more expansive, inclusive curriculum relative to the southern monastic seats, and by the way it wanted to set aside overtly Geluk rituals to be more accommodating, surely this label was also motivated by the institution's foregrounding of "dialectics"; debate-based philosophical inquiry was its raison d'être. Dialectics, through which reason is exercised, belongs to no sect in particular but to all Buddhists.

Another institution that earned the 'ecumenical' label is the annual Jang Kunchö debates. In Tibet, the Jang Kunchö was a celebrated, roughly monthlong winter debating session held annually in Jang, south of Lhasa. The session was dedicated to the study of Dharmakīrti's *Commentary on Valid Cognition*. Despite the austere living arrangements and frigid temperatures, throngs of Geluk monks would descend upon Jang for weeks of intense wrangling and intellection (see Dreyfus 2003:234–

36). As a 1989 issue of the Dharamsala-based magazine *Sheja* put it, in Tibet under Chinese rule the Jang Kunchö was suppressed under a policy that treated "religion as poison," but in India, thanks to the Dalai Lama, it was reinstituted in 1984 and is now held annually.[33] The south's monastic seats take turns hosting the event: Ganden one year, then Sera, then Drepung. The second gathering, which included monks from Dharamsala's Namgyal Monastery and the Institute of Buddhist Dialectics, neared 350. The third drew about 500, and by 1990 more than 2,000 were reported to have attended, but in 1988 a far more dramatic expansion occurred. It was announced that the Jang Kunchö, "which has so far been limited to [the] Gelug tradition, is being opened to other lineages from this coming season as per the expressed wishes of His Holiness the Dalai Lama" (Anonymous 1988b:16). From the January 1989 session onward, all the major learning centers of the Sakya, Nyingma, and Kagyu sections, as well as the Bön order, would be invited. The winter session could now be dubbed 'nonsectarian' (*ris med*), as announcements then called it. This had been a Geluk institution before 1959. Its expansion is motivated by the fact that it is a debate-centered session trained on Buddhism's logico-epistemological tradition. In terms of both the mode and the topic of inquiry, the Jang Kunchö is just the kind of event that ought to transcend differences of sect and lineage. Reason, after all, has no limits.

Though debate as an interactional ritual is rarely singled out in the Dalai Lama's public addresses, the revalorization of debate as a diasporic pedagogy is motivated in manifold ways. First, there is the inseparability of debate from philosophical studies. Debate has not been taken up in India as a "method" that can be unmoored from the philosophical curriculum and "applied" to other domains, despite periodic attempts to suggest this. Second, debate has been introduced in more types of institutions than before, and this is often construed by Tibetans as evidence of change, of reform.

Recalling the design of the debate genre, it is not hard to see which parts might serve as design elements that look consistent with the Dalai Lama's calls for reason's expansion in exile. For critical rationality, one glance at the challenger's multimodal violence toward received doctrine will do, and the "autonomy" of this critical rationality is easily motivated by his objectivity, by the way he is supposed to criticize everything, relentlessly, no matter who the defendant is. But consider especially the defendant in relation to the characterological trope of 'firm'-ness. While perhaps a familiar figure for evoking diasporic "stabilization," "preservation," and survival in exile, it is not difficult to see what it is about debate as an interactional practice that makes this trope so felicitous, for isn't this just how the defendant seems in response to the challenger? 'Firm'-ness is well motivated by the defendant role in debate, not only because his demeanor looks unflappable—'firm'—in many ways (his relative nonreactivity when provoked, his lack of a prescribed repertoire of gestures, that he is seated and does not move, etc.), but also because it is the defendant who performatively stabilizes scriptural tradition. He is to maintain consistency and hold doctrinal tradition together, making authoritative texts 'firm' and acting out this stability at the same time. Those who inhabit the defendant role in India are also diasporic subjects by default, which also helps motivate this likeness in which the defendant in debate exemplifies the ideal diasporic subject in exile.

For whom and under what conditions is this mimetic sympathy between defendant and diasporic subject salient? Not for all actors, nor under all conditions. As should be expected of any discursive practice, debate has been typified in various and divergent ways, and these typifications have a social life of their own. Some younger monks at times seized upon the "sport"- and "exercise"-like character of the practice, citing the challenger's taxing physical accompaniments of clapping, stomping, and pacing. Others suggested that all this bluster is just a way to keep monks alert or ensure they don't forget material. Others had nothing to say. And even when one does secure analogies from interlocutors, whether "naturalistically" produced in situ or "elicited" with the aid of an interview question, these analogies offer no direct window onto speechways or cognitive habits or ideology or culture. Still, there are certain influential metadiscourses that have tried to fix the function of debate as being that of a diasporic pedagogy, in the sense that these discourses have been used to press for debate's expansion to ever more religious institutions on the subcontinent. And this push seems to have worked. The abbot emeritus from Sera Mey, whose words I cited earlier in this chapter, made this analogy between the defendant role and the diasporic subject palpable. When he spoke of the way debate can make participants 'firm' so that "later, [people] can't change [you]," he brought up the Dalai Lama's reforms in India and called attention to the challenges posed by pluralism in exile. Tibetans must learn to field competing truth claims if they want to stay Buddhist and remain Tibetan. The abbot's discourse, and others like it that I heard at Sera, closely resemble an argument the Dalai Lama had been making for decades, even if the Dalai Lama typically spoke of "reason," and not debate per se. For these actors, like the abbot emeritus, it has been the stabilizing power of debate—and more broadly of the exercise of reason—that has prompted the Dalai Lama to disseminate debate to educational institutions that lacked it before 1959.

As debate expands from being a technology that stabilizes institutions (like Sera's monastic colleges) to one that stabilizes a people (Tibetan refugees), its lower-order ideological function of "stabilization" persists. This new, more expansive mimetic sympathy is motivated by qualities in the practice's design and steadied by reflexive activities—many new—located "outside" debate's perimeter, in a dense mesh of other discursive practices. Unlike disciplinary practices like reprimand and corporal punishment, which have often been targeted for reform because of their illiberal design, debate's arguably illiberal elements have been left intact. In spite of debate's agonism and asymmetric design, its apparent failure to allocate "equal rights" to challenger and defendant, its "conservative" drive to preserve doctrinal coherence, the Geluk sect has not refashioned this interaction ritual. What has come to the fore is the way debate permits subjects to exercise an autonomous, critical reason. Certain characterological fractions of the liberal subject—this subject's autonomous, critical rationality—have been selectively foregrounded through second-order reflexive engagements with debate. To counter voices that find Buddhism irrational and backward, and to communicate an equivalence to the modern liberal West, debate is made to exemplify reason and is rescaled. It expands from a practice that does something for an individual monk, college, monastery, and sect to one that works for all monks—even all Tibetan refugees.

PART TWO

# Discipline

# 4

# Public Reprimand Is Serious Theatre

I had originally come to Sera to see how monks wrangle, but when I returned for extended fieldwork I found Geshe-la, the senior monk I befriended two years before, transformed. He had become, his assistant informed me, the college's 'disciplinarian' (*dge bskos / dge skos*), a high-ranking monastic office second only to the abbot. In public, Geshe-la parted crowds. All, save for the infirm and the unsocialized, now scattered upon seeing him, as I discovered during walks with him around Sera's premises. Monks in visual range took cover, colliding with each other as they ducked into restaurants or phone centers or careened down narrow paths. I once caught sight of a frail, elderly monk who could do no such thing. Stung by the disciplinarian's presence, he backed up a few steps and withered in place. His head and shoulders crumpled into a long, abject pose till Geshe-la passed. Geshe-la had been vested with considerable 'authority' (*dbang cha*), and these were signs of respect. Indoors, monks who paid him visits had this way of slinking in and edging down the hall with a sheepish grin till Geshe-la sensed their presence and peremptorily hailed them into his room.[1]

All this conspicuous cross-modal indexing of deference entitlements, figured through an idiom of "fear," was testimony to Geshe-la's new status in the monastic hierarchy. It also suggested, as Geshe-la himself remarked, that monks who inhabit the role of disciplinarian channel during their tenure the college's protector deity, an incorporeal agent who inspires fear, for he preserves moral discipline at *any* expense.

Though his duties are many and varied, the disciplinarian's primary obligation is, as his title suggests, to ensure that the college's moral foundation remains intact. This foundation's integrity is modeled in reportable, normative claims about the disciplinarian's authority. He is likened to a mountain, for instance. Unshakable, his words cascade downhill like rocks, and as rocks tumble down, never back up, so the disciplinarian's authority is unquestioned, and his commands are nonnegotiable for all those in his path.

Methodwise, the disciplinarian operates on the moral dispositions of monks in manifold ways. Administratively, he collects fines from monks who skip courtyard debate and accepts medical slips from those who are ill, for instance. Corporeally, he occasionally metes out punishment through his proxy, an imposing assistant who burnishes a short leather whip. Only rarely did Geshe-la himself strike someone, and then only weakly, as a token show of force.[2] It was especially through verbal means that he carried out his moral charge, which includes a form of public address that he is authorized to deliver.[3] Termed *tshogs gtam,* which translates literally and euphemistically as 'assembly talk' but which is better glossed as 'public reprimand',[4] this speech genre is a key disciplinary practice, a means of "forming or reforming moral dispositions" (Asad 1993:130).

A word about the diversity of disciplinary practices at Sera, first. In *Discipline and Punish* (1979), Foucault led his readers from sovereign spectacles of public execution to modern disciplinary technologies of surveillance and incarceration. His presentation permitted a linear, diachronic periodization, even if the periods were to be understood as disjunctive, not continuous or cumulative in any kind of familiar historiographic sense. At Sera, diverse types of punitive and disciplinary practices seem thrown together in a manner that would tax the stratigraphically minded observer. At Mey college, there is a schoolhouse where young monks pursue subjects like Tibetan literature, English, math, geography, and science. Outside, monks who have misbehaved do frog jumps clockwise around its premises as punishment (clockwise being the direction for circumambulation, so that they pick up a little religious merit along the way). Not far from the schoolhouse is Sera Mey's main assembly hall, where the disciplinarian and his assistant pace up and down the aisles during public gatherings. Sit for a spell and you will hear the periodic crack of the assistant's whip. As the disciplinarian's assistant explained, monks are disciplined for various infractions: for playing, for chatting idly during a sermon, for dozing off. In one assembly, he recounted, a young monk had sculpted some *pak* (roasted barley flour combined with liquid till claylike) into a helicopter and began playing with it. Others tossed around pieces of bread—offering bread, bread that had been consecrated; these were grounds for being struck. The leather is without question more for sound than pain, however; it conforms to "the rule of lateral effects," as Foucault (1979:95) put it ("It is minimal for him who undergoes it . . . and it is maximal for him who represents it to himself"). The whip is a few feet long, but its tip is never used; the instrument is folded in half to dull the blow. A strike or two will typically suffice. Consider yet another kind of punishment, the punishment for playing soccer, a sport categorically prohibited at Sera. Clandestine soccer matches convene weekly. As mentioned before, if monks are apprehended, they must first do prostrations in the assembly hall shared by the two colleges of Sera, Jey and Mey. On the second offense, they prostrate before their own teachers. On the third, they face expulsion. All such formal punishments are penned into ledgers that are kept by the disciplinarian and the head of the regional house (*khang tshan dge rgan*).

## PENAL SEMIOTICS AT SERA MEY

Assembly halls, classrooms, and countless other sites of socialization, each with their own punitive tactics, cannot be reduced to a few cardinal principles or fit into some monolithic disciplinary regime. This diversity notwithstanding, I focus in this chapter on one key disciplinary practice at Sera Mey, the disciplinarian's 'public reprimand'. While Foucault's *Discipline and Punish* has attracted its fair share of critics since its publication in 1979, it deserves renewed attention for its forays into an area that might be called, to use Foucault's own suggestive term, "penal semiotics" (1979:98). By this he meant something quite narrow and historically specific: the program of the reforming jurists in the eighteenth century who sought to replace the sovereign's spectacles of public execution (like drawing and quartering) with a gentler, punitive art that would "rest on a whole technology of representation" (104). In place of rituals that leave "retaliatory marks" on the malefactor's body, marks meant to index the monarch's wrath and power and authority, one finds "serious theatre" (113), where punishment is designed not to exact revenge but to rehabilitate the subject's soul through signs. As Foucault narrates it, this method was rapidly replaced by the modern technology of power, exemplified by the prison and especially by Jeremy Bentham's infamous architectural figure, the Panopticon. But understood broadly, Foucault's entire work can be seen as an exercise in penal semiotics. In exploring public reprimand at Sera Mey, I want to consider how this disciplinary practice can be pedagogical by way of its semiotic properties—how it serves, in Foucault's words, as a form of "serious theatre."

In public reprimand, the disciplinarian seeks to reform the moral dispositions of monks especially through the textual projection, juxtaposition, and evaluation of "voices" (in Bakhtin's sense). Singled out for rehabilitation in the performance from Sera analyzed here is the voice of the "derelict monk," who shirks his duties, chases after money, skips religious assemblies, neglects to take exams in Buddhist doctrine. The disciplinarian juxtaposes morally weighted voices in a manner designed to effect a transformation from derelict to dutiful. This transformation unfolds before the audience as a moral-didactic drama, a kind of "serious theatre," but it is theatre that is often uncomfortably close to the skin.

Uncomfortable, because when the disciplinarian evaluates the voice of the derelict monk, he often appears markedly fierce, both relative to his own typical behavior on other occasions and to standards of interactional etiquette evident elsewhere at Sera. For those who would mistake his affective displays as signs of vulgar, worldly 'anger' (*zhe sdang*), the disciplinarian diagrams his subjectivity as dissimulated, as split into (external) wrathful affect and (internal) benevolent motivation. "Dissimulation"—an effect afforded by a confluence of qualities of the reprimand itself and local talk about personhood and affectivity, as I will suggest—helps motivate readings that the disciplinarian is using a culturally valorized category of affect, a kind of histrionic "anger" used to inculcate moral discipline in others.

Part of the way he communicates dissimulation and indexes this category of affect is through an anonymous, indirect addressivity (Lempert 2012a). In reprimands, Sera Mey's disciplinarian uses language to refer to infractions and moral failings but without naming offenders. To these offenses he instead pins unnamed "voices," Bakhtin's celebrated term for the way utterances (oral or written) index recognizable personae and personae-attributes. At its essence, the notion of voice "addresses the question, 'who is speaking?' in any stretch of discourse" (Keane 2001:271). Though represented speech constructions like direct and indirect quotations in English are the most transparent linguistic means by which interactants project voices—since they project a voice distinct from the animator's, the one who physically produces the message (Goffman 1981)—the resources available for producing voicing effects are, as Jane Hill (1997:109) notes, many and varied.[5] A wide range of indexical signs—register tokens, "accents," deictic forms—can help produce voices, which raises the question of what helps voices cohere. Asif Agha (2005) identifies some of the textual conditions under which signs cohere and become recognizable as types of social personae. Voices can emerge through poetic or metrical contrasts (repetitions and parallelisms of co-occurring chunks of text) and the typification of these contrasts through metasemiotic regimentation, like the addition of proper names (yielding a "biographically individuated" voice) or characterological descriptors (yielding a "social voice"). Text-metrical contrasts—say, the parallelistic alternation of two lexical registers, "militarese" and non-"militarese" in a stretch of talk—can invite one to think that two distinct voices are speaking, even if additional typification is needed to individuate them, to name who these voices are. Metricalized voicing contrasts can also help motivate various kinds of dialogic relations between voices, cases where one voice appears to be responding to or evaluating a second voice.

In reprimand, the disciplinarian seeks to reform the moral dispositions of monks through projecting, juxtaposing, and evaluating morally weighted social voices, like the voice of the "derelict monk" (this epithet is mine, not the disciplinarian's), whose failings are spelled out, sometimes in graphic detail, enough to make the guilty parties squirm; whose subjectivity is exposed to the glare of public scrutiny, but whose voice remains anonymous. No finger-pointing, no proper names. In explaining his art to me, the disciplinarian praised this brand of indirection. The objective is to induce in the wrongdoer's mind the thought "I am the one" about whom the disciplinarian speaks.[6] In principle, the disciplinarian tells me, one can be direct under special circumstances. If the guilty party seems oblivious to the charges, and if one plans to expel him, one is permitted to name names and point fingers, but this must be a last resort.[7] Rather than resort to the blunt instrument of biographic individuation, the disciplinarian populates his discourse with morally weighted voices and invites his audience to consider them and adjudicate between them. Like Hamlet's staging of the play *The Murder of Gonzago,* the disciplinarian delivers a stinging morality play that depends on voicing for its effectiveness.

Outside of public reprimand, indirection is by no means the rule. I saw Geshe-la deliver frank and pointed criticism to subordinates well before he assumed this new post. Tenzin, Geshe-la's then thirty-year-old personal assistant and cook, ever self-deprecating, was on the receiving end of many a moralizing barb; he is lazy, sleeps late, and just eats, Geshe-la would sometimes tell me. As in public reprimand, these remarks were indirectly addressed, fired at me but meant for a copresent target—here, Tenzin. Unlike public reprimand, though, these charges always had a specific and unambiguous human referent. Many of these remarks shaded into a kind of ritualized teasing among intimates, frequently involving puns and epithets. (I became "Michael Limbu" ['Lemon'] for a spell, and after conducting one too many interviews I was dubbed *dri ba dri lan* ['Interview'].) And even after he had assumed the role of disciplinarian, Geshe-la did deliver compliments at times, praising, for instance, Tenzin's elegant handwriting—a valued skill at Sera. But teasing was moral-didactic. It had a disciplinary edge, as evidenced partly by the fact that it was directed especially at subordinates, at junior members in the community, when they were in the presence of older monks or outsiders like me.

Take Chögyel, for instance, who was twelve during my first visit and had arrived just two years before, and who became the focus of a little routine in which I became the surrogate addressee. In Chögyel's presence Geshe-la would delight in asking me whether his English was better than Chögyel's Tibetan—and I should add that Geshe-la would be the first to confess that his English was weak. The imperative: Chögyel must study.

. . .

I hear Chögyel bound up the steps and head straight to his room. The school day is over, so why doesn't he stop in to say hello? Geshe-la explains, breaking the news to me that Chögyel just failed his science exam. When Chögyel joins us, Geshe-la, beaming mischievously, nudges me forward to ask him for his score. "Go ahead," he says. "Ask him." I cannot. I don't want to humiliate him.

In a matter of minutes, Chögyel plummets to the rank of a nonperson. Chögyel's rights of participation revoked, Geshe-la stops addressing him and avoids his gaze. Excluded, he becomes an object of talk, an overhearer of his own abuse. Turning to me in Chögyel's presence, Geshe-la recites a line that masquerades as general moral advice: 'Scholars who don't study don't exist' (*ma sbyang pa la mkhas pa mi srid*). Thrust into the role of student, a surrogate for Chögyel, I suppose, I find myself dutifully penning this line into the little spiral-bound notepad I keep on hand. I always write things down when Geshe-la feeds me lines earmarked as memorable. Contra Chögyel, I am the good student, and the position starts to feel uncomfortable. "Repeat the line aloud," Geshe-la commands, in a break from our usual practice and his usual tone. I do, now feeling a little unnerved myself, and Geshe-la follows up sardonically, again to me: "And *why* is this so?" he pries. With its thin allegorical veil torn off, moral advice becomes overt criticism. He now refers directly to Chögyel's failure, explaining to me—for Chögyel's ears—that this F was caused by one thing: laziness. Chögyel had failed to study.

That evening at dinner Chögyel sits inert, and Geshe-la seems to be smoldering with anger. Unworthy of gaze and direct address, Chögyel remains a nonperson. Says nothing, is asked nothing. From the room's deafening stillness Geshe-la again takes the stage, resuming his morality play. "Take Trinley, for instance," he says, looking at me. He's 'hardworking but unintelligent' (*brtson 'grus tsha po / rig pa skyo po*). Trinley agrees.[8] Now take Chögyel. He's 'intelligent but lazy' (*rig pa yag po / brtson 'grus sdug cag*). Using the compound *spyang*, Geshe-la calls Chögyel 'clever' (*spyang*) outside and 'stupid' (*lkug pa*) within. "He just plays and sleeps, plays and sleeps. He scored only 20 percent on the exam, and the class has just five students in it! Chögyel fared the worst, can you believe that?!"

Over dinner, Geshe-la mints a new nickname for Chögyel. Like most young monks, Chögyel has accumulated many epithets (*ming 'dogs*) that he trades with friends and peers, including 'crooked head' (*mgo kyog*), for certain peculiarities in the morphology of his skull; 'sit down sleep' (*rkub brdabs gnyid khug*), for his propensity to nod off while seated (he confessed to having fallen asleep in the bathroom many times and once leaned so hard on the sink that it came crashing to the floor). I dubbed him *phig phig*, a colloquial expression denoting any gelatinous, jello-like substance (this, for the frenetic way he seemed to move about and for his modest biceps; we teased each other a lot). Then there were the English loans: *scamp*, proposed by an earlier English teacher, presumably for a kind of endearing mischievousness; *mosquito*, for his wiry frame and zippy, "pest"-like behavior—I came up with this one, and Chögyel liked sharing it. To this list, Geshe-la added a new epithet this evening: "fail," which, without the labiodental fricative in his phonemic inventory, became a clunky, plosive /pʰɛl/.

Over Saturday breakfast Geshe-la calls Chögyel by his new sobriquet: "Fail!" Chögyel remains morbidly silent. Geshe-la tells Chögyel to explain to me why he has failed. 'Not study[ing]' (*ma sbyang*) is all that escapes his lips, an echo of that moralizing one-liner Geshe-la had me repeat the day before. Geshe-la now uses directives with Chögyel, telling him brusquely to 'sit' (*sdod*) and 'eat' (*zo*)—bald imperatives that he resorted to rarely. (I heard him once tell a dog to 'take off' [*rgyugs*; the imperative of 'run'], and to another dog that was whining and yelping as we ate dinner he once fired off a piercing 'Shut up!' in Tibetan, and it did. I heard Geshe-la issue the same brusque kind of directive to ten-year-old Pasang when he started dozing off while cleaning offering bowls: 'Wake up!')

Geshe-la drums on the new epithet: "Monday is coming, and Fail will fail again!" At dinner the tide of religious aphorisms rolls in, enveloping me, even though it's meant for Chögyel: 'Without effort, the mind is like stone; with effort, it is like gold' (*brtson 'grus med na rig pa rdo dang 'dra / brtson 'grus yod na rig pa gser dang 'dra*). I sense the tide beginning to recede, though, because now the directives bear the deferential imperative (*dang*) (e.g., 'Please sit' *sdod dang;* not 'Sit' *sdod*). In terms of their stereotypical indexical force, these forms register as less brusque and rude. The nadir had been reached, so he begins inching back up the politeness scale. Meanwhile, where was Chögyel? I find him in another room sunk in the pages of his science textbook, memorizing lines about calories and joules as if they were so many pages of religious text. Chögyel is studying furiously—and ostentatiously—and Geshe admits him back into the ranks of the human. By Saturday, Chögyel could be gazed at and addressed, though addressed only with derisive epithets, directives, and moralizing barbs.

Sunday, the day before he would retake his science exam, Chögyel remains Fail. He is alone in his room, in retreat, absorbed in studying. He skips breakfast. Geshe-la summons him loudly to the table several times, but he doesn't come. Using English, Geshe-la captions Chögyel's state for me with a single word: "embarrassed." Eventually, Chögyel does show his face but only for a few spoonfuls of porridge.

When Chögyel finally leaves for school, Geshe-la confides that he invented the nickname Fail to help Chögyel study, knowing that it hurts him (*gnod kyi 'dug*), and that in hurting him it would spur him to study harder. "Next time he asks for chocolate, I'll use the same strategy," Geshe-la mutters thoughtfully.

. . .

In public reprimand, proper names and epithets are proscribed. Reference must be oblique. This standard of indirection surfaced both in Geshe-la's remarks about reprimand and in his own prescriptive manual on this genre, composed in 2000, and it resonates with the Great Exhortation (*tshogs gtam chen mo*) text recited at Jey, Sera's other college:

> When someone creates a small infraction of the rules of this great and precious college, if such a person is sitting at the head of the row one should look toward the back of it, and if he is sitting toward the east then one should look toward the west. In other words, one should offer [the exhortation] so that others are not aware [of the identity of the perpetrator of the offense], even though one is oneself aware. If that individual does not recognize that [the advice] is being directed at him, then during the second exhortation it is necessary to make others slightly aware [of the identity of the person] by referring oneself to those who sit near him in the row and to his housemates.

If the individual still does not recognize that it is being directed at him, then on the third occasion one must direct oneself at the very person and say, "You have broken such and such a rule," offering [the exhortation] by pointing the finger at him. (Cabezón 1997: 342–43)[9]

This indirection plays a role in communicating the disciplinarian's histrionic anger, I will suggest, though this does not exhaust its significance. This indirection also has the virtue of "lateral effects": it speaks to all because it is addressed to no one. It enhances the scope of the disciplinarian's address, "generalizing" his censure into a moral palliative for the whole monastic community. In this, it is akin to the piercing echoes of the leather strap with which the disciplinarian's assistant metes out mild corporal punishment in public assemblies. That is, there is a certain infectious paranoia that the disciplinarian's low-resolution sketches of social types can induce; with enough scrutiny, you begin to wonder, Is he talking about *me*? You recognize yourself in these nebulous portraits. Second, this indirect addressivity lends to the disciplinarian the impression of an almost preternatural capacity for surveillance, for if the disciplinarian can get the guilty monk to feel that he has been discovered, he can only be impressed by this feat, which bolsters the disciplinarian's authority. And without indexically pinning infractions to real people—to biographically individuated souls—it also means that the indictments, and by extension the disciplinarian, can never be wrong. Together, all these facts conspire to figurate the disciplinarian's own omniscience, or at least omnipresence (How *could* he know this? Maybe he really *can* channel the college's protector deity. Did his assistant spot me, or someone report me?)

Geshe-la needed an agent. He needed the stealth and industry of his assistant to monitor and collect information on Mey monks. The assistant, Jermey, a sturdy twenty-four-year-old monk, did not welcome this job. At nineteen he braved the overland trek from Tibet to Nepal, two days of which were spent trundling forward with a young child slung over his back. To see he had to literally pry his eyes open with his hands. He saw people slip and fall to their deaths and others succumb to frostbite. Were he to face this journey again, he'd prefer a pistol to his temple, he swore. He had been through a lot and shown his mettle. For the job of the disciplinarian's assistant, he had drawn straws with another candidate, a close student of Geshe-la's. Jermey lost. The job was his. Now he is constantly on the move, he complains. "It is a tiring, weighty job," he says. On Tuesdays, Sera Mey's weekly holiday, he travels far and wide in search of wrongdoers: into clearings in the forest where clandestine soccer matches often convene; to swimming areas in the town of Kushalnagar (swimming was forbidden, as monks in the past had once drowned); to movie theatres; to the neighboring town of Bylakuppe, including all of its Tibetan refugee camps; to the police, from whom one could get information. If an assembly (*tshogs*) is poorly attended, he launches an investigation. He tracks missing monks. On most he patiently collects evidence that rarely results in explicit indictments. Instead, this information to which he, the disciplinarian, and perhaps a handful of others are privy, is folded into the public reprimand's text, evidence transposed into character, plot, and narrative.

## PUBLIC REPRIMAND: A CLOSE READING

15 July 2000. Slightly before dawn, perhaps five o'clock. I wake from the sound of scuffling shoes in the corridor, which grow louder and louder and end up, oddly, outside my door. A monk raps his knuckles on my windowpane and shoots a flashlight beam inside. The light darts around the room till it finds the mosquito netting draped over my bed. It settles upon me. Whoever it is out there is obviously pretty startled, because he lets out a screeching whisper to his companion: 'There's a Westerner!' (*dbyin ji cig 'dug.*) Then came the apology, in English, loud and clear: "Sorry!"

They leave. I later learn that they were tasked with rounding up monks who failed to wake up for an early morning assembly (*tshogs*) in the college's main assembly hall; if a monk was caught oversleeping, he'd get whalloped. I knew of the assembly but chose to arrive later to set up my tripod and video camera in a far corner of the room. The hall looks packed—perhaps five hundred monks; at least that's the number quoted to me. I know only that Geshe-la, in his role as disciplinarian, will announce exam scores and that the abbot emeritus will deliver some kind of sermon.

As the event unfolds, I witness a metamorphosis. Geshe-la—the same spry, puckish, hospitable man who has me sit near him whenever we eat together—starts to belt out what I would later discover was the start of a public reprimand. The event lasted a modest eight and a half minutes, but that is not how it felt.

In the lead-up to the public reprimand, Geshe-la announces the results of a recent debate examination on Buddhist philosophy. A list of names and scores in hand, he stands before a microphone that whines and screeches every couple minutes, and patiently reads aloud the results: each name carefully enunciated, each score made plain before the capacity crowd. He begins with the number one (*ang ki dang po*) group whose test scores ranged from 90 to 100. They are invited to stand, are draped with white silk offering scarves, and are handed envelopes lined with crisp rupee notes. The monks are then ushered down the hall's most prestigious artery, the central aisle, which terminates at the foot of a throne on which the abbot emeritus sits. When they reach the throne, each monk bows with surgical precision to touch the crown of his head with the abbot's—a ceremonial embrace of no small distinction. After the names of the top group are read, the disciplinarian begins a slow, methodical descent down his list, ending with the names of those who "failed."[10] By the time he reaches this category of monk, the stream of scarves, envelopes, and salutations with the abbot has dried up.

It is this category of monk, the monk who failed, that becomes the foil for developing the voice of the derelict monk in the public reprimand that immediately follows. In the transcribed segment below, subscripts are used in the free translation column to track voices that are central to the moral-didactic drama: *D* = derelict monks; *E* = earnest monks who try but fail. In the second transcribed segment below, the following are also used: *A* = all audience members; << .... >> = nonmodal voice quality.

1  *'o da de nas*                                                    okay now
   ɔɔ ta   tɛ-nɛ
   oh now that-ABL

2  *brgya cha grwa pa* [1-2 syll] *'dug se zhus pa red*              the [exam] scores have been
   gyaja traba [1-2 syll] dugs   shüü-pɔ          rɛɛ̀              presented(HON.A) in this
   score monk [1-2 syll] like.this say(HON.A)-NZR AUX.~P.FCT        way

3  *a ni de dang da lta ma phebs mkhan yang yog red*                now there are also those_D
   ǝni tɛ taŋ tanda ma-pɛ̈b-ñɛ̈n          yaŋ yɔɔ̀rɛɛ̀             who don't come(HON) [to
   then that and now  NEG-come(HON)-AGNT also AUX.NOM              exams]

4  *da- da lta 'dir*                                                now—now here
   ta    tanda dɛɛ
   now- now this-LOC

5  *brgya cha ma lon mkhan de dang ma phebs mkhan byas kyi yin na*   if [one] compares those_E
   gyaja ma-lön-ñɛ̈n   tɛ taŋ ma-pɛ̈b-ñɛ̈n      cɛɛ̀-gi yin-na    who fail with those_D who
   score NEG-pass-AGNT that and NEG-come(HON)-AGNT do-NZR AUX-COND  don't come(HON) [to exams]

6  *su- su nyen kha che kyi red*                                     who—who is more
   sü- sü ñenga chëwa rɛɛ̀                                          dangerous?
   who who danger great  AUX.~P.FCT

7  *ma phebs mkhan de nyen kha che red*                              those_D who don't
   ma-pɛ̈b-ñɛ̈n      tɛ  ñenga chɛ̈ rɛɛ̀                             come(HON) are more
   NEG-come(HON)-AGNT that danger great AUX.~P.FCT                   dangerous

In these initial moments of the public reprimand, the disciplinarian populates his discourse with two opposed voices denoted through paired nominal expressions: "those who fail" exams and "those who don't come" to exams. He invites listeners to compare the types of monks denoted: one fails because of ability, the other because of neglect. How is the voice of the derelict monk evaluated? The disciplinarian seems charitable. In line 5, in fact, he pays deference to the derelict monk with the honorific variant of the verb "to go," and does the same in line 6 when he asks which category of monks is more dangerous.

In lines 10–11, the disciplinarian represents the speech of the derelict monk. Derelict monks allegedly feel or say that they don't "need" to attend the debating courtyard, a place where monks meet daily to hone their intellect and enhance their knowledge of Buddhist doctrine through argumentation; they also don't need to

8    *'ga' shas gcig 'dug*                                                             there   are   a   few
     < <gashèè  jīg  duù> >                                                            [monks]ᴅ
     few     a   AUX.~P.IEV

9    *dngos gnas drang nas*                                                            really
     ŋööŋɛè traŋnɛè
     really

10   *yar chos rwa la ya'i yong dgos kyi mi 'dug*                                      [who  say,  weᴅ]  also
     yaa    cööra-lɔ        yɛ  yoŋ    go-gi   min-duù                                 don't need to come(NH)
     up-LOC debate.courtyard-LOC also come(NH) need-NZR NEG-AUX.~P.IEV                 up   to  the  debating
                                                                                      courtyard

11   *'o mar tshogs grwa ja dmang ja la ya'i yong dgos kyi mi 'dug*                    oh, [who say, weᴅ] also
     ɔɔ  maa  tsɔ̀ɔ̀  traja  mäŋja-lɔ       yɛ  yoŋ    go-gi  min-duù                   don't need to come(NH)
     oh down-LOC assembly college.tea communal.tea-LOC also come(NH) need-NZR NEG-     down  to  assemblies,  to
                                                              AUX.~P.IEV               college-wide        or
                                                                                      monastery-wide    tea
                                                                                      offerings

12   *de 'dra'i grwa pa a red zer na ni*                                              if [one] asks whether
     tɛndrɛ **grwa**- traba  ä-rɛ̀è          sɛr-na-ni                                 [thoseᴅ who act] that
     like.that mon- monk DUBIT-AUX.~P.FCT say-COND-PP                                 way are mon- monks,

13   *grwa chas cig gyon bsdad yog red*                                               [theyᴅ]       are     there
     tracɛ̀è   jīg  kyö̀n  dɛ̀è  yɔɔrɛ̀è                                                 wearing monks robes
     monk.robe one wear stay AUX.NOM

14   *ma red lab thub yas yog ma red*                                                 [one]  can't  say  that
     ma-rɛ̀è          lɔb  tü-yɛ̀ɛ   yɔɔ̀marɛ̀è                                          [theyᴅ] aren't [monks]
     NEG-AUX.~P.FCT say able-NZR AUX.NEG.NOM

15   *'o 'dir rigs 'di da*                                                            oh, [as for] thisᴅ type
     ɔɔ' dɛ̀ɛ       rig  di  ta                                                        [of monk] here now
     oh this-LOC type this now

16   *dngos gnas drang gnas so so so sos bsam blo cig gtang na yag shos red*          really, [it] is best if each
     ŋööŋɛè traŋnɛè  sösosösö     sämlo jīg dāŋ-na < < yagshöö rɛ̀è> >                 [personₐ] individually
     really       individually  thought one send-COND best   AUX.~P.FCT               thinks some [about this]

17   *don dag khyon nas mi 'dug ga*                                                   [it] doesn't make any
     tödaà   kyö̀nɛè  min-du-gaa                                                       sense, right?
     meaning any    NEG-AUX.~P.IEV-CSQ.INT

attend daily religious assemblies.[11] When the disciplinarian introduces the derelict monks in line 8, there is also what Hill (1997) refers to as an "intonational shadow" in the form of a gravelly voice quality. This quality belongs to a cluster of nonmodal voice qualities that include especially tight, strained, harsh, and shouted, all of which appear to signal degrees and shades of "anger" in this reprimand. Throughout, the disciplinarian tends to key these voice qualities either directly to the voice of the derelict monk or to the "character zone" (Bakhtin 1981), the swatch of discourse in which this voice makes its appearance.

With the voice of the derelict monk on display, the disciplinarian elicits an evaluation from his audience, whom he positions as moral adjudicators. Should these derelict monks be considered monks? He leaves his audience little time for deliberation. A response comes from himself in the form of the voice of a "neutral observer" (the impression of "neutrality" derives from the nomic auxiliary verb *yog* [*ma*] *red*, conveying the sense of generally known truths; this is juxtaposed with the evidential auxiliary *mi 'dug* in the preceding lines 10–11). The neutral-observer voice coolly notes that the derelict monks *do*, in fact, wear monk's robes. One can't technically say that they *aren't* monks, the voice concedes. Yet the disciplinarian allows suspicion about the derelict monks to hang in the air undispelled.

There are two parallelistically contrasted voices. The first consists of the derelict monk's represented speech. The second is a neutral-observer voice that appears to adopt a dialogic stance toward the first voice. In line 16, the disciplinarian then invites each and everyone in the hall to think about this case—an invitation that is something of a refrain during the reprimand. The sequence that occurs here, and that recurs across the event, is as follows: the disciplinarian first invokes the voice of the derelict monk, deploys a second voice to comment on it, and then enjoins his audience to "think" about the matter well—to adjudicate among the juxtaposed voices, to select who is right. Any hope that the derelict monk will be acquitted is soon quashed, however, for the disciplinarian weighs in with his own evaluation in line 17, though with a token measure of audience involvement in the form of a confirmation-seeking question: '[It] doesn't make any sense, right?' The verdict? That derelict monks are spurious social types and don't deserve to stay at the monastery.

How delicately the disciplinarian has thus far proceeded! He began with a charitable display of deference toward the derelict monk, then launched an inquiry into the voice's moral status. At the close of this inquiry the disciplinarian is still rather removed from the verdict he reaches. He holds up the figure of the derelict monk for public scrutiny and invites the audience to evaluate it. He does not appear to confront the voice of the derelict monk himself, not yet.

The list of charges leveled at the derelict monk gets longer in subsequent lines:

18  *yang med na*
    yaŋ mɛɛ̀-na
    also NEG.AUX-COND                                          not only that

19  *u- u- dge 'dun gi las hyed hyed 'dug ga*
    ɔ- ɔ- gendün-gi lɛ̀ɛ̀jèè cɛ̀ɛ̀   dùù-gaa                    uh-    uh    there's
    uh- uh monk-GEN work do   AUX.~P.IEV-CSQ.INT               monastic    service
                                                               work to do, right?

20  *las ka hyed sa gcig la c tshud cig lta dgos red*
    lɛ̀ɛ̀ga cɛ̀ɛ̀sa jĩg-lɔ      ē-tsũ̀ũ̀       jĩg tā   go   rèè    [they_D] need to try to
    work place a-LOC/DAT DUBIT-include a  look need AUX.~P.FCT   see whether [they_D]
                                                               can get  into  a
                                                               workplace

21  *de nas lta rogs hyed kyi ma red*
    tɛnɛ tarɔɔ̀       cɛ̀ɛ̀-gi ma-rèè                            then [they_D] don't try
    then look.after do-NZR NEG-AUX.~P.FCT                       to look [for that
                                                               work]

22  *yang med na*                                                               not only that
    yaŋ mɛɛ-na
    also NEG.AUX-COND

23  *tshogs- tshogs chos rwa 'grim sa der yar phebs dgos red*                    [they$_D$] need to
    tsɔ̃ɔ̃-    tsɔ̃ɔ̃   cööra   drimsa  tee    yaa   pēē   go   reè              go(HON) up to
    assembly- assembly courtyard visit.place there-LOC up-LOC go(HON) need AUX.~P.FCT   religious assemblies,
                                                                                the debating
                                                                                courtyard, places to
                                                                                go to

24  *de nas phebs gi ma red*                                                    then [they$_D$] don't
    te-ne pēē-gi      ma-rcè                                                     go(HON) there
    then  go(HON)-NZR NEG-AUX.~P.FCT

In part of this sequence (lines 23–24), the disciplinarian again pays deference to those who don't come to religious assemblies or go to the courtyard, yet his deference ends here and is soon replaced by condemnation. About a minute later the disciplinarian again invokes the voice of derelict monks whom he characterizes euphemistically as 'very odd'. He then shares a narrative about these monks, during the course of which this surprise becomes shock, and the shock, contempt.

In this narrative, the disciplinarian describes an incident in the debating courtyard. One evening he arrived in the courtyard and noticed that many monks were absent. Monks who miss courtyard debate must pay a twenty-five-rupee fine (no small sum, especially for repeat offenders). Concerned, the disciplinarian approached the class leaders in the courtyard to ask them about the absences. The class leaders must record the names of truant monks so that fines can be assessed. To the disciplinarian's astonishment, the class leaders declared that all the monks were present and accounted for. It dawned on the disciplinarian that the class leaders had been turning a blind eye to the derelict monks to save them from their mounting fines. While the class leaders are spared criticism, criticism is heaped on the derelict monks at the narrative's close:

83  *'di gras 'dod pa med na 'gro bzhag na 'grigs kyi red ta*                   if [you$_D$] lack the
    < <dindreè   döö-ba  mɛɛ-na    dro    shaà-na    dri-gi    rɛtaa > >        desire [to come], it's
    this.kind desire   NEG.AUX-COND go(NH) leave-COND alright-NZR AUX.~P.FCT-   right if [you$_D$] leave
                                                                   DIR.ASR      [the monastery]!

84  *grwa pa grwa kyang yin zer*                                                [you$_D$ say], '[we$_D$] are
    < < traba tra   kāŋ  yin-s > >                                              simple monks'
    monk monk only AUX.P.FCT-QT

85  *grwa pa grwa kyang yin na zhogs pa'i ga re yin na'i shog ta*               if [you$_D$] are simple
    < < traba tra   kāŋ  yin-na   shɔg-bɛɛ     kare yinɛ shöötaa > >            monks, then come to
    monk monk only be-COND morning-GEN whatever come(NH).IMP                    whatever is going on
                                                                                in the morning!

86    *grwa ja mang ja yong dgos kyi yog ma red*              [you~D~ say] there's no
      < < traja       māṇja yoṇ    go-gi    yȝȝmareè > >      need to come to
      monastic.tea communal.tea come(NH) need-NZR AUX.GNM-NEG  monastic and general
                                                              tea asemblies

87    *rkub tshugs a*                                         [you~D~] stick [it up
      < < gūp dzuùg-aa > >                                    your] ass!
      ass  insert-IMP.INJ

The phrase 'simple monk' denotes a valorized category of monk, who is unattached
to material things and leads a virtuous life. The stretch of represented speech containing 'simple monk' in line 84 is attributed by default to the derelict monk; that
is, it is what derelict monks purportedly say about themselves. This resonates with
the issue of the fines that they have had to pay for missing debate sessions. Though
their pockets have been emptied from steep fines, the derelict monks have the au-
dacity to take pride in their newfound penury. In this reading, they flaunt their
poverty as evidence of their elevated religious status—proof of their commitment
to a "simple", nonmaterialistic lifestyle. Whatever the specific readings members of
the audience may find in this invocation of the 'simple monk', the disciplinarian's
rhetorical arithmetic is simple and unforgiving. He juxtaposes a valorized type of
monk, the simple monk, with the negatively valued derelict monk, yielding the following: if derelict monks really want to be 'simple', virtuous, authentic, the path they
have chosen is dead wrong. Here, he has not just compared morally weighted figures.
He has also constructed a makeshift syllogism and confronts the voice of the derelict
monk more directly.

     In line 86, the disciplinarian again represents the speech of derelict monks. These
monks purportedly argue that there is no need to come to the college-wide or
monastery-wide tea assemblies. Here, the disciplinarian's treatment of this voice
reaches a peak of intensity: 'Stick [it up your] ass' (line 87), he belts out.[12] Earlier,
he had invited his audience to weigh and adjudicate the voice of the derelict monk.
And in the preceding lines, he began to confront derelict monks with an argument
about why they should change. In line 87, he hurls an invective at them in the imperative mood. Not surprisingly, this entire evaluative sequence, which occurs immediately after the close of the narrative, is shadowed with a nonmodal voice quality. This voice quality, associated by default with the animator (the disciplinarian),
is again keyed to the character zone occupied by the derelict monk.

     In the remainder of this event, the disciplinarian's strategies for handling the voice
of the derelict monk are many and varied. At times, he juxtaposes fragments of
widely accepted religious doctrine with the behavior exhibited by the derelict monks.
At a certain moment, for example, he tropes on a famous line from Śāntideva's
revered work on the life of the bodhisattva:

As long as space abides and as long as the world abides, so long may I abide, destroying the suffering of the world. (Santideva 1996:143)[13]

The disciplinarian uses this line to chastise monks who chase petty pleasures and abandon the life of virtue, thereby failing to 'remain' in the world for the sake of serving others:

| 152 | *grwa tshang ser ra smad (.) zer ya de* | as for those from Sera Mey monastic-college, |
| | tradzaŋ        sëramëë-pə   ser-ya   te | |
| | monastic.college Sera.Mey-NZR say-NZR that | |

| 153 | *ji srid nam mkha'* | if, for as long as space [exists,] |
| | jisii        nāmkā | |
| | as.long.as   space | |

| 154 | *de srid tu gnas dgos kyi yod na* | [bodhisattvas] need to remain [in the world] |
| | tesii    tu      nëë    go-gi    yö-na | |
| | till then LOC/DAT remain need-NZR AUX-COND | |

| 155 | *'o 'di gras 'dir sdod shig ta* | well, in this way, [you$_D$] stay put! |
| | ɔɔ' dindree dee     döö shii-taa | |
| | oh like.this this-LOC stay IMP-DIR.ASR | |

The disciplinarian does more than spotlight the failure of derelict monks to live up to Śāntideva's ideal; insofar as derelict monks themselves accept the authority of Śāntideva's classic text—and they do by default—they live hypocritical lives. They are not being reasonable.

The appeal to reason is more overt at times. Just before the sequence transcribed above, the disciplinarian begins by appealing to his own authority (e.g., in line 144, he says: 'I told you it is virtuous if you go to the debating courtyard a bit, right?') but then justifies this by rattling off two reasons for attending the courtyard: First, if you go to the courtyard, you won't need to pay fines. Second, you will be able to accumulate religious merit that will serve you well in this and future lives. Derelict monks seek to satisfy their own interests rather than serve others, but even here they rely on a faulty calculus. If they want to satisfy themselves, they have clearly chosen the wrong means.

Late in the event, the disciplinarian indicts the derelict monks through simile. He likens the derelict monk to a class of incorporeal beings termed 'hungry ghosts', pathetic beings known for their selfishness and avarice and for the obstacles they create for earnest Buddhist practitioners. Yet shortly after he makes this damning comparison, the whole mood of the reprimand lifts, if only momentarily. The disciplinarian shifts topic and mentions that a new set of exams—written exams—will be administered in a few days. As he initiates this topic shift, he resumes the poise and deference projected at the outset of this event (subscript $A$ = audience members; $I$ = disciplinarian):

186   *da da lo nas bris rgyugs gtang zer*                  now, [I₁ said] 'written exams [will

        ta   thalo-nee   trigyuù      dāŋ-s        be] given from this year onward'

        now this.year-ABL written.exam do-QT

187   *gtang rogs gnang zer zhus pa yin zer*          [I₁]  said(HON.A)  'please(HON)

        dāŋ  rɔ̀nan       shüü-bɔ       yin       take [these exams]'

        do  PRC.INJ(HON)-QT say(HON.A)-NZR AUX.P.FCT

188   *zhus pa gzhir bshag zhal bshad gnang song*      [you_A] agreed(HON) [to take the

        shüü-bɔ        shirshaà shèèshèè   nāŋ    sõŋ    exams] based on what [I₁]

        say(HON.A)-NZR base.on  accept(HON) do(HON) AUX.~P.PEV   said(HON.A)

Gone is the intonational shadow cast by the nonmodal voice qualities. Gone are the voice of the derelict monk and the damning comparisons with hungry ghosts. In their place, the disciplinarian seems to lay out for his newly reinvited guests a sumptuous spread of honorific forms. Everyone in the room, derelict monks included, are now given a second chance—a chance to *come* to exams. This moment, which again occurs very late in this event, is fleeting, for shortly after this moment there is another brief phase in which the disciplinarian summons and harshly evaluates the voice of the derelict. Yet at the very end of the public reprimand (forty-two lines later in the transcript), there is a sustained phase in which the derelict monks—the same monks who were previously reprimanded for not paying their fines—receive deference as they are asked to do what they ought to do: pay up.

231   *de nas chos chad- chos chad bsdu ya de tsho*     then, as for the religious

        tene  cööcèè-     cööcèè    düü-ya    te-dzo    fines, the collection of

        then  religious.fine- religious.fine collect-NZR that-PL   religious fines.

232   *gang ga log hur thag 'bad thag*                 everyone, diligently

        kangalɔɔ     hürdaàbadaà

        everyone   diligently

232   *ga re zer dgos red*                    'how should [one] put it'

        ˈkare  ser go     reè`

        WHQ  say need ~P.FCT

232   *yar gnang rogs gnang*                 please(HON)         hand

        yaa       nāŋ     rɔ̀nan       over(HON) [the fines]

        up-LOC/DAT give(HON) PRC.INJ(HON)

At the close of the earlier narrative, the derelict monk is told to stick it up his ass; here, he is delicately asked to pay the fines he owes. In line 232c, the disciplinarian uses the honorific variant of the precative injunctive mood marker (*rogs gnang*), together with the honorific variant of the verb 'to give' (*gnang*). Notice also the disciplinarian's disarming remark about his own alleged dysfluency in line 232b ('How should I put it?' he adds softly). The disciplinarian appears to be prescriptively modeling the transformation of the derelict monk's voice from derelict to dutiful, demonstrating how deference awaits the derelict monk who commits to changing his ways. This shift in deference and demeanor is maintained till the end of the event. Here are the disciplinarian's closing words:

239   *hyas na ta da lta zhus pa nang bzhin*

      cg̈ena   ta̠ ta̠nda   shü̠ü-bɔ         nɔŋshin

      therefore now now   say(HON.A)-NZR like

      *therefore, now—now as [I've₁] said(HON.A)*

240   *da lo brgya cha ma lon mkhan*

      tha̠lo    gya̠ja  ma-lö̠n-ñ̈en

      this.year score  NEG-pass-AGEN

      *those₁ who failed this year*

241   *dus sang nas brgya cha lon pa cig brgya cha yar spar ya*

      tü̠üsaŋ-nɛɛ    gya̠ja lö̠n-bɔ   jig gya̠ja ya̠a   bär-ya

      next.year-ABL score  pass-NZR one score up-LOC increase-NZR

      *please(HON) contemplate(HON) how to increase [your₁] score and pass next year*

242   *'di gras gi 'dug se dgongs pa 'i nang bzhes rogs gnang*

      di̠ndreè-gïi  du̠ts   gɔ̠ŋ-pee       naŋ shɛ̀ɛ     rɔ̠ɔnaŋ

      this.kind-INS like.this mind(HON)-GEN in  accept(HON) PRC.INJ(HON)

243   *e ni 'o*

      ɔ̄ni  ɔ̠ɔ

      then oh

      *then oh*

244   *da zhus ya da ga yin*

      ta̠ shü̠-ya         ta̠ga   yı̠n

      now say(HON.A)-NZR just.that AUX.P.FCT

      *now that's all [I₁] have to say(HON.A)*

245   *gang yang zhus pa gang yang btab pa ci kyang nas*

      ka̠ŋ shü̠ü-bɔ     ka̠ŋyaŋ  dɔ̠b-(b)ɔ   ji̠ kä̠ŋ-nɛɛ

      what say(HON-A)-NZR whatever plant-NZR whatever-ABL

      *whatever [I₁ have] said(HON.A), whatever [virtue I₁ have] sown,*

246   *bka' 'drin skyong bar shog*

      gɔ̄drin    gyö̠ŋ-waa        shö̠ö

      kindness(HON) protect-NZR-LOC/DAT OPT.INJ

      *may it serve to safeguard kindness(HON)*

In this coda, the disciplinarian pays deference to both categories of monks—those who failed but tried, and those who failed because they didn't show up. At the end, as at the beginning, the disciplinarian uses honorific forms liberally. And in his closing dedication, he frames what has transpired as if it had been a wholly benevolent act, consolidating its virtue and gifting it to all sentient beings: "May it serve to safeguard kindness."

In sum, the disciplinarian seeks to (re)form the dispositions of monastic subjects primarily through a kind of moral-didactic theatre in which the dramatis personae consist of unnamed social voices, and these are evaluated in diverse ways. At times the evaluations come in denotationally explicit form (e.g., when the disciplinarian asks: 'It doesn't make any sense, right?'). At times, they come in the form of prosodic accompaniments (esp., the nonmodal [e.g., harsh, strained, etc.] voice quality), applied especially to the character zones in which the derelict monk appears. Sometimes the evaluations are inferable only through the text-metrical juxtaposition of voices. And then there is variability with respect to the types of juxtaposition created by the disciplinarian. At times, he formulates pointed analogies (e.g., derelict monks are like hungry ghosts). More often he set representations of the speech and behaviors of the derelict monk against the very values that they, as Buddhist monks, (should) uphold, as if to expose their logical inconsistencies in a bid to change the way they think and behave.

## HISTRIONIC ANGER

Has the disciplinarian been angry, though? What kind of affect has he manifested throughout this event? Consider a few distributional facts about some of the semiotic resources for conveying "anger," namely the nonmodal voice qualities (harsh, tense, etc.) and the segmentable linguistic elements (especially the expletives).[14]

These were not distributed evenly across phases of the event. The expletives do not appear at the event's beginning and end, and there are only scant traces of nonmodal voice qualities in these positions.[15] At the beginning and end of the reprimand, the cluster of "angry" nonmodal voice qualities is all but absent. The disciplinarian used a nonmodal voice quality (gravelly and then tight) on just two words (lines 8 and 16, indicated earlier). In the closing forty-seven seconds of the reprimand, the voice quality is mostly modal, with some tenseness. While it waxes and wanes during the body of the reprimand, the left and right peripheries are nearly clear of nonmodal voice qualities. (In the body of the reprimand, there are two roughly forty-five-second-long stretches of modal voice quality, the second of which, tellingly, consists largely of an announcement made about upcoming exams; it involves a phase of discourse in which the voice of the derelict monk is absent.)[16]

Read globally, as a whole that comprises several parts, the stretches of discourse laminated with nonmodal voice quality are bracketed by text-segments (albeit of shorter relative duration) that lack it. Moreover, the disciplinarian began the event with charitable displays of deference; charitable, because he offered deference to those who didn't deserve it—derelict monks. Honorifics become dense toward the phase's conclusion, too, where he seemed almost hyperbolically benevolent. Signs that might otherwise index a morally transgressive affective state are hence cushioned by contiguous but contrastive text-segments. The disciplinarian constructs a global, tripartite text structure in which the "middle" text-segment stands out as being affectively incongruous. To the extent that the disciplinarian's behavior seems to violate standards of appropriate demeanor in the middle (monks aren't supposed to hurl invectives), it begs for an explanation.

A range of explanations are possible, of course. Perhaps the disciplinarian has momentarily succumbed to the 'afflictive emotions' (*nyon rmongs*), like desire and pride and ignorance; included in this canonical list is vulgar 'anger' (*zhe sdang*), against which Buddhists are taught to be vigilant. In this reading of the tripartite text structure, he begins placidly, loses his cool, then recovers it at the close of this event, returning his audience to the status quo ante. Or perhaps the disciplinarian's affect was itself affected, a controlled detonation, as it were, designed to bring down the hardened habits of derelict monks. Has this been, in other words, an expression of a cultural type of virtuous, "histrionic" wrath?

It is the second reading that was suggested to me, namely that of a category of anger distinct from vulgar aggression. Beyond the discursive properties of the reprimand, there are certain ideas and ideals about this special, virtuous form of dissimulated anger, including an aphorism that came quickly to my interlocutors at Sera: 'Face, darker than a craggy mountain. Mind, whiter than a snow mountain'.[17] This aphorism asks monks to dissimulate—to sever affect from 'motivation'. (By 'motivation' here I mean *kun slong*, a Buddhist term denoting the seat of moral action).

A reincarnate lama at Sera Mey I knew glossed the aphorism's term 'face', tellingly, as 'external display' (*phyi logs pa'i rnam pa bstan yag*), which he counterposed to an underlying, 'benevolent mind set' (*phan pa'i bsam pa*). The aphorism about the craggy and snow mountains comes up in interviews with the disciplinarian, in a prescriptive manual on public reprimand that he authored, and in conversations with other monks at Sera Mey. This aphorism distinguishes inner states from outer signs. Wrath is to be displayed, not felt. This lama unpacked the aphorism with these words:

> *kho rang gi phan pa'i bsam pa 'di ga re nang bzhin dkar po cig 'khyer dgos red zer [-s]*
> */ a ni dge bskos kyi phyi logs pa'i rnam pa bstan yag 'di / gdong rdza ri las- rdza ri yog*
> *red pa / rdza ri- nag po zhib po zhig yog red pa / 'di las nag pa'i dpe gdong drag po byas*
> *byas / a ni kho yar skul brda byed dgos red zer.*

> [As for] his [i.e., the disciplinarian's] benevolent mind-set, [the aphorism] says that no matter what happens, purity must be maintained. Now as for the disciplinarian's external display, "face, [darker] than a craggy mountain"—craggy mountains, right? Craggy mountains are extremely dark, right?—[It] says that he needs to address [others] with a menacing expression even darker than that.[18]

The disciplinarian himself offered a similar explanation and constructed an analogy between his affective behavior in public reprimand and the wrathful displays of Buddhist protector deities.[19] Protectors, like Buddhist tantric deities, are said to have an immutable core of enlightened consciousness. Untainted by worldly passions, they can exhibit hyperbolic and transgressive affective states, including anger. By his own analogy and by other evidence, the disciplinarian's reprimand is a vehicle for exhibiting virtuous, histrionic wrath.

Multiple forms of reflexivity conspire to overdetermine the disciplinarian's affective displays as an appropriate act, a kind of violence that can shape moral dispositions. In terms of production, this cultural category of affect is not made linguistically manifest at the level of lone utterances, nor is there a single linguistic or prosodic feature—or even a cluster or configuration of such features—that uniquely indexes this affect's presence. This affect has no signature; harsh voice quality may be used here, an invective and furrowed brows there.

What properties of the disciplinarian's discourse and configuration of independently presupposed contextual facts motivate the construal that this cultural category of affect, this histrionic wrath, is in play? First, there is indirect addressivity. Affect indexicals of "aggression" are directed at social voices, not named addressees; this contrasts with vulgar aggression, which canonically has real-world referents—specific persons—as its indexical focus and visceral motivation. Second, a tripartite global text-metrical structure figurates the "containment" of affect indexicals of anger, framing them fore and aft with conspicuous (even hyperbolic) displays of deference. Affective "containment" helps motivate interpretations of volitional "control," helping distinguish this state from the vulgar, uncontrolled aggression proscribed by Buddhism. Third, there is a widespread ethnodramaturgical discourse on the need for "dissimulated" anger, on the need for an inner-outer fractionation of the emotive subject. Disciplinarians (and all those authorized to engage in histrionic anger) are asked to disjoin "inner" states from "outer" signs, as conveyed in the aphorism of the pristine mind within and the menacing "face" without. Fourth, and perhaps the most obvious presupposition of all, surely such a high-ranking monastic official, who oversees the moral discipline of others, no less, must be capable of keeping 'afflictive emotions' (*nyon rmongs*) like anger in check!

This affect's stability as a cultural type—the conditions under which it appears and becomes recognizable to interactants—rests on distinct but mutually reinforcing types of reflexivity both immanent "in" and "external" to events of public reprimand. The primary resources and media for signaling this "anger" (the expletives, the directives, the nonmodal voice quality laminated over stretches of discourse) acquire a higher-order affective meaning when considered in relation to distinct forms of reflexivity.

Besides the issue of recognizability, that is, how people identify this as a *kind* of anger, I should also note that this cultural category of affect is also not said to be specific to reprimand. The disciplinarian and other monks I spoke with at Sera often formulated a homology: the disciplinarian is to the disciplined as challenger (in Buddhist debate) is to defendant as teacher is to disciple. Figured here would seem to be a local-cultural "emotional regime" (Reddy 2001), a "set of normative emotions and the official rituals, practices, and emotives that express and inculcate them" (129). Distinct domains of male-monastic socialization are chained to each other, each said to require communicative violence to produce moral subjects. In debate, challengers issue taunts and deliver claps that resemble physical strikes. Good religious teachers are strict with their pupils, scolding them when necessary and applying mild forms of corporal punishment. Several domains of socialization appear strung together, as if they were all of a piece, even if they are *not* of a piece when it comes to the history of their reanalysis and reform.

# 5

# Affected Signs, Sincere Subjects

*I am very apt to think, that great Severity of Punishment does very little Good, nay, great Harm in Education; and I believe it will be found that, cœteris paribus, those Children who have been most chastis'd, seldom make the best Men. All that I have hitherto contended for, is, that whatsoever Rigor is necessary, it is more to be us'd, the younger Children are; and having by a due Application wrought its Effect, it is to be relax'd, and chang'd into a milder Sort of Government.*

—JOHN LOCKE

With what emotion and tactics should monks reform the moral dispositions of others? For some Tibetan monks in India, this is a live and at times vexing question. In a range of male socialization practices in the monastery—public reprimand, courtyard debate, the meting out of corporal punishment—Sera monks are asked to exhibit a kind of anger. But this affective state must itself be affected. It exists under the strictures of a morally inflected dramaturgy summarized well by the aphorism that contrasts outer wrath with inner benevolence, "dark," menacing, rocky mountains with "white," snow-covered ones. Distinguished from vulgar, worldly anger (*zhe ldang*), histrionic anger targets a monk's moral habitus. It extinguishes his arrogance and kindles humility. Like the ideal of speaker "sincerity" (Keane 2002; Trilling 1972), the self implied is split into an inside and an outside, but, unlike sincerity, one must *disjoin* rather than align inner and outer states.

For its apparent insincerity, but also for its uncanny resemblance to "real" aggression, this histrionic anger—anger performed, not felt—has come to trouble certain Tibetans in exile. It may not be troubling in debate, where ritualized violence has been left intact, but it is troubling in disciplinary practices like reprimand and corporal punishment, some of whose features have been undergoing reanalysis by Tibetans who aspire to ideals associated with the modern liberal speaking subject, such as rights, autonomy, and directness. This partial emulation of the liberal subject can be seen vividly through comparison, through juxtaposing, as I do below, disciplinary practices at Sera Monastery in Bylakuppe with those of the Institute of

Buddhist Dialectics in Dharamsala. The institute's name itself suggests its attempt to break from the past, from "traditional" monasteries like Sera. At the institute the globalizing liberal subject seems to rear its head, displaying its attributes of rights and autonomy, clarity and sincerity, which the monks there strain to emulate. These attributes are no random assemblage but a bundle of morally weighted ideals concerning language, affect, and personhood, whose genealogy is best understood in relation to a globalizing modernity, including liberal-democratic notions of autonomy and rights, as well as to the ideals of denotational "clarity" and "sincerity" that have been communicative desiderata since at least the seventeenth century. These ideals, conveyed across transnational networks involving human rights advocates, religious aid agencies, foreign Tibet activists, and others, have become objects of partial emulation in exile projects that court sympathy. Practices of courting sympathy with those abroad can sometimes change the way one makes monks at home, at monasteries like Sera.

## HOW VIOLENCE BECAME A PROBLEM

Setting aside the disquieting application of pain to the body in corporal punishment, it is not hard to appreciate why monks might worry more generally about disciplinary practices like reprimand and corporal punishment: the practices' failure to presume the disciplined subject's rights and autonomy; their failure to be "clear" when communicating what has been done wrong or even who, specifically, has done it; their failure to put trust in a monk's capacity to control himself; the whole asymmetrical, hierarchical tilt of these encounters, which makes them look alarmingly unequal and violent. If all this seems incompatible with Buddhist principles of nonviolence and compassion, and liberal-democratic principles with which these principles are designed to resonate, might this not jeopardize the projects of sympathy on which the exile government's ethnonationalist struggle in part rests? Might this not disturb foreign supporters, whose gaze—real or imagined—could see in these behaviors a "culture" that deviates from the culture and politics of compassion and nonviolence promoted by the Dalai Lama? Such concerns, and the scrutiny of Buddhist institutions these concerns inspire, cannot be understood apart from the exile government's positions toward violent resistance in Tibet and the engagement with liberal-democratic ideals, which stem from the early days of exile. While the problem of violence, not to mention the overdetermined pragmatics of writing about violence in Tibetan culture and society, can be traced especially to the Tibetan Government-in-Exile's shift in strategy in the mid-1980s, its international campaign and the Five Point Peace Plan, it began much earlier.

As leader of what would crystallize into an exile "government" in India—the Central Tibetan Administration of His Holiness the Dalai Lama (CTA)—the Dalai Lama peremptorily announced at his first press conference in June 1959 that there would be no return to the old society. (He would later remind the world that he had tried to introduce land and tax reforms in Tibet some five years before his departure but had been stymied by Chinese Communists.) "Democracy Day" was instituted on 2 September 1960, and in an address on the anniversary of the Lhasa uprising on 10 March 1961, the Dalai Lama spoke of plans for a democratic constitution. Circulated in 1963 in both Tibetan and English, this constitution was really a provisional charter that would become actionable once Tibet's independence was won. (This, to the dismay of critics in the Tibetan exile community who complained that the document had no teeth, that it did not insist on democratic reforms *now*, in exile.) By its letter, the constitution envisaged the Tibetan polity as a "unitary democratic state founded upon the principles laid down by the Lord Buddha," a state that would "adhere strictly to the Universal Declaration of Human Rights" and offer citizens "equality before the law" and the "right to life, liberty and property."

This sounding off of hallowed liberal-democratic ideals—albeit in the subjunctive mood of a world desired but yet to be—was in part designed to be overheard by member states of the United Nations. It betokened a commitment to principles of representative governance shared by those outside the Communist Bloc, who, it was hoped, would advocate for Tibet's cause. Critical among such members was the United States, whose Cold War interests inspired it to offer a measure of covert CIA support for Tibetan resistance fighters from 1956 to 1973, and while the precise circumstances under which Tibet's constitution was drafted remain unclear, John Kenneth Knaus (1999) has written that Ernest Gross, a former American ambassador who offered council to the Tibetans, had a hand in crafting it. About the democratic sensibilities of the Tibetans, Gross (1961:139) mused in the October 1961 issue of *Foreign Affairs*:

> Although they did not know their Locke, Mill and Jefferson, and had traditionally accepted an autocratic form of government, Tibetans by nature are a democratic people. Mountain, space and a feeling of closeness to God produce an instinctive sense of equality and regard for human dignity. Self-reliance is a necessity of life in Tibet. These facts of their nature soon became evident in India.

In the Tibetan constitution, it was Buddhism that had shaped their dispositions, not the stark environment or an ethos of Emersonian "self-reliance." Tibet's draft constitution trumpeted the Buddha's authority and his teaching's basis in "justice, equality and democracy," as the preamble read. The Tibetan text was bolder, opening with florid epithets in praise of the Dalai Lama, followed by a cascade of lyrical Buddhist-themed verses, as if what followed were a doctrinal treatise.

Even though the Buddha may have discovered liberal-democratic truths long before Locke, Mill, and Jefferson, this invocation of the Buddha's authority did not mean Tibetan Buddhism was immune from reform. The very liberal-democratic ideals used to reimagine governance were turned back upon Buddhist institutions in exile,[1] if only partially and fitfully. In the midst of the refugee crisis of the early 1960s and the ferment this disorder provided, the Dalai Lama sounded the need for reforms in language that often resonated with liberal-democratic ideals. Women, for instance, should be allowed to participate equally in Buddhism. Buddhist education ought to be extended to all and should no longer be the preserve of elite monk-scholars, the Geshes. Conditions in exile may have eroded traditional divisions of rank, region, and sect, but all this offered an opportunity, he argued, a chance to rediscover one's essential unity, and unite. From a 1963 conference convened by the Dalai Lama to preserve and advance Tibetan Buddhism, to which representatives of all Tibet's Buddhist sects were invited, came the stated aim to heal age-old sectarian wounds (Office of H.H. the Dalai Lama 1969:190–96). The effects of such efforts (not all attributable to the Dalai Lama, even if the convention is to defer to him) were often quite substantial. They included an initiative to modernize the Geluk sect's philosophical curriculum, launched at Buxa in 1966; the opening in 1968 of a university-styled institution initially called the "Institute of Higher Tibetan Studies"; the inclusion of Buddhist lessons—including lessons in elementary dialectics and epistemology, which monks study—in primers meant for *all* Tibetan schoolchildren; the founding in 1973 of the self-consciously modern "Buddhist School of Dialectics" (in Mcleod Ganj, renamed the "Institute of Buddhist Dialectics" in July 1987), which, taking traditional Geluk monastic seats like Sera as its foil, aspired to transcend sect and hierarchy and run on austere principles of individual responsibility. Elements of these initiatives resonated with the post-Enlightenment and liberal-democratic aspirations being voiced in the domain of exile politics and its ethnonationalist struggle. Enjoin all to exercise reason and think critically about received doctrine, as if to adjure, with Kant, "Sapere aude!" Redistribute Buddhism: give everyone—men and women, clergy and laypeople—equal opportunity to learn and participate in Buddhism; it is their right. Overcome sectarianism and petty differences in doctrine. Let meritocratic principles replace the automatic respect for the received status of *tulkus,* reincarnate lamas; karmic inheritance may vary wildly from individual to individual, but one's knowledge, and the respect it commands, must be demonstrated in *this* life.

It should be apparent that efforts to remake Geluk institutions were well under way before the mid-1980s, when the Dalai Lama and the Tibet question began to enjoy unprecedented international visibility. This is not to suggest some simple, linear continuity from 1959 to the present, as if these initiatives were all of a piece; there were different motivations and actors involved, not to mention a good deal of ambivalence. There is a history here that I cannot address. I simply wish to stress how old these discussions are, discussions about how Buddhist education ought to work, how best to inculcate and reform dispositions, how to create, through ped-

agogy and curriculum, the right kind of Tibetan Buddhist subject. All of this discussion, as mediated through the guiding force of the Dalai Lama, was in the shadow
of an ethnonationalist struggle and the engagements with liberal ideals it required.
Still, the role of human rights discourse in the 1980s was different from this discourse's role in the 1960s, or the early 1970s, at least in terms of the degree of urgency it created surrounding the need to reform disciplinary practices.

The exile government's international campaign of the mid-1980s was, in many
respects, precipitated by a crisis. In 1959 the strategy for mobilizing international
support had been largely to work on the United Nations by seeking out member
states that would raise the Tibet question. A letter from the Dalai Lama to the UN
secretary-general on 9 September 1959 marshaled facts about Tibet's sovereignty
and read off a train of abuses that were said to amount to genocide. A second letter in 1960 cited a damning report to the International Commission of Jurists prepared the same year by the Legal Inquiry Committee on Tibet. That report, like the
prior year's interim report—neither disinterested, as later critics would observe—
cited grave human rights abuses and acts of genocide. The UN for its part passed
resolutions in 1959, 1961, and 1965 that put the abuses on record but did little more.
Meanwhile, and more substantively, the US State Department continued clandestine support for the Tibetan resistance, even if it planned as early as the mid-1960s
to phase out this assistance (Shakya 1999:360). In 1971 the People's Republic of
China was admitted into the fold of the UN and US-China relations began to thaw
under the Nixon administration. Geopolitically, the United States and China shared
strategic interests in curbing Soviet expansionism. Beijing was anxious about its disputed Sino-Soviet border, Washington about mounting US setbacks in Vietnam.
From the 1970s till the mid-1980s, relations between the two appeared to be on the
mend, and while US support for Taiwan periodically strained ties between Washington and Beijing, "human rights"—in Tibet or elsewhere in China—did not, and
would not until the mid-1980s (Harding 1992). For Washington, the Tibet question was no priority at all.

Within the PRC, liberalization in the post-Mao era offered renewed hope for the
Tibet question in the form of a series of official Dharamsala-Beijing contacts that
began in 1979, followed by fact-finding delegations to Tibet by representatives from
Dharamsala, and overtures by Beijing for the Dalai Lama to return home, albeit under conditions that he and the exile government could not accept. The Dharamsala-Beijing meetings collapsed finally in late 1984, leaving Dharamsala at an im-
passe: neither a UN-based approach nor direct bilateral talks with Beijing would
suffice (Shakya 1999; Roemer 2008). In what is reported to have been a series of
high-level strategy sessions held by the CTA between 1985 and 1987, the exile government settled upon a strategy to make Tibet matter again, especially through securing the support of the United States. A deliberately international campaign, it
put the Dalai Lama forward as political emissary for the first time.[2] He had already

been traveling and speaking internationally, but now he would take Tibet's political message directly to the West. As this campaign gained traction, Dharamsala became a node in what would become a vast network of nongovernmental and intergovernmental organizations and Tibet support groups (Frechette 2002; Roemer 2008; Goldstein 1999).

As part of this international campaign, the Dalai Lama–led exile government discursively conceded independence for autonomy and parceled out the Tibet question into smaller issues—human rights, religious freedom, environmental protection, women's rights—that were taken up by prominent NGOs like Amnesty International and Human Rights Watch, and by Tibet-specific lobbying groups like the International Campaign for Tibet and Students for a Free Tibet. In Gangchen Kyishong in Dharamsala, new Tibetan NGOs, like the Tibetan Women's Association in 1984, became part of this expanding international network. In the CTA's Information Office (renamed the Department of Information and International Relations, DIIR), a Human Rights Desk was created, and in 1996 this became the more substantive Tibetan Centre for Human Rights and Democracy, TCHRD); an Ecology Department was added in 1990, later becoming the "Environment Desk" and evolving from there into other forms; a Women's Issues Desk emerged in 1993 in the lead-up to Tibetan participation in the Fourth World Conference on Women at Beijing in 1995.[3]

If unwinding the Tibet question into so many distinct strands risked making the whole campaign fray, especially since the overarching aim of independence was no longer there to ensure its coherence, the threads were braided back together in the signature proposal of this period, the Five Point Peace Plan. Unveiled by the Dalai Lama before the US Congressional Human Rights Caucus in Washington in 1987 and expanded before the European Parliament in Strasbourg in 1988, the plan's points included "respect of human rights, democratic ideals, environmental protection, and a halt to the Chinese population transfer into Tibet." As for autonomy, the PRC would continue to manage Tibet's foreign affairs, but in all other matters Tibet would self-govern. And "Tibet" did not mean the smaller, PRC-delimited "Tibetan Autonomous Region" (TAR) created in the mid-1960s, but also the ethnically Tibetan areas traditionally called Amdo and Kham, which stretch into the Chinese provinces of Qinghai, Sichuan, Gansu, and Yunnan. And Tibet would be demilitarized, a "zone of peace" that would separate India from China.

The proposal went nowhere with Beijing. In Tibet, protests erupted, and violent crackdowns began in 1987, with Lhasa coming under martial law in 1989, the year of the Tiananmen Square tragedy. In 1991, Dharamsala declared the Five Point Peace Plan no longer binding. Apart from the question of its political effectiveness, the international campaign's visibility invited new forms of scrutiny, and self-consciousness. It raised questions about whether and to what degree Tibetan culture and society—as evidenced in miniature at Dharamsala, where the Five Point Peace Plan was crafted—really did respect democracy, the environment, human rights, and so forth. This made the very topic of "violence" a difficult one.

In the domain of exile Tibetan politics, the question of whether violent means should be categorically rejected, as the Dalai Lama has insisted through his "Middle Way" approach, has been decidedly fraught. The Tibetan Youth Congress (TYC), Dharamsala's largest nongovernmental organization, founded in 1970, has long styled itself the "loyal opposition" (J. Norbu 2004:15) and criticized the Dalai Lama's Central Tibetan Administration for its rejection of violent resistance, its willingness to trade independence for autonomy, and its sluggish pace of democratization. A series of publications and often incendiary opinion pieces penned by TYC's cofounders, notably Jamyang Norbu, a former guerilla fighter and maverick writer who endured mob violence from Dharamsala Tibetans who could brook no dissent, have countered the pacified histories of Tibetan culture to stir exile Tibetans from their "pacifist inertia" (J. Norbu 1997:20). A 1981 play by Norbu explored the Tibetan uprising in the region of Lithang, for instance, while *Warriors of Tibet* (Norbu 1986) traced the life of a Khampa warrior. Let us not forget, wrote Norbu (1997) in one biting commentary from 1997, that when the Dalai Lama escaped in March 1959 he was escorted by gun-toting Tibetan resistance fighters.

Regarding Thubten Ngodup, a former monk and resistance fighter who immolated himself during a Tibetan hunger strike in 1998, Norbu (1998) noted Ngodup's frustration with the nonviolent, Middle Way approach less than a week before his martyrdom; after Ngodup's death, some official publications erased this frustration and replaced it with statements that suggested he actually backed the Middle Way path. As Carole McGranahan (2010) observes, not only did hunger strikes like that fateful TYC-organized "Unto Death Hunger Strike" of 1998 draw criticism from the Dalai Lama, but, more deeply, Ngodup's past, his participation in the CIA-supported Tibetan resistance, was not even remembered. His past was a "public secret" (Taussig 1999), something widely known that nevertheless cannot be remembered for its dissonance with the official policy of nonviolence. "What veterans like Ngodup are encouraged to forget—a history of war—is directly correlated to what the world is encouraged to remember—a nonviolent Tibet" (McGranahan 2010:187).

Violent exchanges among monks can be disquieting, too. Even if this violence is qualified as ritualized or figurative and restricted to a few sites of socialization, it risks being snapped up as evidence of Tibetan "culture," of durable—for some, essential, ahistorical—group-specific beliefs and values. In scholarly literature on Tibetan society and culture, such culturalist readings are common and have served both critical and apologetic historiographic ends. For every work that calls up memories of Tibetan armed resistance or truculent monks or full-scale military campaigns—campaigns led by former Dalai Lamas no less, like the Fifth Dalai Lama in the seventeenth century or the Thirteenth Dalai Lama, who tried to quash the Qing in early twentieth-century Lhasa (Sperling 2001; Maher 2010)—there are other works that prove the opposite. These reassure us that the Great Fifth pacified his opposition through his charisma and moral superiority, transforming Tibet into a demilitarized "spiritual democracy" (Thurman 2008:28–34), or that Tibetan religious education reflects a "worldview" based on compassion and nonviolence (e.g., Goldstein-Kyaga 2003). The mirror-image symmetry that much of the literature on Tibetan religious culture and history can exhibit, as if each were tacitly indicting the other, as if there were clear, diametrically opposed sides, gives away the shadow dialogue—the slow-motion, high-stakes dispute over who Tibetans are and what their religion is.

At places like Sera, from the standpoint of someone like Geshe-la, such efforts to reform how monks discipline and punish are doomed; they do not mix well with Tibetan sensibilities about how to make monks. Others feel an urgency in reforming these dimensions of monastic life, but let us not forget that such tensions play out in the domain of observable resemblances, and here, as always, there is plasticity. As with debate, there are certain things about public reprimand that surely can be held up as evidence of things modern. Forget the way that monks scatter and hide when the disciplinarian enters visual range, and the way public discourses make his authority sound uncontested. Forget corporal punishment, which is not easily rehabilitated. Focus instead on the disciplinarian's use of argument in his reprimand, his appeal to reason, and the indirect addressivity that seems to leave the project of reform to the disciplined subject himself. In prodding his audience to "think" carefully about what he says, the disciplinarian seems to suggest that monks can think and adjudicate and, in a sense, self-govern. Their fate is in their own hands. The disciplinarian thus could be seen to concede a measure of "autonomy" to those he wishes to reform, just perhaps not enough to dispel a fundamental question: Who is *he* to stand up there and use anger on me?

## DISCIPLINE: VIEWS FROM SERA

At Sera, I hear no apologies for public reprimand and few for corporal punishment. I catch up with Geshe-la the same day of the reprimand and ask him what happened in the assembly hall that morning. He breezily dismisses the event as a 'public reprimand' (*tshogs gtam*). I jot down the name—a sign of my interest—and sensing my interest, he tells me some days later, again, nonchalantly, to bring my recorder to an event at Sera's joint assembly hall (*lha spyi*), where monks from both colleges meet. He does not tell me why I should attend, only that I should. There, before a mass of seated monks, he delivers a long, braying reprimand at the top of his lungs. After the event he asks me for my recorder without explaining why. Behind his closed door bursts of laughter erupt as he plays the tape back to himself.

Geshe-la was not against the use of force. He was not categorically opposed to violent resistance in Tibet and elsewhere and felt that war with China is inevitable. He once recounted Hindu-Muslim tension that broke out a year or two back in the neighboring town of Kushalnagar. Some guy was creating a commotion in the street, but an Indian policeman stepped in and settled things in a snap. Smiling broadly, Geshe-la described how the police just waltzed over to the man, whacked him on the head with a baton, tossed him into a car, and drove off. Everything became so 'still' and 'peaceful' (*'jam thing thing*), he concluded, now laughing riotously. Still and peaceful—pacified—that's what physical punishment can do for young monks. The best teachers don't shrink from applying pain to the body, Geshe-la told me during my first trip to Mey. Such punishment can exhaust the drive for disruptive behavior (*zang nge zing nge rdzogs 'gro gi red*). It was precisely in this context that he made a point of telling me that he and most others at Sera do not blindly accept everything the Dalai Lama says. About the need to curb corporal punishment at Sera Mey in particular, a reform he attributes to the Dalai Lama, he was unequivocal: nobody at Sera would accept this. Few would, it seems.

Dondup is a plucky fourteen year old who joined Sera recently, rarely attracts criticism, and seems to do rather well in just about everything, including in his classes at Sera Mey's school. I ask him which of his four schoolteachers he likes best. He names the teacher. "How come?" I ask. He rattles off his traits: he stands while teaching, speaks clearly, is a good teacher. And, adds Dondrup, not missing a beat, he 'strikes' students from time to time.

Tenzin is Geshe-la's personal assistant and has lived at Sera for about two decades. Tenzin seems to share Geshe-la's views on punishment and mentions an excellent reincarnate lama whom I will call Dawa Rinpoche. "Why 'excellent'?" I ask. Though Tenzin is quick to voice skepticism about reincarnate lamas generally—just as Geshe-la does—he respects this lama because his teacher had been excellent. Again, why "excellent"? In response he explains that Dawa Rinpoche's teacher had been strict with him and used corporal punishment.

Dawa Rinpoche has a number of disciples and lives in a modest, private residence not far from Tenzin's regional house. I pay him a visit, and he confirms what Tenzin says. He was an unruly kid, he confides, and earned a beating from his teacher once or twice a week. His teacher would mend any minor wounds he inflicted, and then send him off for a treat. Food rations at Sera in the early 1980s were meager, and the quality poor. His teacher would put some money in his hand and send him off to enjoy a plate of steamed meat dumplings or a bowl of noodle soup. Now a teacher himself, someone who turned out well, Dawa Rinpoche presents his own life history as evidence of this method's effectiveness. Pedagogically, you can't be nice and just rely on words. 'If you gently tell [your students] things like, "You(hon.) need to behave well," "[You] need to do this," they won't be scared, right?' (*'jam po byas nas khyed rang yag po byed dgos red da / gcig byed dgos 'di 'dre lab na / khong tsho zhed kyi mi 'dug ga*). Some monks don't listen. They neglect their studies and go for long walks and play soccer. Some brazenly skip out for an entire day and return in the evening with their faces sunburned from hours spent playing around outdoors. That's why teachers are said to use a stick (*rgyug pa gcig*) on their students. Beat (*rdung*) them, beat them, beat them—he repeats this three times, with exaggerated vowel lengthening that seems to model the durative aspect of discipline—"and they turn out well." Apply pain to the body, and you can right the habits of monks.

For the disciplined, not unlike the unflappable defendant, there is an expected demeanor of reception that runs counter to instinct: say and do nothing when assailed.

· · ·

Twelve-year-old Chögyel makes an offering before an altar but spins around and turns on me. He threatens to pinch me with the ends of two foot-long sticks of lit incense, incense weaponized into blazing pincers. He whines and snarls and busts out a few faux kung fu moves, complete with the most dramatic and implausible stunt, the feigned back flip. "Jackie Chan!" he shouts, captioning his antics. He is a big fan, as I learned when he pointed out a movie billboard on a day trip to nearby Mysore. He loves World Wrestling Entertainment, too, and once dropped the names of a few classic tough guys: "Hulk Hogan," "The Undertaker." Our encounters tend to descend into playful roughhousing when older monks are not around. I introduce him to the childhood game of slapsees, where we face off against each other, hands outstretched and level. He hasn't quite mastered it, so I score a number of open-palmed smacks to his knuckles. He winces and laughs and lets out the response cry of pain, *aya!*

So why shouldn't monks cry out when struck in public assemblies? Two years later I quiz Chögyel on how monks take pain when the disciplinarian's assistant metes it out in assembly halls. (He confesses that he has felt the sting of the assistant's leather strap a couple times. That they are neighbors, have the same teacher, and belong to the same regional hostel doesn't seem to have earned him any reprieve.) There is no 'custom' of crying (*ngu ya gi lugs srol yog ma red*), though if it smarted enough, one probably would blurt out *something*. (Tenzin listens in by the doorway and smiles, amused by my line of questioning and Chögyel's thoughtful, dead-serious response.) You sit silently and bow your head. You accept. Chögyel enacts what he describes. He strikes a pose that looks remarkably like that elder monk I saw on the road, who melted into an abject, deferential posture as the disciplinarian passed.

· · ·

An aphorism surfaces in talk about corporal punishment: 'A child's virtue lies on the tip of a whip' (*phrug gu yon tan rta lcag rtse la yod*).[4] The saying has a wide social distribution. Younger monks I spoke with recognized it at once, and some reported that the school's principal himself had taught it to all the students when school started. Dawa Rinpoche explains it for me: beatings can help inculcate virtue in the young; that's why virtue is figuratively located on the tip of a riding crop. In some cases, histrionic anger alone can stand in for physical force, he adds. When a teacher begins to manifest signs of anger—the idiom here is *gdong nag po,* literally 'dark face'—this can 'automatically induce in this student the capacity to assume responsibility'.[5] A willingness to study comes "automatically," a reflex of the teacher's affective act. Dawa Rinpoche tells me of a close friend and fellow teacher who handles students like this. He never strikes them. He doesn't need to. He just flashes a baleful expression so piercing that it strikes fear in his students and spurs them to behave well. He immediately qualifies this, adding that this reflex is made possible by cultural conditioning: 'This is the character of us Tibetans'.[6]

Trinley—the same Trinley who sneaks off to play soccer and who has fared poorly in philosophical studies—holds a minority view. He complains to me one day that his legs ache from frog jumps. (I refrain from asking him what he did to earn laps around the school.) Another time he points to some marks on his elbows, signs, he says, of having had to crawl around on all fours as punishment. His point? Too much punishment is counterproductive. Treating monks 'gently' (*'jam po byed*) is better, and as proof he tells me of a kid from Mey's schoolhouse who was initially a good student. His teacher was rough with him, and now the poor monk is chronically anxious (*sbug sub dog po*) and unwell (*skyid po mi 'dug*). When I return for extended fieldwork, I asked Trinley again about punishment, and he reports that policies are now changing; in place of corporal punishment, efforts are being made to make monks work off their misdeeds through community service. The reforms he mentions are more complex and the attitudes toward them far more ambivalent than he lets on, but the trajectory of change he traces out did recur in conversations with those closely involved in the school system. Corporal punishment has not disappeared, but it has come under increased scrutiny at Sera.

Lobsang is a layperson who used to work for Mey's school. He tells me of orders he received directly from the top, from the highest echelons of Sera's administration. He was instructed to punish students who misbehave: 'If [a] student doesn't behave well, please beat [him]', he was told.[7] This does not mean that teachers themselves must do this. Schools do have a "discipline master" (that's the English term he uses, the Tibetan term being *'grigs gtsugs bkod pa*) on their premises who is, in a sense, the disciplinarian's 'substitute' or 'representative' (*tshab*) in the school. Mey's disciplinarian does not rule the schoolhouse. His jurisdiction is outside the school's perimeter, in the debating courtyard, in assemblies, and in all other venues within the monastic college. Lobsang adds that he graduated from the Tibetan Children Village (TCV) school in Dharamsala, and when he was a student there corporal punishment was normal. Two or three years after his graduation in the mid-1990s, all that changed, however. The school became 'Westernized' (*phyi rgyal lugs srol rang chags pa red*) and discouraged corporal punishment. He senses something similar afoot at Sera. Regarding the Tibetan penchant for corporal punishment, he wonders why Tibetans at Sera should buck mainstream Western pedagogical wisdom in the first place. Maybe Tibetans are just different, he muses. Maybe Tibetans are wild and obstreperous and cannot listen or think clearly. I hear similar views from the disciplinarian's assistant, Jermay. Ethnoracial stereotypes of Tibetan incivility are invoked and contrasted with a more mannered West, hence the need for beatings to socialize Tibetan children. (Images of untamed, uncultivated Tibetans have a long history, and analogous stereotypes seemed to surface in discussions of etiquette, like one monk who complained about the way Tibetans tend to eat with their mouth open and barge into people's rooms without knocking.)

Dondrup is a middle-aged monk and an administrator in Sera Mey's school. Like the lay teacher Lobsang, Dondrup says he knows corporal punishment meets with disapproval in the West, so when he talks about it with me he demotes it to the status of a cultural 'tradition'. 'This is a Tibetan tradition of ours, yes?' (*nga tsho'i bod lugs srol red pa da*). (He then makes light of this purported cultural divide by joking that in the West you make wrongdoers pay fines, and that if you tried to levy people at Sera for money, you wouldn't get much!)[8] Like so many others, he charts a trajectory of change, of decline in usage. As he narrates it, corporal punishment has been decreasing in frequency and intensity as a consequence of the West's gaze and the self-scrutiny this gaze has triggered in many Tibetans:

*nyes dag sdug cha da btang gi ma red..deng sang / nyes dag zhe drag mang po btang gi ma red.*

Severe beatings aren't done nowadays. Beatings aren't done much.

*deng sang da phyi rgyal da lta gin lta gin byed dgos red pa / de gyad nyes pa gtong ya til tsam nyung du phyin pa red da / phyi rgyal gyi lugs srol la da 'di 'dra'i nyes dag gtang (ya) zhe drag yog ma red pa.*

Nowadays the West has been watching [us], right? Beatings have decreased somewhat, see. In the Western tradition, beatings like this aren't common, right?

*da phyi rgyal gyi mi 'di 'dra'i 'ga' shas gyis / zhe drag zhe drag gtong rgyu yog ma red / phrug gu klad pa la skyon shor gyi red / 'dra mi 'dra zer nyan yog red pa da / 'di 'dra'i bsam blo btang nas da nga tsho zhe drag nyes pa gtong gi yog ma red.*

Now there are some Westerners who say things like "[You] shouldn't beat [kids] too much. [Beatings] will harm a child's brain." Having thought over things like this, now we don't punish much.

In response to the gaze of a superaddressee, the West—for which I serve as the local proxy in this interview—Tibetans have reconsidered their practices and mended their pedagogical ways, he suggests. Misdeeds are now countered in new ways. Public forms of penance come to the fore, practices that are at once individualizing and glaringly public. Corrective operations are still trained upon the body, yet these disciplinary spectacles offer no visible participant role akin to "aggressor." They are carried out by no one in particular. Dondrup cites two such methods. The first requires young monks to crawl around on their knees, sometimes in a clockwise manner around the school, as if this were a religious act of circumambulation, and the school being the object of reverence, it would seem. The second is full-body prostrations, a physically taxing spiritual exercise that is a standard part of a monk's repertoire. You raise your hands above your head, clasp them together as in prayer, then descend while stretching forward and outward, palms gliding out and stroking the floor in front till you are flat, outstretched, trunk and limbs hugging the ground. Prostrations are typically done before a venerated object, like a statue of a Buddha or deity, and may be accompanied by visualizations and prayer. Whatever else these practices figurate (self-purification, the accumulation of merit), they tend to foreground the wrongdoer and background agents who impose discipline. They privatize discipline while keeping the performance public as a new kind of serious theatre. And, of course, there is always the plausible deniability that comes from this being cast in a religious idiom. It is punishment for the *benefit* of the wrongdoers, after all.

Again, these reforms are said to have come as a response to the presence of a critical, ever-watchful superaddressee, which hints at the existence of a vast, interdiscursive project of recalibration and sympathy. If addressivity—the presence of others, even if only virtual—is said to explain the emergence of such reforms, this means that the whole occurrence becomes like one big interaction. It imputes recipient design upon reform. While Dawa Rinpoche explains why it is useful to apply force to the body, especially the untamed bodies of the young, he knows that this isn't so in 'foreign countries' (*phyi rgyal lung pa*), and tells me this, just as Dondrup had. My interlocutors are quick to note that these practices do not harmonize with sensibilities in the West about how to make people, and while many speak in defense of these practices at Sera, their practical orientations toward them are far from simple.

Dawa Rinpoche does not actually resort to corporal punishment with his students. From observation and from what he tells me, I learn that he prefers to reason with his students when they fail to show up or study. He reminds them that he teaches voluntarily, that they attend voluntarily, that it is *they* who have elected to study with him. "If you lack interest, stop coming." Admonishing his students like this works but doesn't last, he admits. The effect wears off after about two weeks. Even Geshe-la, Mey's disciplinarian who balks at reforms attributed to the Dalai Lama, has a complicated stance on disciplinary practices. Despite his staunch defense of corporal punishment, he relied heavily during his tenure as disciplinarian on fines that he imposed on monks who failed to show up at courtyard debate. Geshe-la's assistant meted out punishment in assemblies, but he himself relied overwhelmingly on the force of speech. I did once see him chase down a monk in public and swat him a few times with his prayer beads, but this was rare; I never saw Geshe-la strike anyone. Speech was his strength, and he had a biting humor that could undo people far more effectively than muscle.

Geshe-la, like Dawa Rinpoche, like nearly all my mature interlocutors, knows that Sera's methods look inappropriate to many foreigners. In this respect, the very fact that the school's principal and others must cite a "traditional" aphorism promoting corporal punishment, a saying whose authority is lawlike—a transcendental truth, unanchored in time and space—hints at just how beleaguered efforts to apply pain to the body are. Stridently "traditional," the aphorism betrays the precarious state of disciplinary practices at Sera. Precarious, not only because the labor of social and cultural reproduction must overcome entropic forces (Urban 2001), which are always at work, but also because of a superaddressee, "the West," whose proxies—Christian aid agencies that financially support Sera and sometimes monitor its operations, foreign English-language teachers who work at Sera for short periods of time, a few foreign tourists, the occasional researcher like me—are felt to eye disciplinary practices with concern. For Tibetans who worry about what Buddhism might look like to a larger world (cf. Herzfeld's 1997 discussions of "cultural intimacy"), who worry about the consequences for the sympathies on which they depend, these practices may seem to trace out unwittingly a picture of a subject who *lacks* the very rights and autonomy that exile Tibetans have demanded in their ethnonationalist struggle with China. The discomfort toward and precariousness of these methods aside, at least within the field of Tibetan Buddhist education in India, Sera has staked out a conservative position on corporal punishment relative to places like the Institute of Buddhist Dialectics in Dharamsala. Sera refuses to give up entirely on this mode of punishment.

## MONASTIC DISCIPLINE, SOUTH TO NORTH

When asked about changes under way in exile, Geluk monks in India often spatialized difference, distributing it unevenly in a diasporic cartography that divides north from south. In Dharamsala, I hear my Tibetan interlocutors comment on the alterity of 'the South' (*lho phyogs*), as it is plainly and monolithically called. (No corresponding term for 'the North' [*byang phyogs*] is regularly used, partly because places like Dharamsala are unmarked for certain facets of exile life.) For Geluk monks in Dharamsala, the toponym "the South" suggests monasteries—"traditional" monasteries. Go to the monastic seats of southern India, and you'll find evidence of the past in great measure, they say.

The field of Tibetan Buddhist religious education in India is heterogeneous, as you can sense from the names that monasteries like Sera choose to bestow upon themselves in print, names that sometimes invite comparison with "modern," "secular" institutions of higher education.[9] Some schools self-consciously model themselves on universities and their research institutes; others, like Sera Monastery in southern India, seek to preserve the monasticism of old. As I crossed the courtyard outside the Dalai Lama's residence in Dharamsala, I sometimes felt as though I was moving imperceptibly from one extreme to the other, as if on a Möbius strip. On one side stood Namgyal Monastery, founded by the Second Dalai Lama in sixteenth-century Tibet. Its Indian incarnation prides itself on its preservation of the past, including the arts of ritual chanting and sand mandala creation, which it has showcased on stage during several international tours. Namgyal shares this courtyard with the Institute for Buddhist Dialectics, whose name bespeaks its modernist mission. Opened officially on the Dalai Lama's birthday in 1973, a time when the future of India's monastic seats seemed tenuous, when new recruits were few, and existing ranks thin, the "School for Buddhist Dialectics," as it was called until July 1987, would offer a new, hybrid form of Buddhist education designed to attract youth from the Tibetan schools. According to the school's charter, penned in the mid-1970s by the late former principal and confidant of the Dalai Lama, Geshe Lobsang Gyatso, this school would integrate "traditional methods of study followed in the great monastic universities of Tibet with present-day methods of teaching and administration" (L. Gyatso 1978a:8).

Relative to "traditional" southern Indian monastic seats like Sera, the Dharamsala institute positioned itself from the start as 'ecumenical' (*ris med*), as beyond the parochial attachments of sect. In this it assumed the mantle of its predecessor, Buxa Lama Ashram. Buxa was called 'ecumenical' (*ris med*) for the way it housed more than just the Geluk sect. Buxa was, officially, a preserve for the whole of Tibet's Buddhist patrimony, even if, in terms of numbers, it was disproportionately Geluk, and the other sects had consolidated their monks elsewhere. When, in August 1973, the Dharamsala-based English-language monthly, *Tibetan Review*, announced the inauguration of the Buddhist School of Dialectics with its class of twenty-nine novices, it also happened to note that this was a Geluk school, a sect "to which the Dalai Lama belongs" that "is well-known for love of logic" (Anonymous 1976a:7). The school was not pleased, and its principal wrote the editor (L. Gyatso 1973:32):

> Your news report on the Buddhist School of Dialectics (*Tibetan Review* August 1973) does not give a true picture of this institution. Your news report implies that the Buddhist School for Dialectics is an institution exclusively meant for the Gelukpa sect. On the contrary, however, this institution was conceived with the aim of embracing all monks of any sect. Advertisements were placed by the Office of the Private Secre-

tary to HHDL in the two major Tibetan-language publications, *Sheja* and *Tibetan Freedom*, inviting all monks irrespective of their sect to join the school.

Monks at Dharamsala's institute readily admit that their school has not lived up to its ecumenical mission. In content and architecture, their curriculum remains decidedly Geluk-centered, following Drepung Loseling college in particular—Loseling's curriculum is what the principal, Geshe Lobsang Gyatso, knew best. Still, they do break from places like Sera partly by including, or at least aspiring to include, a modest selection of literature from other sects during advanced phases of study. It is not uncommon to find a few young lamas of other sects enrolled at the institute as well. At the time of my fieldwork, I learned of plans for a new title to be given to graduates: 'ecumenical scholar' (*ris med slob dpon*), in contrast to the traditional Geshe (*dge bshes*) degree issued by monasteries like Sera.

Monks from the Institute of Buddhist Dialectics often marvel at the sheer size of the southern Geluk monastic seats, and some lament their own modest enrollment numbers. They posit a correlation between size and the quality of courtyard debate. The more monks, the more rigorous. With courtyards dense with debaters and bristling with intellectual energy, the southern monastic seats can forge first-rate scholars. None question the South's rigor, though some suggest that these massive monasteries do have their shortcomings. Besides the more difficult living conditions in the South, monasteries like Sera are said to be at chronic risk of disorder by virtue of their numbers. That is the view of the institute's current principal, who praises the South for its rigor but notes the need for stricter discipline there. Stricter discipline is needed not just because there are more monks to manage but because many are young. Unlike the institute, whose enrollment is limited to the mature, early adolescent and even preadolescent monks can be found at monasteries like Sera. Some are as young as five. As a widespread ethnopsychological discourse would have it, the young are plagued more than the mature with the "afflictive emotions" (desire, pride, anger), against which Buddhists must be vigilant. Prone to disorder and incivility, the South needs stricter discipline.

## THE INSTITUTE OF BUDDHIST DIALECTICS: THERE IS NO REPRIMAND HERE

When I lend Tashi, my research assistant who trained at Dharamsala's Institute of Buddhist Dialectics, a recording of the Sera Mey reprimand, I term the event just as I heard Sera's disciplinarian term it: *tshogs gtam* ('public reprimand'). To my question of whether 'public reprimand' (*tshogs gtam*) is practiced at the institute, Tashi replies with a flat, categorical no; but after reviewing the tape, he qualifies his position. He seems perplexed and surmises that this practice must have been altered in exile:

*tshogs gtam de a ni tshogs gtam chen mo dang gcig pa yin zer a yin bsam gyi 'dug / tshogs gtam 'di—spyir stangs bshad na nga tsho bod pa'i tshogs gtam lab ya 'di 'gyur ba tog tsam btang yog red lab kyi 'dug ga / deng sang khag khag red / sngon ma dang mi 'dra.*

[I've] been thinking, is it really the case that the *tshogs gtam* [from Sera Mey] is the same as *tshogs gtam chen mo?* This *tshogs gtam*—generally speaking, it is said, isn't it, that what we Tibetans call *tshogs gtam* has been changed somewhat. [It] is different today. [It is] unlike the past.

Tashi distinguishes *tshogs gtam* from its grander, adjectival-bearing relative, *tshogs gtam chen mo* ('great'), the latter denoting a more "traditional" disciplinary ritual that José Cabezón (1997) translates as the "Great Exhortation." In fact, Tashi once saw a Great Exhortation during a trip to Sera Jey monastic college in southern India and found the event quite odd. How do these two genres, *tshogs gtam* and *tshogs gtam chen mo,* compare? Tashi says that the Great Exhortation is 'like a religious text' (*dpe cha nang bzhin*), something 'to be recited' (*mar skyor ya gcig*). Its words never change.[10] He counterposes the Great Exhortation's fixed, frozen, "traditional" style of reprimand with the more labile, extemporaneous reprimand that I had recorded at Sera Mey, and suggests that the extemporaneous type captured on my tape is similar to what he had experienced when he was a monk at the Institute of Buddhist Dialectics—at least when the former principal, the late Lobsang Gyatso, affectionately referred to by his students as Gen-la, was alive. Gen-la would often deliver such speeches at the institute's assemblies, he explains. In this kind of public reprimand, you address real things that happen, historically specific infractions.[11] In this respect, Sera Mey and the institute seem 'identical' (*gcig pa gcig kyang red*) to Tashi.

Identical it may seem, but Tashi is reluctant to call the institute's brand of reprimand 'public reprimand' (*tshogs gtam*) at all, and I should note that both he and the disciplinarian from Sera Mey agree on one metadiscursive fact: the word *tshogs gtam* can be glossed with the verb phrase 'to scold' (*bshad bshad gtong*). It suggests something punitive. Despite the similarities he feels between Sera and the institute, when it comes to naming what goes on at the institute, 'scolding' does not seem apt to him. In place of *tshogs gtam,* Tashi prefers the verb phrase 'to give advice' (*slob gso rgyag*), a label suggestive of a more well-mannered and didactic communicative encounter.[12] In speaking about the former principal's 'advice', Tashi occasionally uses the honorific equivalent, 'to offer advice (hon.)' (*bka' slob gnang*); this verb phrase denotes an asymmetrical role configuration, one higher, one lower, but makes the event sound rather gentle.

It is no surprise that Tashi prefers the word 'advice' and exhibits discomfort with 'reprimand'. In fact, descriptors like 'to give/offer advice' resonate with the Institute of Buddhist Dialectics' official discourse on its operations and aims. When asked what makes the institute different from places like Sera, the institute's monks voice an egalitarian ethic: they are a community of peers unified by their passion for Buddhist philosophy. Unlike the Geluk monastic seats of southern India, they eschew hierarchy and nonmeritocratic privilege, prizing instead individual autonomy—precisely the kind of environment in which 'advice' would seem appropriate. This does not mean that status differences really are neutralized, naturally. While reincarnate lamas may not enjoy separate residences, personal assistants, and special treatment vis-à-vis the curriculum, they can keep private donations made to them. (One young lama I interviewed had a laptop, a luxury at the institute.) In public assemblies, seating arrangements flatten status asymmetries among monks, relative to those at Sera, though not completely. At the institute's religious assemblies, senior monks and reincarnate lamas deserve to sit toward the front, near the altar area—though this is more a matter of courtesy and only rarely would junior monks be forced to move. While this front-to-back axis figurates differences in relative status, senior monks and lamas sit on just one cushion, the same height as everyone else. The institute's principal and religious teachers enjoy special, thronelike seats, but equal seat height among students helps minimize differences among them, despite their differences in seniority and religious status. On balance, the divide between junior and senior, ordinary monks and reincarnate lamas, is weak compared to that in the South, a fact touted as a hallmark of the institute.

'Advice', it turns out, is prescribed in the institute's first charter (L. Gyatso 1978a and b; see also 1987). In this work, which is part history of the institute, part aspiration, the principal charged that the Geluk monastic seats of southern India were too mired in the past to attract Tibetan youth (L. Gyatso 1978a:3, 1978b:17). In recounting how he arrived at the institute's egalitarian ethic, he wrote: "I promised from that day on to be simply an equal member in a community of equals and to treat all students with undifferentiated kindness, enjoying only the same rights that they have and working side by side with them," a commitment allegedly bolstered during meetings with the Dalai Lama (L. Gyatso 1978a:6, 10).

This commitment has consequences for the office of disciplinarian. Indeed, the Institute of Buddhist Dialectics *needs* no disciplinarian at all. Or so wrote the former principal: there is "no need to appoint any type of disciplinarian or monitor"; the school will rest solely on "personal discipline" (L. Gyatso 1978a:11). At first there was indeed no disciplinarian per se. Gen-la was the principal, and he alone did disciplinary things. At morning assemblies, for instance, he might criticize monks, and sometimes the criticism had a trajectory that moved from the particular to the general, morphing into religiously framed 'advice' (*bka' slob*), a moral-didactic lesson. Gen-la started to delegate this disciplinary activity, and in 1984 he finally relented and created the office of 'disciplinarian' (*dge bskos*). Senior students would be recruited to serve this role (L. Gyatso 1987:9). From the start the office had little weight relative to monasteries like Sera, a fact noted by the institute's current principal, who tells me that the disciplinarian here has 'no special authority' (*dbang cha chen po khyad yog ma red*). As an index of their diminished status, the institute rotates disciplinarians frequently—every six months, not every year. "Acting like a school prefect, he is appointed for a period of six months" (L. Gyatso 1987:9), the 1987 prospectus read, careful to stress the affinity with secular schools. When you become a disciplinarian at the institute, not a whole lot changes, either. There is no dramatic shift in status. It does change your relations to peers. In public, peers may now address you as 'Disciplinarian', and your seat in assemblies would be more statusful; this would be signaled through increased seat height, which continues to be used as a gradient icon of relative status, just not for distinguishing categories of student. Unlike the way monks would react to Gen-la and the other religion teachers, nobody scattered and hid when they saw the disciplinarian at the institute.

What of reprimand, of *tshogs gtam*? Asked if *tshogs gtam* exists at the institute, its disciplinarian responds much as Tashi does: 'Public reprimand? We don't have anything special like "public reprimand". The most important thing is self-discipline.'[13] He expands on this:

> *da gtso bo gal che shos 'di / slob phrug so so gi sgrig 'dzugs / so so rang gis dang blangs byas nas so sos khyer dgos ya 'di / nga tsho gi da / gtso bo 'di- 'o 'di byed dgos red pa.*

> Now the most vital thing [is] [a] student['s] control of himself. This need for each person himself to take [responsibility] individually [and] voluntarily, now that's—that's the primary thing we must do, right?

The institute's core proscription is simple, he insists: don't waste time in your studies.[14] Individual responsibility is paramount, and with this responsibility comes the need for "direct" criticism,[15] as the disciplinarian explains when he contrasts the public reprimand of monasteries with the institute's milder and more direct methods:

> *tshogs gtam zer nas nga tsho'i dgon pa khag la yin na tshogs gtam mang po gtang ya yog red pa / 'di . . . 'dir nga tsho yog ma red / nga tsho kha thug kha thug yin na khyed rang 'grig gi mi 'dug khyed rang 'grig gi mi 'dug zer [-s] lab gyi red / dper na phrug gu gcig gi . . . grwa pa gcig gi . . . (gal srid) sypod pa til tsam ma 'grigs pa gcig byung na / yang na pha gi tshogs la 'grig gi mi 'dug zer [-s] lab dgos red / dri ba btang shog zer [-s] /yang min na khyed rang da lta dge bskos shag la shog zer [-s] / skad gtong.*

> [As] for what's called "public reprimand," a lot of public reprimands are done at monasteries, right? This—We don't have this. If we are really direct, [we] say: "You are not appropriate, you are not appropriate." For example, if a kid . . . a monk . . . should happen to exhibit some inappropriate behavior, then either over at the assembly one needs to say: "[That's] not appropriate." [You] ask questions. Or else [you] summon [him], "You [hon.], go now to the disciplinarian's room."

When you have the offender before you in private, the institute's disciplinarian spells out what the offender did wrong. Mistakes should be plainly listed, and individuals confronted. Language identifies offenders and clarifies what the offenses are. No theatrics. Disciplinarians can—and sometimes do—call out individuals in public.

Not so at Sera, as Sera Mey's disciplinarian had impressed upon me when he explained how public reprimand departs from "ordinary" modes of communication, where directness and bluntness are dominant norms. 'Now nowadays in these times, whatever most people say ends up being blunt, right?' (*da deng sang dus tshod 'di'i nang mi tsho kyi phal cher gi da gcig / skad cha ga re bshad nas dmar shed yong gi yog red pa*). He continued:

> *deng sang 'di ma bshad na go gi yog ma red pa / go ba 'di gal che byas bshad dgos red ta / [ . . . ] / gzhan skad cha go ba bshad chog gi ma red / gtam zer [-s] zer gyi 'dug ga? / tshogs kyi gtam zer [-s] / gtam zer dus ga re zer na dpe bshad ya ma gtogs kha thug bshad chog gi ma red / dper na cha bzhag gi yin na / khyed rang dpe cha ma ltas pa byed 'khyam 'khyam sha stag 'gro bsdad kyi yod na / 'ga' zhig gis zer dgos red /.*

> Nowadays if [one] doesn't speak [bluntly], others won't understand, right? [One] needs to speak in a way that promotes understanding, see. . . . [In public reprimand] one cannot speak [to] others in an [easily] comprehensible way. It's called *tshogs "tam"* [*gtam*, lit., 'speech', 'discourse'] because only allegorical speaking is permitted. One can't speak directly. For example, if you were not studying scripture but just going around taking strolls, [in public reprimand], [one] must say "some people." [One] must say "some people."

To illustrate, he used me as his example, explaining that if I were a derelict monk he'd avoid uttering my name in public reprimand and refer to me only with an amorphous "some people." Again, while it is possible to pin offenses on offenders with proper names, this strategy remains a last resort. The disciplinarian should instead induce recognition of wrongdoing in the guilty individuals through metaphoric, allegorical, and generally indirect means. Yet even as he articulated the norms of indirect addressivity that should govern public reprimand, Geshe-la, Sera's disciplinarian, acknowledged that most people nowadays are blunt when they speak, and demand speech that's easy to understand. Public reprimand does not work that way. Through a bit of creative etymologizing, Geshe-la made this point by directing my attention to the head noun of the term for reprimand, *gtam* in *tshogs gtam*. This lexeme is the same as *gtam* in the term *gtam dpe*, which may be glossed variously as 'proverb', 'maxim', 'aphorism', and 'adage'. What these sayings denote is attributable to nobody and is about no one in particular. They impart their moral wisdom through felt resemblance to the here-and-now context in which they are deployed. Just as proverbs operate on people through analogy and allegory and hence a strong measure of "indirectness," so the disciplinarian should avoid directly linking the denotational text of reprimand with the real-world transgressions that he "really" means to address. It is against a rising tide of directness that the indirectness of reprimand stands out. Geshe-la made this quality of his disciplinary theatrics sound somewhat embattled, and for many it is.

At the Institute of Buddhist Dialectics, the methods of punishment contrast sharply with those at Sera as well. If it is the first offense and if the offending monk usually behaves well, one may excuse him, explains the institute's current disciplinarian. But if he routinely behaves badly, you punish him (*nyes pa gtong gi red*). As for punitive measures, Lobsang Gyatso's charter permitted only "gentle advice" (L. Gyatso 1987: 9; *zhi 'jam slob gso,* Gyatso 1978b:29): "I teach by giving just enough instructions in a gentle way" (L. Gyatso 1978a:11). The disciplinarian's role is described in the 1987 prospectus: "While inflicting punishment we always try to discipline students in a gentle way without resorting to fines or thrashing" (L. Gyatso 1987:9). As the current disciplinarian says, when punishment is meted out, it typically comes in the form of community service. The offender is tasked with extra kitchen duties or sweeps the assembly hall.

The monastic subject is to be directly but delicately counseled, not scolded, let alone corporally disciplined. This kind of "analogical" punishment (Foucault 1979:104–5) presses the face of the errant individual back into the pages of the social contract: an antidote to selfishness, a reminder of the primacy of the social order. Such punishments march the wrongdoer back to sites of collective welfare, to assembly halls where people gather to pray or kitchens where food for all is prepared. In sum, the objective for administrators and disciplinarians is to be civil and gentle and clear. They should persuade, not punish. These tactics suggest the fundamental autonomy and competence of the monastic subject. Tug on Tashi's seemingly innocent descriptor 'to offer advice', and a modern, autonomous, rights-bearing Buddhist subject seems to surface, a subject defined against the "traditional" Geluk monastic seats of the South and of Tibet's pre-1959 past.

Equally telling are Tashi's remarks on the fate of the 'Great Exhortation' (*tshogs gtam chen mo*) in exile (see Cabezón 1997). Besides being a fixed and scheduled recitation, it is delivered, he explains, in a highly marked and rather odd register of Tibetan. I ask him what it's like. To illustrate, Tashi stands and begins imitating the sounds of the Great Exhortation reprimand he once witnessed at Sera Jey college in South India. In a nonmodal voice quality and with loud, long, droning monosyllables—*ohhhhhh, ahhhhhhh*—Tashi begins pacing up and down the floor of the hotel lobby in Dharamsala where we meet. To his parodic performance of the Great Exhortation's register Tashi adds a telling caption. He confesses that he could salvage little sense from the disciplinarian's speech. It was unintelligible.

His performance complete, Tashi explains how public reprimand changed after 1959. It was the Dalai Lama who had pressed to reform the *tshogs gtam chen mo* in exile, who urged disciplinarians to speak 'clearly' and 'precisely' (*T* = Tashi; *M* = author):

T    *'di sku mdun gyis thengs ma gcig gsung song / a ni tshogs gtam chen mo gtang dus a ni / dpe 'di dras yar phyin mar phyin byas / a ni skad dbyangs mi 'dra ba brgyab / a ni 'di dras byed dgos kyi ma red zer / a ni kho rang don dag tag tag mar bshad na -*

The Exalted Presence [epithet for the Dalai Lama] once said(HON) this. So, "when [the disciplinarian] performs the *tshogs gtam chen mo*, [he] moves up and down [the aisle], and affects a different tone of voice. [He] doesn't need to do that. If instead he were to speak with precise meaning"-

M    *a la'i a la'i sku mdun gyis de dras bka' slob gnang song nge*

really, the Exalted Presence offered(HON) that kind of advice(HON)?

T    *gnang song*

[He] did(HON)

M    *a la'i*

oh

T    *'di 'dras byas na 'grig kyi red zer / snga mo'i tshogs gtam chen mo gtang stangs byed dgos ma red zer [-s]/ 'di 'dras gsung song*

"It would be appropriate if the [the disciplinarian] were to do that [i.e., to speak precisely]. [He] doesn't need to follow the traditional procedure of the *tshogs gtam chen mo*." That's what [the Dalai Lama] said(HON).

M    *ga re byas nas byed dgos ma red / don dag ha go ya khag po*

Why doesn't [the disciplinarian] need to do [the traditional reprimand]? The meaning [is] hard to understand?

T    *don dag ha go ya khag po red / 'o da byed stangs 'di gyad ma gtogs la [...] byes tshang a ni / de dmigs gsal don dag zer [-s] ge mi 'dug zer [-s] de la 'di dras zer [-s] zer nas . . .*

The meaning is hard to understand. It is merely a style of behavior, right? So [the Dalai Lama] said, "that [practice] doesn't make any sense."

Later in our interview Tashi again cites the Dalai Lama, who purportedly declared: '[Disciplinarians] don't need to engage in activities like the Great Exhortation.'[16] Disciplinarians in exile must be 'clear' (*gsal po*) and 'precise' (*don dag tag tag*). Tashi thus assigns responsibility for change to the Dalai Lama, who is independently renowned as a modernist reformer. Again, the Dalai Lama is a voice of authority and moral guidance, to whom one can and should defer. Irrespective of the historical question of what role the Dalai Lama has played in redefining disciplinary practices in exile, Tashi's remarks suggest that the Dalai Lama was engaging facets of a modernist language ideology.

In sum, the institute features an assemblage of practices and policies whose effects serve to figurate a (relatively) modern liberal subject, a subject defined against the "traditional" southern Geluk monastic seats in the field of Buddhist education. These include (a) a diminished place for the disciplinarian (e.g., as prescribed in the principal's charter, and as indicated in interview data and in the institute's current rotation policy for disciplinarians); (b) the charter's valorization of 'personal discipline' and preference for 'gentle advice'; (c) the institute's reliance on analogical punishments (e.g., kitchen duties) that suggest a social contact among persons conceived as autonomous individuals; (d) an egalitarian sentiment articulated in the charter and expressed in the monks' standards of appropriate behavior (e.g., their professed disregard for relative age, seniority, and received religious status—axes of status differentiation that matter at southern Geluk monastic seats); (e) likewise, unlike the South, the lack (at least officially) of special privileges (with respect to dress, resources, lodging, etc.) for monks with received religious status (namely those recognized as reincarnate lamas). Piece these together, and we are left with a composite sketch of a subject who bears a family resemblance to the subject of modernity: a subject freed from external constraints, vested with natural rights and faculties, over whom none shall rule without consent. This subject may be only delicately prodded with 'advice', not struck.

Tashi's remarks suggest that liberal mimicry is under way at the institute. Though the moral-didactic theatre of public reprimand in the South, with its unnamed voices and histrionics, registers for Tashi as the "same" as the institute's reprimands in Dharamsala (based on his recollections of the former principal's past reprimands), he feels uncomfortable calling reprimand at the institute 'reprimand' (*tshogs gtam*) at all. As for the "traditional" species of reprimand, the Great Exhortation (*tshogs gtam chen mo*), its scripting, staging, and opaque register feel antiquated. In evaluating the Great Exhortation, Tashi summons the Dalai Lama's voice, sounding the call for "clarity" and "precision" in exile and the need to avoid empty ritual—the latter being a frequent topic in the Dalai Lama's public addresses to Tibetans in India and one that betrays more than a hint of Protestantism. In his public addresses to Tibetans in India, the Dalai Lama has repeatedly warned against externality and empty ritual. He has placed under scrutiny popular religious practices like prostrations, mantra recitation, and the lighting of butter lamps. Without reasoned faith as backing for these and other practices, they become mere habit, and refugees risk succumbing to exile's corrosive pluralism. The Dalai Lama has promoted a recalibration of inner and outer, a new regime of sincerity and transparency that would seem to make affective dissimulation—histrionic anger—of questionable value. Plus, there's the more glaring problem of what histrionic anger looks like. It looks remarkably like "anger," just the thing that could undo the message the Dalai Lama has helped to craft and disseminate widely, namely his promotion of nonviolence and compassion to the level of universal truth—an "essence" that is Tibet's gift to the world (Lopez 1998) and, simultaneously, a cutting, ethnonationalist riposte to China. In brief, Tashi culls his various remarks and observations, fashioning them into a diasporic narrative in which modern reprimand derives from an opaque ancestral register. He charts a moral trajectory of communicative change. *Tshogs gtam* emerges from *tshogs gtam chen mo,* clarity from opaqueness, sincerity from histrionics—modernity from tradition.

Comparing Sera and the institute is but one way to bring into sharp relief the ongoing discussions and tensions among Tibetans over how to produce monks, tensions that index the presence of globalizing liberal ideals. These two institutions in the field of religious education (and others I have not discussed, like the Central Institute of Higher Tibetan Studies—now a full-fledged university—in Sarnath, near Varanasi) have come to inhabit roles homologous with "West" and "non-West" as they recursively play out the agonistic drama of "becoming modern" within the compass of a religious-educational field. If this heterogeneous field of Buddhist education is in turn set within the social space of the exile community, this field's internal, relational drama of "traditional"-(into)-"modern," Sera-(into)-institute, reads as a story line of a group composed of both modern and vestigial parts, that, as a whole—as a people—is evolving. In suggesting that the field of education is organized in a way that induces a certain emplotment—a story line about the evolution of a people into modern subjects—I do not mean to suggest that the recent history of monastic pedagogy in the diaspora can be reduced to one of pure mimesis and replication. As should be apparent from the Dalai Lama's discourses considered earlier, ambivalence and critique are directed at those whom Tibetans feel obliged to (at last partly) resemble. In his promotion of modern Buddhism, the Dalai Lama has argued that Buddhism is compatible with the West's Enlightenment and the sciences that emerged from it, but he has also added that Buddhism can complement and even complete this world-historical evolution by adding Buddhism's signature contribution—its "inner science"—to what has hitherto been the West's reductive, materialist orientation toward knowledge.

Despite all that seems to separate the South's Sera from Dharamsala's Institute of Buddhist Dialectics, other dimensions of contrast exist, the most glaring of which is relative age and centers on a specific demographic: senior monks socialized into Tibet's monasteries of old. For older Geshes I interviewed who had trained in Tibet, including Geshe-la, there was little question about how to make monks. Corporal punishment had been typical in Tibet's monastic life, and my older interlocutors did not apologize for this; some seemed to even bemoan the loss of respect that has come from the softening of discipline in exile. A senior Geshe from Dharamsala's Namgyal Monastery, for instance, was originally from Tibet's Ganden Monastery and now teaches and helps monitor daily courtyard debates at Namgyal. As I was video-recording two young preadolescent Namgyal monks debating in the courtyard one afternoon, Geshe-la saw me and decided to pop by to observe their performance. He began sparring with the defendant, a feisty monk who could not have been more than ten. (I once played this sequence back to my Tibetan research assistant, Tashi. He was reduced to laughter when he heard the little defendant's flagrant disrespect for this senior Geshe. While all sorts of breaches of etiquette are permitted in debate, for someone so senior and who is the very highest rank of Geshe—a Hlarampa Geshe—a modicum of deference is owed.)

In an interview I later ask this Geshe about the young monk he interacted with in the courtyard. "These young monks don't listen," he grumbles. "In Tibet you could discipline them." As he says this, he raises his hand above his head as if to show how you'd strike such an upstart. "They used to respect the teacher," he says next, lowering his head to model the other role, the role of the disciplined, in what was once a cultural reflex of deference. Here in Dharamsala things aren't like that. So 'there is no punishment here, right?' (*nyes pa gtong gi yog ma red pa*), I ask. "That's right, here we just let the students 'be.'" Opinions like this are common among older Geshes and do not depend on the category of educational institution with which one is affiliated. Even the late Geshe Lobsang Gyatso of the institute—the same Geshe who prescribed only "gentle" punishment at the institute—is reported to have used corporal punishment on monks from time to time, when nothing else worked. Common to elder Geluk Geshes is a tendency to lament the decline of respect and the correlative ascendance of rights for those who do not yet deserve them.

To the extent that diasporic Tibetans in India try to materialize ideals of communicative autonomy, rights, sincerity, and clarity, we might expect such disciplinary violence to look anachronistic, perhaps heralding a sea change in penal semiotics in Tibetan monasteries. What is more, we might expect a challenge to public reprimand's foundation, its dramaturgy. Referentialist ideologies, which view language as a neutral and autonomous medium for describing states of affairs in the world, have long been hitched to ideals of sincerity, in which one strains to align inner states with outer signs. In aligning the two, in speaking clearly and sincerely, we lay bare our interiority for our interlocutors (Keane 2002). Sincere speech is speech that "adds and subtracts nothing in *words* that was not already there in *thought*" (Keane 2002:74). In laying bare our thoughts, we convey a sense of our "autonomy," since sincere words "display their freedom from any external compulsion" (75); they are not said out of deference to others, to the past, to tradition. It is in this sense that these communicative practices prepare the ground for civil communication among purportedly autonomous and agentive social actors, each endowed with rights of participation and allowed to speak his mind. Jürgen Habermas imagined that these rights were hewn into metapragmatic bedrock. They made up the "ideal speech situation"—the procedural symmetry conditions presupposed in rational communicative behavior, a kind of species-level competence. Writers like Habermas have neglected the way subjects must be fashioned out of concrete materials if they are to be seen and recognized. In practicing the craft of liberal mimicry, Habermas gave a particular form, shape, and esthetic to interaction, based on the cardinal principle of symmetry, the performance of which invites one to jump scale, to leap from mercurial face-to-face discussions to enduring truths about human capacity and nature. For theorists like Habermas these intuitions about critical, rational communication are not the result of some historically specific regime of language and personhood. But this is precisely what it is, and the very design of the institute is best understood as an effort to accommodate that regime. The disciplinary methods at the institute, which are relatively "modern" through being self-consciously pitted against "traditional" monasteries like Sera, are best understood in relation to a project of sympathy, where Tibetans practice the craft of liberal mimicry to court affective sympathies from spectators—or at least not disturb them with their difference. Just as debate has a dense, cross-modal poetic architecture, where lots of sign-partials come together to trace out a picture of what the ritual purports to accomplish, so at the Institute of Buddhist Dialectics we have a superabundance—again, hypertrophic, formal plenitude—of mutually reinforcing semiotic effects that leave little to chance. The institute offers an assemblage of discursive practices and policies, some of whose effects reinforce one another and invite us to see a figure that looks fractionally like a modern liberal subject.

# Conclusion

## The Liberal Subject, in Pieces

How liberal is this liberal subject that encroaches on Sera, an Indian avatar of a fifteenth-century Tibetan monastery, and sweeps through the Institute of Buddhist Dialectics, a place nearly as monastic and just as devoted to centuries-old philosophical texts? Remember: These are places populated by men who wear robes, in principle renounce the world, and spend their days poring over Buddha's teachings. In such places the liberal subject looks uncanny, and deliberately so. Buddhism's specificity—all the things that make it different—should obtrude and break up the impression of this subject's identity, for this is no act of replication. The Dalai Lama may seem to echo liberal aspirations and encourage fellow refugees to emulate this subject's behavior, but it was the historical Buddha who is said to have discovered reason and rights, autonomy and freedom, long before Locke, Mill, and Jefferson. "Buddhism says you are your own master." "Universal Responsibility." "Every human being wants happiness and does not want suffering." Liberal, Buddhist. Two parallel lines that converge at their vanishing point, or perhaps, as the Dalai Lama put it during moments that were at once critical and apologetic, it is Buddhism that completes the West's Enlightenment. It offers a rigorous "inner science" that both complements the West's materialistic science and compensates for modernity's "lack of sympathy, compassion" (Anonymous 1976b:21). Far from slowing modernity's march, Buddhism rounds out the West's science and straightens its course.

This craft of liberal mimicry cannot be reduced to pastiche, syncretism, or bricolage, nor is it just something that happens when discourses or cultures collide. It is a craft that involves the pragmatics of modernity. That mimesis can "do" things, that it can function pragmatically, is now a familiar proposition. Homi Bhabha, for instance, wrote of the way imperial Britain created inferior copies of its constitution for subject states like India. Exhibiting the "*ambivalence* of mimicry (almost the same, *but not quite*)" (Bhabha 1994:86; emphasis in original), these ersatz copies were meant to keep colonial subjects dependent. From the side of colonial subjects, many have detailed the craft and pragmatics of mimicry, like Paul Stoller, who wrote of Igbo craftsmen who "carved satiric images of white men and Europeanized Africans (collaborators)," and of Hauka spirit possession in Niger and Yoruba *ouimbo* masquerades (Stoller 1995:76, 122). I have highlighted the mimetic dimensions of monastic reform in India, showing how such reforms echo liberal-democratic aspirations, and how this is meant to help actualize the aspirations of an ethnonationalist project, a project in which Tibetans in exile have felt obliged to cultivate strategic allies in the West by looking a little bit like the ideals to which these allies aspire. Critical allies like the United States had from the start discouraged the Tibetan exile government from framing its cause in terms of lost independence and sovereignty. Tibetans largely heeded this advice, but they also resisted it, fearing that it would jeopardize their chance of getting their country back. In addition to developing legal and historical arguments that proved Tibet's nationhood and right to self-determination, the Tibetan exile government had to appeal to the doctrine of universal human rights and demonstrate some degree of commitment to liberal-democratic institutions. Given the transcendental anchoring of these institutions—the fact that they are supposedly universal, unmoored from time and place—they deserve everyone's natural, unforced respect.

Respect came at once, and from no less than the Dalai Lama. After crossing into India in 1959, he acknowledged to his people and to the world that Tibet's old society had, indeed, been "backward." In exile, as in a future, free Tibet, Tibetans would need to respect modern institutions and become more open and democratic. This was never a concession that Tibet's religion had been backward, though, because at its core Buddhism already had what Western democracies prized. Buddhism was always already modern. The task was to peel back the layers that obscure Buddhism's liberal-democratic core, to expose the religion's essence so that Tibetans could behave accordingly and foreign spectators could feel reassured that the Tibetans' aspirations converged with their own. I have suggested thus far that this new labor, which reflects on and worries about what debate and discipline look like, is an attempt to materialize the liberal subject for certain addressees, spectators, and overhearers. It is the liberal subject that Tibetans seem to invoke when they promote and curtail, preserve and transform, interaction rituals like debate.

And yet if there is a liberal subject here, it is a subject in pieces. In pieces in the sense that different *fractions* of the liberal subject have come to be thematized in relation to debate, reprimand, and corporal punishment, and these fractions—rationality, rights, autonomy, clarity, sincerity—entail different *positions* for institutions in the field of Tibetan Buddhist education in India. Over this diasporic history, debate's design has been left largely intact. The challengers' martial idiom persists, as does the whole asymmetric tilt of the practice. Selected from among its qualities is, rather, the way the practice criticizes received doctrine in a manner that suggests a commitment to an autonomous, critical rationality; and the way the exercise of this critical rationality in turn "stabilizes" the subjectivity of monks. Recast as a modern diasporic pedagogy, debate is spread liberally. Its social domain expands, incorporating new categories of Tibetans, like nuns who lacked the opportunity to benefit from the debate-based curriculum in the past. Today, all Tibetan refugees should learn to reason about Buddhist doctrine rather than allow their religiosity to devolve into mere habit, empty ritual, blind faith.

As debate-based education expands, the more general field of Buddhist education contracts and nucleates. The three Geluk monastic seats of South India—avatars of the central Tibetan monasteries that enjoyed enormous sway for some three centuries before Tibet's violent annexation—have reemerged as central institutions. Whatever else debate's expansion does, it also tries to shrink the field of Tibetan Buddhist education in India, recentering it around the Geluk monastic seats of old. Fears about the reproduction of Geluk hegemony in exile come easily to many outside the sect's fold, even though for decades the Dalai Lama has done so much to promote a more ecumenical, nonsectarian (ris med) stance toward Tibet's religious diversity. Ecumenicalism aside, there is no doubt about where the best place for debate-based education can be found. In his public addresses, the Dalai Lama has sometimes said flat out that the Geluk sect currently offers the best debate-based training, and everyone knows that the monastic trinity of Sera, Drepung, and Ganden is the best the Geluk sect has to offer. (So much so that it was widely rumored at Sera that monks of other sects, notably those from nearby Namdroling Monastery, of the Nyingma sect, sometimes join the Geluk monastery for a spell to hone their skills at debate before returning to their home monastery.) None of my monk interlocutors, not even those from the Institute of Buddhist Dialectics in Dharamsala, questioned the monastic seats' status when it came to the issue of where the most rigorous, debate-based philosophical study can be found. Geshe-la from Sera dismissed degrees earned at the Institute of Buddhist Dialectics. Degrees from the institute are *like* Geshe degrees, sure, but they should not be confused with bona fide degrees earned from monastic seats like Sera in the south. To the extent that monastic seats like Sera excel at debate, and debate in turn exemplifies a modern commitment to autonomous, critical reason, Sera would seem to belong to a pedagogical vanguard. Does it not seem that Sera enjoys a privileged place in the field of Buddhist education along a cline of diasporic modernization, then?[1]

Even if such consolidation has been under way,[2] at least since Sera's expansion in the 1980s, the result has not been a unified field with a single undisputed center, not even if we restrict attention to Geluk and Geluk-centered educational institutions. This is so because in so many other respects Sera looks conservative compared to places like the Institute of Buddhist Dialectics. Sera is "backward," or, depending on where one stands, "conservative," along several other dimensions of comparison, dimensions that involve interaction rituals other than debate, and fractions of the liberal subject other than autonomous, critical rationality. At Sera, hierarchy is conspicuous, and corporal punishment still in evidence. Administrators and monk educators at Sera seem to pay relatively little heed to the natural autonomy and rights of the monks. Histrionic anger and indirectness in reprimand pass largely unremarked at Sera, but these have disturbed disciplinary sensibilities at Dharamsala's Institute of Buddhist Dialectics, where antidramaturgical ideals of "direct"-ness and "sincerity" have come to the fore. When it comes to disciplinary practices like public reprimand and forms of punishment, the institute does everything it can to break from "traditional" monasteries like Sera. The institute has done much to flatten hierarchy between monks and construct instead their fundamental autonomy, rights, and equality. In sum, in terms of attributes like sincerity, clarity, autonomy, and rights—a cluster of attributes that bears a family resemblance to those of the liberal subject—it is the institute, not Sera, that belongs to the vanguard of Buddhist education in exile. And this is to say nothing of the Central Institute of Higher Tibetan Studies,[3] which, on a cline of modernization, has always stood far from places even as modern as the Institute of Buddhist Dialectics. A self-consciously modern university, it was originally hitched to Varanasi's Sanskrit University and was granted "deemed university" status by the Government of India in 1988. In 2009 it left the orbit of its peer institutions forever when it became a full-fledged university, the "Central University of Tibetan Studies."

Fractions of liberal and illiberal subjectivity are variously distributed across these different institutions, which suggests that there is no unitary liberal subject on the march in the field of Buddhist education. In fact, we may wonder whether the fractions of the liberal subject that do exist are substantive enough to overcome the dissonant illiberal elements and become recognizable. It may be that many Tibetans do not even feel that a measure of modernity has come to monastic life in exile. I want to close with this corrosive question, which applies to all the sightings of the liberal subject reported in this book and which cannot in principle be answered: Who is it, in essence, who is apprehended? Are liberal attributes so pronounced that the subject seen is that of a Tibetan agent "emulating" the West, or so indistinct that it is a Buddhist host who allows a few innocuous foreign qualities to creep in? Which voices, if any, predominate in this dialogue? What kind of emulation is this? Sympathy *with whom*?

For my interlocutors from Sera and even from the institute, all my sightings of the liberal subject would raise suspicions for obvious reasons: the failure to explain practices like debate in terms of established religious frameworks; the undue focus on the "superficial" design of these practices rather than their deeper religious purpose; the preoccupation with differences among Buddhist educational institutions in India rather than their shared kinship and genealogy. Perhaps most troubling is the very identification of the liberal subject as "liberal." Where are all the agents monks cite and credit? And not just the panoply of incorporeal deities and protectors that make up the Buddhist imaginary, but especially His Holiness the Dalai Lama himself, whose enlightened agency in the diaspora cannot be overstated. Monks invariably animate his voice to help explain why Buddhist education looks the way it does now, in exile. All such agents seem to have vanished into a world of steely, secular, homogeneous time where a new protagonist reigns, a Western liberal subject who moves at will and triumphs over the local (see Chakrabarty 2000b).

For exile Tibetans who live outside the monastic fold, the liberal subject can look just as insubstantial but for very different reasons. If, as the Dalai Lama has long suggested, monasteries like Sera are not unlike the modern university, where people exercise their critical, autonomous rationality, then surely quite a few Tibetans from the exile settlements would want to join, just as they aspire to enter higher education in India and abroad. So why is it that, as we shall see, the monasteries have largely been avoided by Tibetans from the exile communities and flooded instead by recent waves of refugees from Tibet? If we turn as well to some of the public discussions about whether monks make good schoolteachers in secular Tibetan schools, and whether the monastic curriculum ought to be more expansive by including secular subjects of study, we can begin to sense how nonmonastic Tibetans from exile communities presume an insurmountable divide between "secular" and "religious" education, despite the Dalai Lama's long-standing efforts to bridge it.

## MONASTERIES ARE NOT SCHOOLS

The sheer effort invested in modernizing Buddhist education—however modest such adjustments and reforms may look from afar—seems compensatory; it betrays the beleaguered status of monastic education in India, its perceived backwardness. Many Tibetans in India simply cannot see places like Sera or even Dharamsala's institute as anything other than "traditional," part of a world forever linked to Tibet's pre-1959 past and incompatible with modern, "secular" education in India. For these Tibetans the liberal subject in monasteries really is in pieces, not fractions but fragments.

This becomes apparent when we retrace Sera's move from Buxa Duar to Bylakuppe and consider a critical demographic shift that occurred during its expansion in the 1980s. Buxa may have been the crucible in which the Geluk monastic curriculum was first "reestablished" in exile, but it was also a place of experimentation. For a brief period the whole curriculum was dissolved and then recomposed as part of an experiment in modernization. Buxa, it was decided, should be recast in the mold of a university—an experiment that was short-lived but prefigured the creation of Sarnath's Central Institute of Higher Tibetan Studies (or the Institute of Higher Tibetan Studies, as it was earlier called). Buxa's experiment in reform and the later creation of the institute in Varanasi were credited to resolutions that came out of a critical five-day-long conference held in November 1963 for leaders of all the Buddhist sects. There the Dalai Lama "stressed the need for change in the old system of education which continued to be followed by Tibetan religious scholars," and one resolution had been to convert Buxa into a "centre of learning for Tibetan Buddhist Philosophy accessible to all" (Office of H.H. the Dalai Lama 1969:197–98). To ready Tibetan monk scholars for this new Buddhist education, a handful were selected and sent in 1965 to Mussorie for a special teacher-training program. In November 1966 the new curriculum developed in Mussorie the prior year was implemented in Buxa.

The reforms at Buxa were disorienting. The experiment suspended the traditional graduated curriculum in which the philosophical subjects—the Perfection of Wisdom, Middle Way philosophy, and so forth—build on each other in linear, lockstep manner. Now each of the five main, traditional subjects (*gzhung chen bka' pod lnga*) would be an autonomous topic of study, and just as geography is distinct from geometry is distinct from English, so each monk student would wind his way through the five major subjects (including some nonreligious subjects, classified traditionally as *rigs gnas*) in the compass of a single day. Moreover, no longer could a monk choose the teacher he preferred; teachers would be assigned, as in any ordinary secular school. Though this educational experiment was deemed a failure and abandoned, for some it seemed to serve as an important 'preliminary' rite (*sngon 'gro*) (Tshewang 2003:23) for the later, successful initiative in Varanasi.[4] The institute in Varanasi began to function as early as November 1967 and was officially opened in January 1968. For others the abortive attempt at reform was evidence that the traditional educational system still had value in the diaspora, or at least that there were no convincing alternatives.

In 1966, the same year Buxa tried out its new curriculum, the Council for Religious and Cultural Affairs became alarmed about the health conditions there. Tuberculosis was rampant and claimed many lives, a problem brought to the attention of the Ministry of External Affairs, which oversaw life at Buxa Duar. Recognizing the hazards of leaving the shoots of Tibet's religion in terrain as harsh as Buxa's, the Tibetan Government-in-Exile sought a new home for this diminished, weakened community. Buxa would be divided up based on sect and monastery and redistributed across India. Bylakuppe in Karnataka State (then Mysore State) would become Sera's new home. (For a while it had seemed that the exile government would secure a more hospitable site elsewhere in India, but the south ended up being the only option.) Bylakuppe had already housed the exile community's first agricultural settlement, which began functioning at the end of 1960. In late 1969 an advance party of around three hundred monks moved into Mundgod, clearing land and making preparations for what would become Drepung and Ganden monasteries. In Bylakuppe, Sera was allotted a plot of two hundred acres from the state government, and, as with Drepung and Ganden, a small number of Sera monks arrived from

Buxa as an advance team, paving the way for the transfer of more than three hundred Sera monks that occurred shortly thereafter (Anonymous 1977; Council for Religious and Cultural Affairs 1986).

Buxa had been no refuge, but the prospect of moving south was hardly comforting. Moving south would mean starting again in another inhospitable environment. The oldest Tibetan refugee settlement was nearby and could lend a hand—they had suffered enormously in clearing land and setting up the first Tibetan agricultural settlement in India in the early 1960s—but Sera monks from Buxa would still need to create a monastic habitat from nothing. As one senior Sera Geshe recounted in an interview, Sera's monks took shelter at first in inauspicious dwellings: military tents. The elements ate at the fabric till the tents leaked—a detail on which he seemed to linger. A metaphor, perhaps, for an anxious train of thought: would the canopy of Sera hold, and if so, for how long?

The concern was warranted, for even after Sera managed to rekindle monastic life and learning in Bylakuppe, the embers quickly started cooling. Bylakuppe's Sera, just a few hundred monks strong, started to suffer from attrition. Here they had carved out a niche and restored a semblance of routine, so where were all the new recruits? Few from the settlements in India chose to join their ranks in any substantial way. From some reports, those that did join in the 1970s tended not to remain monks beyond adolescence. They were young and would stay for a spell, benefit from the limited schooling introduced there in the early 1970s, and then abandon their robes and return home.[5] No signs of Tibet's mass monasticism of old were evident in the early 1970s.

The fate of Sera changed dramatically in the early 1980s. The opening of the Tibet-Nepal border in 1980, coupled with liberalization in Tibet, made it possible for Tibetans to get visas to visit relatives in India. Sera's expansion is reported to have begun in earnest in 1983, when refugees fresh from Tibet began to stream into the subcontinent. As Sera expanded, a demographic chasm opened, however. The vast majority of recruits at Sera Monastery in India are now the post-1980 generation of new refugees, referred to—sometimes pejoratively—as 'new arrivals' (gsar 'byor). Sera Mey's entrance ledgers, which record the age, place of origin, date of arrival, and regional house selected for each monk that arrives, suggest an overwhelming majority from Tibet and just a handful from the Tibetan settlements in India.[6] The records' earliest entries date to 1978, but place of origin begins to be noted in 1982, and then only fitfully (for only 32 percent of all entries between 1982 and 1989). From 1990, place-names are indicated with more regularity, and beginning in late 1994 place-names are found on nearly all entries. Of all 1,398 entries in which place of origin is listed, stretching from 1982 to 2000, only 44 came from destinations within India—just over 3 percent. Of these 44, only 4 hailed from Dharamsala.[7] A larger number of recruits hailed from Nepal (159, or 11.4 percent), though 78 percent of this demographic group began arriving in 1998. As for Tibetans from Tibet, roughly 21 percent (289) came from areas clearly within the Tibet Autonomous Region (TAR)—slightly more if one includes recruits who listed areas near the Nepal-Tibet border. The majority of these recruits had roots outside the TAR. Lithang (*li thang*), traditionally located in the cultural region of Kham and now in Sichuan Province, drew the largest proportion of recruits (33.3 percent, or 465 / 1398), almost all of whom joined Pomra regional house, Mey's largest.[8]

Why so few monks from the exile settlements? The causes are no doubt many. Geoff Childs (2004, 2008; Childs et al. 2005:343) reports a sharp decline in fertility rates among exile Tibetans in India and Nepal, from 6.3 births per woman in 1987 to 1.7 by 2000, which may help explain both the low numbers of recruits from the exile community and increased monastic recruitment from ethnically Tibetan areas in the highlands of India and Nepal, where fertility rates are higher. Childs finds indirect evidence of the effect of fertility decline on monastic recruitment in the Tibetan Government-in-Exile's 1998 demographic survey, which reports that "less than five percent of all males aged 5–14 who were born in exile are now monks, compared to between ten and 12 percent in each of the 15–19, 20–24, 25–29, and 30–34 age cohorts" (Childs 2008:144; Central Tibetan Administration-in-Exile (India), Planning Council 2000). In addition to fertility, Childs cites foreign patronage of Tibetan exile monasteries (and of reincarnate lamas, in particular; see also Frechette 2002), which has facilitated monastic expansion and intensified recruitment. But Childs also sensed something more diffuse and perhaps most important of all, a widespread attitudinal shift among exile families, a shift away from monasteries toward more secular avenues of education. "As one young man put it," writes Childs (2008:144), "becoming a monk is only considered an option for those children who fail at school, are not adept enough to learn a vocation, or cannot start their own business." Tibetan monks far outnumber nuns—over 93 percent of the Tibetan monastic population in India consists of males, as the demographic survey suggests, and most reside in the south. In the 1998 survey, nearly 77 percent reside in southern India and number 7,715,[9] but few recruits hail from exile settlements there. The Tibetan settlements neighboring Sera in Bylakuppe have been sizable, yet few Tibetans from these communities can be found within Sera's ranks. Official estimates from 1980, several years before Sera's expansion, suggest that Karnataka State as a whole had some 15,000 nonmonastic Tibetans, from which Sera could have expected many male recruits. It received very few.[10] Whatever the causes, the result is clear: it has been the so-called new arrivals from Tibet who have expanded Sera's ranks and enabled this monastic seat to reemerge as a force within the field of Buddhist education.

That so few recruits have come from Tibetans born in exile communities in India has not been lost on the Dalai Lama. In a 1999 address in Hunsur, not far from Sera and site of the Lower Tantric College, the Dalai Lama urged parents to take an interest in Buddhism to ensure that they can transmit Tibet's religious patrimony to their children. He then turned to the failure of Tibetans in India to join monasteries like Sera:

> phu gu'i bsam blo'i nang sangs rgyas kyi chos de slob sbyong byed dgos kyi 'dug / de gnad 'gag chen po 'dug bsam pa na / slob sbyong byed sa'i bsti gnas la dad pa skye rgyu dang / de la zhugs 'dod yong gi red / de 'dra med na da lta dgon pa gang 'tshams yod na yang / 'di tsho'i nang gsar pa zhugs mkhan ma byung na ltag chu chad pa'i rdzing bu lta bur 'gyur nyen yod / bar skabs nga rang tsho'i nyams myong la bltas pa yin na / dper na smad rgyud grwa[11] tshang dang / gdan sa khag tsho'i nang la slob gnyer byed mkhan phal mo che bod nas gsar 'byor tsho ma gtogs / nga rang tsho'i gzhis chags nang la skyes te 'tshar longs byed mkhan gyi mi rabs nang nas nyung shas ma gtogs mi 'dug / nga tshos mthud ka rgyag stangs dang / mtshams sbyor byed stangs yag po ma shes pa'i 'thus shor phyin 'dug / dgon khag nas gsar zhugs pa tshor dmigs bsal gyi lta rtogs byed srol med pa dang / khyim tshang khag dang / slob grwa'i dge mkhan tshos 'grel bshad lam ston byed rgyu gang ci nas 'thus shor 'gro gi med dam bsam gyi 'dug. (T. Gyatso 2000a:vol. 3, pp. 649–50)

If, in the minds of children, [they] think, "[I] need to study Buddha's teachings, that's crucial," faith will develop in the sources where one can study, and desire will arise to enter them. Otherwise, even though there are now quite a few monasteries, if nobody new enters them, there is the risk that these [monasteries] will become like ponds cut off from a reservoir. If you consider our own experience over time, such as in the Lower Tantric College and the various monastic seats, most of the people studying there are new arrivals from Tibet. Of the generation born and raised in our settlements, there are just a few. We've been hindered by not knowing how to establish contact and forge ties [with youth from the settlements]. From the side of monasteries, there is no custom of giving special help to those who have newly entered. [I] wonder whether families and schoolteachers have been completely hindered in explaining and guiding [youth].

Children who have finished primary studies at school and want to learn more about Buddhism ought to be able to do so, the Dalai Lama advises, even if this does not mean monastic education. Laypeople, male and female, can always attend places like the largely nonmonastic Central Institute of Higher Tibetan Studies, he goes on to say. He warns that even those who carry karmic predispositions (bag chags) from past lives, seeds that ripen and inspire one to study and practice Buddhism, may end up losing interest, if external conditions conspire against them. For this, parents and educators bear responsibility, but monasteries, too, need to look after new recruits in order to curb attrition (e.g., T. Gyatso 2000a:vol. 3, p. 650). It cannot be true that Tibetans in India do not join the monasteries simply because they "lack interest"; many things have eroded ties between refugee settlements and Tibetan religious institutions, and all such factors must be investigated, he urges. About the weak commerce between settlements and monasteries, the Dalai Lama is measured and diplomatic. Though he leans here somewhat more on parents and schoolteachers, he allocates blame to both sides of the monastery–settlement divide.

Monk educators within Sera can be far less charitable. In speaking about the demographic shift toward "new arrivals" from Tibet, some of my interlocutors wrote off those from the surrounding Tibetan settlements, at times casting them as myopic, economic climbers who would trade Buddhist cultivation for this-worldly mobility, Tibetan identity for Western trappings.

A younger Tibetan Geshe recounted stories he had heard about the anxieties and hardships of the 1970s, hardships he was spared, having joined in the 1980s. The older monks from the Buxa community were distraught in the 1970s because few new monks were joining the monastery from the Indian settlements:

> gsar pa ma slebs tsang / a ni grwa pa rgan pa tsho la / sems la dka' ngal dpe yog red zer gyi 'dug ga /da nga tsho- nga tsho rang ma gtogs yog ma red / gsar pa yod nyan 'og la yog ma red / da rjes ma grwa ba'i rgyun chad 'gro gyi red zer [-s] / dpe bsags sa red bsam byas / dka' ngal zhe drag byung ba red za.

> It's said, right, that the older monks were really distraught because new people weren't arriving. [They] thought, "Now us—there's just us. After us there's no one new. So later the lineage of monks will be cut off. [We're] in deep trouble." It's said [they] suffered a lot.

According to official published estimates, in 1980, Sera Monastery's two monastic colleges totaled 653 (Information Office 1981) (393 at Jey, 260 at Mey), which is perhaps slightly more than twice the size of the founding community in South India. In 2000, they boasted around 4,500 monks—almost a ninefold increase. Though India's Sera Monastery pales in comparison with Tibet's Sera before the Chinese annexation, which had around 10,000 monks, its present size is considerable. I asked this Geshe about all these monks from Tibet: 'It's said that there are very few monks born in India [here]'. To which he chimed in and ratcheted up the emphasis: 'Extremely few, extremely few. Incredibly few'.[12] "Ninety percent must be from Tibet," he says. Indeed, he continues, of Sera's monks, there can't be more than 10 percent from the refugee settlements in India, and probably not even that. So what are these Tibetans in the settlements doing?

> rgya gar la skye bsdad nyan mang che ba de tsho so so'i nang tsha la yog red pa / pha ma tsha la yog red pa / a ni nang la 'gro / tshong brgyag / a ni gos thung dug slog gon / a ni yar mar 'khyams di 'dre byed yag la interest che 'dug ga.

> Most of those born in India stay at their own homes, right? [They] are at their parents' place. Then [they] go out, sell things. [They] put on [nice] pants and clothes. [They] go around taking walks like this. These are the kinds of things that interest them.

Among those from the settlements who do decide to join the monastery, few study doctrine, he noted. 'If 10 percent of Sera's monks hail from India's Tibetan settlements'—and here he overestimated—'probably only 3 or 4 percent really study', he says. 'What about the other 6 percent?' I ask. 'Now as for the [other] 6 [percent], just hanging out, going here and there . . . how should I put it . . . it's called "time pass" in English, right?'[13]

"Time pass"—an Indian-English barb for people who idle away the time. Tibetans from Tibet, in contrast, are cast as industrious, courageous, determined. While a story unto itself, this divide between new Tibetan migrants and older settlers in the south and elsewhere suggests two basic facts. First, despite the soaring populations of each of the monastic seats, the Geluk sect has had limited success in promoting its form of education in India. The Geluk monastic seats are not the institutions of choice for Tibetan refugees from the settlements in India. Second, the fact that recent Tibetan refugees from Tibet fill the monastic ranks of places like Sera to the near exclusion of exile Tibetans contributes to an ideological correlation: Tibetans from the Indian settlements pursue largely "modern," "secular" avenues of education, while those from Tibet fill the ranks of "traditional" centers of learning, most of which are geographically displaced avatars of Tibetan institutions understood to be repositories for Tibet's patrimony. In spite of efforts by some Tibetan monasteries to demonstrate compatibility with facets of modernity, Tibetans born and raised in South Asian exile communities seem largely unconvinced.[14]

## MONKS ARE NOT SCHOOLTEACHERS

In 1976, the *Tibetan Review*, a Dharamsala-based English-language monthly, then edited by the late Dawa Norbu, led its April issue with an ambitious editorial, "The State of Tibetan School Education."[15] The piece bemoaned the lack of Tibetan teachers for Tibetan children. Indian instructors far outnumber Tibetans. What is more, the few Tibetan teachers that do exist are "almost all" lamas, a fact it blamed on "a discriminatory policy that Dharamsala pursued in the mid '60s," where only monks were invited to participate in the teacher-training school opened in Dharamsala. In the mid-1960s two teacher-training programs were convened, and, indeed, only Tibetan monks were invited to participate. Monk scholars were perhaps natural candidates to be instructors in the Tibetan language, even if they did need some training in modern pedagogy. The presumption, according to the editorial, was that monks were akin to Jesuit fathers and could be made into teachers just as effectively. "Jesuit fathers are not only professionally trained teachers"; they are also "very much in touch with realities of life and society," the editorial read. "Tibetan lamas," it concluded bluntly, "are not" (D. Norbu 1976:4). The *Tibetan Review* is renowned for trying to create space for dissent from the exile government, and at least the semblance of a public sphere—no surprise, given the *Review*'s ties to the Tibetan

Youth Congress. Here it seemed to defy everything the Dalai Lama had been trying to suggest about Tibetan Buddhism since the early days of exile. Why do Tibetans "lack the intellectual curiosity which is the spirit of Western education and
which is the key to human progress"? "Perhaps," came the response, "the absolutist
postulates of Buddhism, like other religions, made the possible development of a
scientific spirit of enquiry impossible" (D. Norbu 1976:3). So Buddhism is "*like* other
religions," not unique as the Dalai Lama has long suggested? Stodgy and unscien-
tific, an *obstacle* to modernity? Monk teachers may know their material well and
even teach well, but they have a "one-dimensional approach to life," they "scare
young children . . . by dishing out horrifying details of hell," and they cannot cultivate the "close and friendly teacher-student relationship" that facilitates learning.
The editorial ended with six suggestions, the first of which was uncontroversial: "The
quality of non-Tibetan teachers must be improved." The second was incendiary:
"The practice of employing only lama teachers must be stopped," and they must be
replaced by "more versatile lay teachers" (D. Norbu 1976:4–5).

　The April editorial drew fire, and some support, in the form of letters to the editor, which the journal published in subsequent issues in 1976. The *Tibetan Review*'s
editorial got the ratio wrong, one argued. Monk teachers do not in fact grossly outnumber lay Tibetan teachers, as the editorial alleged, and anyway there ought to be
at least *some* representation of monks at schools. Another suggested that having
monk teachers in schools was a pragmatic, stopgap measure. That way you could
keep Tibetans in schools till Tibetan lay teachers are trained (Rigzing 1976). Geshe
Lobsang Gyatso himself, the principal of the Institute of Buddhist Dialectics, wrote
in to bat down the charge of discrimination. He had been a beneficiary of teacher
training in the 1960s, after all. In the early years of exile, it had been "exceedingly
difficult to find qualified teachers among monks, let alone among lay people" (L.
Gyatso 1976:24). Monks wanted to lend a hand and were sometimes obliged to do
so. If there was discrimination against lay teachers, monks weren't the ones guilty
of it.

　Several letters flagged a difference between monk and lay teachers that the April
editorial had failed to mention. Monk teachers are just as competent as lay teachers and probably even better in some ways, one wrote, but that's not the source of
tension. The "main grudge against lama teachers is being 'Strict'" (Dorje 1976). But
that's a good thing, the letter argued. Discipline builds character. "An army discipline is very much needed in a school," another wrote. "A school with a loose discipline will never produce good students" (Migyur 1976). An anonymous letter titled "Suppression by Lama Teachers" disagreed. Monk teachers are "the most cruel
ones!" it protested. "There is not a lama teacher who hasn't beaten or wounded a
student" (Anonymous 1976d:22). Another letter complained about this complaint:
"From the outward [sic] they [the lama teachers] seemed to be very harsh and rude
in having been strict disciplinarians but inwardly they were without any bad in-

tention and personal grudge." "They believe and practice the principle of 'Spare the rod and spoil the child', which is particularly common in [the] Tibetan way of imparting education" (Gelek 1976:36). Another letter writer, incensed by the anonymous letter, accused its author of being "a well known and a well paid enemy of Tibet and Tibetans" (Wangyal 1976) and noted with satisfaction that he obviously got the beating he deserved!

This whole debate, which played out over several months, had, of course, been incited by a Dharamsala-based English-language journal keen on providing space for dissent. As such, it offers no clear window onto how Tibetans in India think about monastic education in relation to schools, but at the very least it hints at just how unconvincing monastic aspirations to modernity can be for Tibetans outside the monastic-educational fold. None of the responses to the April editorial, positive or negative, questioned the gulf between "religious" and "secular" education, monks and schoolteachers. None seemed to embrace the Dalai Lama's claims about the modern liberal character of Buddhism, its avoidance of blind faith and embrace of an autonomous, critical rationality.

In its December 1976 issue, the *Tibetan Review* (Anonymous 1976c) made an announcement about monastic education that again presumed this gulf between domains of education. Titled "Modern Education for Monks?" it reported how Dharamsala's Council for Tibetan Education decided to petition the Central Tibetan Schools Administration (CTSA) to supply teachers to the newly founded Geluk monastic seats in Mundgod and Bylakuppe. Monks needed to learn modern subjects—hardly a new argument; the Dalai Lama had long pushed monastic communities to train monks in new skills, especially language skills, in exile. Let us not forget that just decades before the Geluk monastic seats had been at loggerheads with modernization. In the mid-1940s, for instance, they opposed the opening of a modern school at Gyangtse (*rgyal rtse*) that featured courses in English, math, and science. They lobbied the Tibetan government and planned to close it by force, if it came to that (Goldstein 1989:419–26). At Sera in South India, instruction in nontraditional topics did begin, but it was not until Sera's expansion in the 1980s that "real schools" were built, first at Jey, then at Mey. In these new school buildings, young monks assemble in classrooms and learn subjects like English, geography, and math. Set within Sera, these schools enjoy their own built environment and administrative apparatus. New literacy practices and pen-and-paper exams at Sera may bring educational methods of learning and assessment into traditional monastic education, but there is no question about the separateness of this kind of 'school' (*slob grwa*). Well demarcated and circumscribed, Sera's schools have been placed *within* each monastic college, which keeps monastery and school distinct, the latter subordinate to the former.

That a seemingly minor issue like whether monks make good schoolteachers could incite such reactions—a couple of the letters expressed outrage—hints at a truly incendiary issue that the April editorial did not raise. It is an issue that haunts all talk about monasteries and modernity: did Tibet lose its freedom because a conservative clergy had thwarted modernization and supported a policy of isolationism in the early twentieth century?

Tibet's "failure to modernize" has been a familiar problematic for exile Tibetan intellectuals, and few spare Tibet's religion. The following year—to cite but one example—the *Tibetan Review* published an article on this issue, "Religion: A Major Cause of Tibetan Disunity," by the Tibetan scholar Samten Karmay (1977). "Let us see," Karmay asked, "to what extent this much vaunted religion has benefited Tibet" (25). He proceeded to tick off a series of ill effects caused historically by Tibet's religion to demonstrate "that in the past sectarian strife and self interest had in one way or another undermined national unity and integration" (25). Karmay closed with a cutting exhortation: Tibetans should "read history rather than rely upon the sporadic babbling of the superstitious and obsolete Nechung Oracle" (26). Didn't this sound awfully like Chinese Communist discourses that railed against superstition and used this backwardness as a rationale for violence against Tibetans? Some wrote in and said so. In one riposte, the author accused Karmay of echoing the enemy's propaganda and undermining the Tibet cause. Roiling beneath the surface of all these relatively minor, seemingly secondary questions about monastic reform in the diaspora—whether the curriculum at places like Sera should expand, whether monks should learn new subjects—are fierce currents that threaten official histories and may even erode the exile leadership under the Dalai Lama. All of this suggests just how fanciful sightings of the modern liberal subject can seem to many Tibetans in exile.

Once we resolve "the liberal subject" into its fractions and ask about the conditions under which it materializes, it becomes obvious that the story here is not that of some clash of discourses, structures, or ideologies. It is a commonplace that "liberalism" does not name a monolithic doctrine but is rather a tangle of arguments about and aspirations toward what it means to be human. Still, we too often neglect to explore the practical work of materializing this subject in particular times and places, in real-time discursive interaction. The liberal subject lives vicariously through discursive practices, if it lives all. It takes these practices as its host. To explain the labor involved in animating this subject, in bringing this subject to life, I have directed attention both to the semiotic qualities of ritual and to processes at work outside the ritual perimeter, where repeated, reflexive efforts to discover affinities in the design of these practices afford glimpses of an agent *here* who seems to have come from afar: the liberal subject on its globalizing career. Immanent and concrete though this subject can sometimes seem, the liberal subject is cursed with all the precariousness and contingency of a voice, in a Bakhtinian sense. A "virtual locus" of personhood (Urban and Smith 1998), this voice may be heard here and there, it may seem to stem from a specific source, but there is no durable substrate, no agent from which this voice is issued. It is always an echo. The liberal subject and its various qualia are "seen" and "heard," more precisely, by virtue of second-order reflexive engagements with the shape, design, and texture of sign use in inter-action ritual.

And all this takes time, labor, and materials. For the liberal subject to material-ize in interaction ritual, people must be shown—repeatedly, persuasively—how local patterns and textures of sign use in the space-time envelope of the ritual event ex-hibit larger-scale and even transhistorical ideals about what it means to be human. For debate, for instance, to seem as if it involves the exercise of an autonomous, critical rationality, demonstrable signs of this otherwise intangible faculty must be found and pointed out to others. Like other fractions of the liberal subject, critical rationality must be transformed into concrete manifestations so that it can sum-mon what it exhibits, not unlike the ritual work an effigy is made to do in what was once called sympathetic magic.

Given how distributed the assemblages that afford such likenesses are—they are not localized in the "meaning" of any one ritual text—it is no simple matter to change what an interaction ritual looks like, and no simple matter to ensure that new like-nesses last. While the resemblances that can be discovered in interaction ritual are not as mercurial as, say, the train of figures you can see in clouds as they morph and file across the sky, they have a protean quality that makes them hard to stabi-lize. From one angle I could make out the silhouette of a liberal subject in the Ti-betan diaspora, but when I turned my head a few degrees it was gone. I sensed this subject when monks spoke of Buddhism's scientific sensibility, its difference from monotheistic faiths like Christianity, the fact that monasteries are like modern uni-versities, like my own. Then somebody would come along, like Geshe-la, who bris-tled at Dharamsala-based reforms and was proud of Tibet's old monastic culture, and disrupt everything. Others drew my attention to Sera's illiberal attributes, not as a way to push back against foreign imposition, but, if anything, to hasten reform.

I once ran into a British English-language instructor who had been living and teaching at Sera as part of a program that sends language instructors to the mon-astery for six-month stints. In one of our first conversations, unprompted by me, he asked if I knew about the use of corporal punishment at Sera—and not only the variety used in the school and public assemblies but private punishment by teach-ers that he said resulted in real injury. He aired some rumors about a couple egre-gious cases; this disturbed me, naturally, and that seemed the point. He seemed to want to strike up in-group commiseration about Sera's backwardness.

One morning I was walking past Mey's school when I noticed a clutch of monks buzzing around a foreign woman in the school's sandy courtyard. I learned that she was a journalist researching human rights at Sera. Hers was a lightning tour, the purpose of which was to gather evidence of human rights violations in Tibet through interviews with recent refugees. "Can somebody ask him if he experienced 'torture' in Tibet?" I overheard her say. As she was bringing up rights discourse and all that it entailed, I wondered whether she had heard about corporal punishment at Sera. What I witnessed in monastic assemblies was nothing even remotely like torture, but it did look enough like "corporal punishment" to be called that, and that alone is no trivial classification. Tibet advocacy groups had cited corporal punishment at Chinese schools in Tibet as one of China's many human rights abuses. Three years before this journalist's visit, Dharamsala's own Tibetan Centre for Human Rights and Democracy published a report on the state of education in Tibet and condemned corporal punishment at Chinese schools. Citing the United Nations Convention on the Rights of the Child (CRC), the report wrote: "In violation of article 28 of the CRC, teachers under the Chinese administration reportedly resort to extreme forms of punishment defiant of the most basic standards of human dignity for little or no apparent reason" (Tibetan Centre for Human Rights and Democracy 1997). Representatives of Christian aid agencies that support Sera periodically visit the monastery, and Tibetans told me these visitors aren't keen on the monastery's disciplinary methods either. And there are Tibetan educational reformers from places like Dharamsala who have agitated for reform at Sera as fervently as anyone.

This is not to suggest that educators and administrators at Sera have felt pressure to change just because people are literally watching them. The changes in progress that I witnessed at Sera—changes slowed by ambivalence and plenty of foot-dragging—seemed less a response to actual copresent agents than to reflect a more diffuse concern about how their monastic pedagogy might look to potential spectators. This concern seemed to have been learned. It seemed to have been transmitted to them somehow—by contagion or by cautionary words about what others might think—from Dharamsala, a place that has experienced more scrutiny than any other Tibetan settlement in India. If one can speak of pressure for reform at Sera, especially among educators and administrators, it was pressure to engage in a kind of preemptive self-fashioning, a prophylactic liberal mimicry in which one acts so that if someone somewhere were to march down to Sera to check up on how Tibetan monks treat each other, there would be no gross inconsistencies in word and deed, no chasm between the Dalai Lama's Buddhist-modernist creed and procedures for making monks of men, in a word, no embarrassment for the Tibetan Government-inExile. This mimicry had none of the intensity or commitment evident at a place like Dharamsala's Institute of Buddhist Dialectics, but just enough, perhaps, to make the aspiration to modernity seem sincere.

## INTRODUCTION

1. Shakya's (2001) review of Lopez's (1998) *Prisoners of Shangri-La: Tibetan Buddhism and the West* is provocatively entitled "Who Are the Prisoners?" and his answer is, in a word, the West. Shakya correctly points out an empirical lacuna: the neglected issue of exactly how Tibetans in exile (to say nothing of those in Tibet) have registered the constructions of Tibet and its religion described by Lopez, if they've registered them at all. Shakya prematurely resolves this question by declaring that somehow Tibetan subjectivity has remained impervious, that "the majority of Tibetans living either in exile or in Tibet are not conscious of the western discourse on Tibet, and they continue to practice their faith as they did in the past, albeit mutatis mutandis" (186). In a sense, Shakya's response resonates with the now well-rehearsed critiques of Said's (1978) *Orientalism* (and of Foucault, from whom Said drew much inspiration), in the sense that Shakya complains that those subject to such constructions have been ceded little "agency." There is no space here to consider the storied debates over structure and agency, ideology and practice, not to mention more recent critiques of "agency" that call attention to its Protestant-inflected liberal-humanist genealogy (Keane 2002, 2007; Mahmood 2001). Citing Shakya's review with approval, Powers (2004) raises the ante, wondering aloud whether Lopez ever set foot in India. Powers notes that he "asked a number of Tibetans what 'Shangri-la' meant to them" (152). It meant very little, he discovered, though had he asked about, say, 'Lamaism' (*bla ma'i chos* [*lugs*]), to which Lopez dedicated considerable attention, he might just have garnered some interesting responses! Recall that no less than the Dalai Lama himself defended his religion against the charge of "Lamaism" in public addresses to Tibetans in India as early as 1960 (see chapter 3), and he did so even more visibly in his 1962 autobiography, *My Land and My People,* in both the English (Ngawang Lobsang Yishey Tenzing [1962] 1997:203) and the Tibetan versions (bla-ma 1962:291); for an unorthodox defense of Tibetan Buddhism as "Lamaism," see K. Dhondup's (1978) inter-

view with Tsultrim Kesang. Leaving aside the question of how Tibetans "really" think and feel, it scarcely requires argument that many of the reforms proposed for Tibetan Buddhist religious institutions in India—the way monks learn, the way they should be disciplined, the benefits reincarnate lamas should enjoy—have not emerged ex nihilo or as mere culture-internal developments of earlier trends (e.g., the nineteenth-century nonsectarian [ris med] movement in Tibet) but out of complex interdiscursive engagements with the West. Addressing these matters with care means avoiding steamroller approaches to discourse that neglect the dynamics of uptake and the pragmatics of emulation, as well as approaches that react to the alleged "power" of such discursive formations by retreating into the presumed inviolable integrity of subjectivity. In this respect, this book is meant to address precisely the lacuna noted by Shakya and builds on a number of works that do the same (e.g., Frechette 2002; Adams 1998).

2. This is not a matter of dissimulation and "strategic" or "agentive" self-presentation, as vulgar readings of Goffman would suggest. There is no place here to address the conception of the subject presupposed in Goffman's writings. Recall, for instance, Gouldner's (1971:381) early, unsympathetic critique, where he argued that the actors in Goffman's dramaturgical microsociology were all "busy contrivers of the illusion of self," and that this was really just a portrait of one sociohistorical category of person: the late capitalist bourgeois subject who has experienced a "transition from an older economy centered on production to a new one centered on mass marketing and promotion, including the marketing of the self."

3. Of course these feelings are often fleeting and depend on many things, including the sense of place. In places like Dharamsala, a hub of transnational traffic for things Tibetan, these feelings are more likely to surface, for instance.

4. One must take care in retelling the narrative of the Dalai Lama's role in promulgating democratic ideals in top-down fashion, because pressures for democratization in the exile environment of India have been widely distributed and complexly motivated (see, for example, Sangay 2003:123); one need only recall the Tibetan Youth Congress's strained relations with the Central Tibetan Administration (CTA) on matters of democratization to recognize this.

5. Oxford English Dictionary Online, s.v. "sympathy," http://www.oed.com (accessed 30 January 2011).

6. This is not really a "symbolic act," if by symbol one understands a sign that stands for its object from some comfortable remove, because the fate of sign and object are intertwined to the point of causal influence. For Tylor (1913:116), this connection was an error of thought: "Man, as yet in a low intellectual condition, having come to associate in thought those things which he found by experience to be connected in fact, proceeded erroneously to invert this action, and to conclude that association in thought must involve similar connexion in reality."

7. For thoughtful semiotic and linguistic perspectives on ritual effectiveness, see, for example, Tambiah 1981; Silverstein 1981b; Parmentier 1997; Keane 1997; Stasch 2011.

8. While this sense of "sympathy" is not drawn from Hume and Smith, they certainly did have an appreciation of the role resemblance and contiguity play in sympathetic communication. For Hume, more than Smith, the psychological mechanism of sympathy works through a kind of emotional contagion, where a sensory impression of a passion triggers the spectator's idea of that passion, which in turn triggers the conversion of that idea back into

an impression of a like-passion in the spectator. For Smith, more imaginative labor is required of the spectator, who transposes ego into alter's situation as part of the sympathetic process (which explains, among other things, how one can sympathize with the dead, with agents who are not there and offer no initial affective stimuli). Nevertheless, neither Hume nor Smith pays heed to the dramaturgical and strategic ways in which agents can project affinities to facilitate sympathetic communication.

9. Compare with J. G. Frazer, fifteen years Peirce's junior, who resolved Tylor's sympathetic magic into the Law of Similarity ("like produces like") and the Law of Contact or Contagion ("things which have once been in contact with each other continue to act on each other at a distance after the physical contact has been severed") (J. Frazer 1963:12).

## CHAPTER 1. DISSENSUS BY DESIGN

1. Observing that a monk's primary allegiance is to his 'college', not to his 'monastery' (*dgon pa*), Dreyfus (2003) considers these poor glosses. He prefers to call the latter "monastic seat" and the former "monastery."

2. "Pasang" is a pseudonym, as are all personal names used for monks at Sera.

3. *byes kyi za khang 'gro dgos ma red / smad za khang yog red.*

4. On the tragic murders and fallout from this episode, see, for example, Mills 2003; Dreyfus 1999; Central Tibetan Administration-in-Exile (India), Dept. of Religion and Culture 1998; Blo bzang rgya and Sparham 1998.

5. Information on Buxa is drawn from the oral narratives of Geluk monks interviewed in Dharamsala and Bylakuppe, and from a range of textual sources, including Central Tibetan Administration 1968; Office of H.H. the Dalai Lama 1969; Tshewang 2003; Bose and Gopal 1978; Bose 2008; Chopra, Chavan, and India Ministry of Home Affairs 1969; Krull 1968; Kusari 1981; Lahiri and Dasgupta 2001; Ray 1990.

6. A small number of nuns were present, as were a few monks of the Bön order. By 1960, Buxa's official population was 1,325—overwhelmingly from the Geluk sect. The total population breaks down as follows: Geluk, 1,190 (90 percent); Sakya, 80 (6 percent); Kagyu, 40 (3 percent); Nyingma, 15 (1 percent) (Office of H.H. the Dalai Lama 1969:181). The other sects had other places where their monks could resettle. Kagyu and Nyingma monks had relocated elsewhere, especially Bhutan, Nepal, and Sikkim.

7. As Newland (1996) observes, the noun *yig cha* denotes 'records' or 'documents' (cf. Goldstein, Shelling, and Surkhang 2001:995). Newland glosses *yig cha* in a more restricted sense as 'debate manual'. This gloss could be misleading if by "manual" one envisions a portable text-artifact that supplies readers with denotationally explicit instructions. Put another way, "manual" risks ceding too much autonomy to the book itself. At Sera and other Geluk institutions, extensive extratextual mediation is needed. The *yig cha* literature requires the mediating exegesis of a teacher to render it accessible, and it is enlivened and explored through daily courtyard debate. One should thus view these text-artifacts as one key part of a socially distributed circuit of learning, a circuit that includes oral commentary and daily public argumentation. For these reasons, 'textbook' is perhaps a more conservative gloss for *yig cha* (e.g., Hopkins 1999:11), but even here one should hold in mind a type of textbook that presupposes the mediating authority and exegetical prowess of a teacher (e.g., a book

that lacks "summary" sections and "self-tests" at the conclusion of each chapter, sections that presuppose the capacity for individuals to learn through solitary reading).

8. *rje btsun chos kyi rgyal mtshan.*

9. *mkhas grub dge 'dun bstan pa dar rgyas.*

10. I report here only prescriptive and proscriptive discourses on allegiance. I make no argument about the social distribution of these discourses or the consequences that follow for monks who violate them. The very issue of doctrinal "allegiance" must be handled delicately, because it is caught up in a broader argument about what kind of religion Tibetan Buddhism is, and what kind of sect the Geluk is, in particular. On these issues, see chapter 3. For discussions of these and related issues, see, for example, Cabezón 1994; Need 1993; Dreyfus 2003. I thank José Cabezón for pressing me to qualify claims about allegiance.

11. *paN [n] chen bsod rnams grags pa.*

12. I exclude the tantric colleges here, which are spatially and otherwise distinct from their associated monastic seats. I should stress that this larger-scale, intermonastic dyadicism is not homologous in all respects with the smaller-scale, intramonastic dyadicism. That is, not all members of the three allied colleges share the same textbooks (the exceptions being Sera Mey college and Drepung Gomang college), so the two large-scale collegiate alliance groups cannot be said to be opposed to each other doctrinally in the same way and to the same degree as the two colleges of each monastery clearly are. For at least four out of the six colleges, however, spatial propinquity is inversely proportional to doctrinal propinquity. Nor do I wish to suggest that the degree of allegiance between the partner colleges is *proportionate* to the degree of intracollegiate allegiance; in fact, when I heard disparaging remarks made about other monastic seats (e.g., that their philosophical curriculum or method of debate was less rigorous), the disparaged monastic seat was treated as an undifferentiated whole. Still, spatially contiguous colleges within the confines of a single monastic seat are categorically made to differ doctrinally: the textbooks they uphold always differ.

13. The profile of participants tells another story. Though I did not investigate this, I was told that players tend to be relatively young (no older than thirty) and overwhelmingly to be drawn from two less-statusful categories of monks at Sera: school-going adolescents and workers (i.e., those who failed to perform well enough to continue in the debate-centered philosophical curriculum and are hence required to discontinue their studies and take up some form of monastic labor). Matches do not always fall along Jey-Mey lines, of course; other principles of division are used, including the divide between "school-goers" and "workers." These divisions, along with the complex orientations toward sport and philosophical studies, raise issues about the kinds of masculinities being negotiated and cultivated at Sera. As these issues do not bear upon processes that interest me in this book, I do not address them. For recent anthropological work on Buddhist monastic masculinities, see, for example, Makley 2007:225–84; Bernstein 2010:178–215.

14. While the stabilities of organization surveyed in this chapter center largely around the philosophical curriculum, as if that were the exclusive source of gravity, the division of Sera into two colleges serves as a resource for more than curricular ends; it serves at times as a resource for pursuits like soccer that seem to work at cross-purposes with the philosophical curriculum. The relations between the practices detailed above should not be conceived as a closed circuit of mutual and reciprocal motivation, even if they do jointly con-

spire to overdetermine the ideological significance and effectiveness of debate as a rite of institution.

15. *mngon rtogs rgyan, abhisamayālaṃkāra.*

16. If one were so inclined, one could try to reduce the opposition of scripture class and debate to a kernel opposition between, say, mnemonics and dialectics. But this would be neither a synchronic opposition nor an equipollent contrast (where each element of the pair has equal but contrastive value). Once we set these discursive practices in their temporal habitat, in the compass of a day—or a week, month, or larger temporal unit in the monastic calendar—and once we consider the relative markedness of debate itself, it can easily be appreciated that it is mnemonics that predominates, that enjoys the status of the default, relatively "unmarked" class of philosophical practices at Sera. It is not only that monks, young and old, in the heat of the curriculum begin and end their days with mnemonic activities—memorization and recitation of memorized material—suggesting that these practices are "primary" by virtue of their privileged, temporal placement; debate itself, which occurs twice daily, from nine to eleven in the morning and seven to nine in the evening, broadcasts its marked status by the way it tropically departs from "ordinary" social-educational behavior, as public ritual so often does. It is the quotidian, the "literal," that is the foil, the ground from which public ritual spectacularly departs.

17. This is akin to the way linguistic anthropologists distinguish "text" from "text-artifact," and "interactional text" from "discursive interaction" (Silverstein and Urban 1996; Silverstein 1997).

## CHAPTER 2. DEBATE AS A RITE OF INSTITUTION

1. *gsang phu sne'u thog.*

2. *tsong kha pa.*

3. *rngog lo tsa wa blo ldan shes rab.*

4. *phywa pa chos kyi seng ge.*

5. Debate, as Tillemans (1989) rightly stressed, is an *activity* (cf. Dreyfus 2008:45), and his amalgam "debate-logic" is meant to remind readers of this fact. In suggesting that Geluk "debate-logic" can be seen to "embody a system of moves, responses, rights and obligations in a rigidly-structured game," Tillemans (268) acknowledges the need for an account of the pragmatics of debate, even if he does not supply one. Like the vast majority of writers on debate, he does not use transcripts of naturally occurring debate data to motivate his claims:

> The examples which I give from *Bsdus grwa* texts are not generally direct quotations, but are simplified versions of passages to found in such texts and are *completely typical* of what transpires in actual debates. In controversial cases, I give passages on which my examples can be based. (287 n. 7; emphasis mine)

Transcription is not, of course, some theoretically neutral pen-to-paper capture technology, as linguistic anthropologists and sociolinguists have long appreciated (Ochs 1979; Briggs 1983; Edwards and Lampert 1993; Urban 1996; Haviland 1996; Duranti 1997; Edwards 2001). No such pretensions about transcription are harbored here. Still, as Duranti (1997) ably summarizes, fields such as conversation analysis, interactional sociolinguistics, and linguistic anthropology have found transcription invaluable, in part because many of the behavioral regularities exhibited in discursive interaction are not easily reportable by interactants (see especially Silverstein 1981a).

It is in this context that Kenneth Liberman's work on debate as "dialectical practice" has been a welcome development (e.g., Liberman 1992, 1996, 1998, 2004, 2008). Given the entrenched approach to Tibet's logico-epistemological tradition by way of text-artifacts, a textualism that Liberman sees as orientalist, it is no surprise that he should stress his focus on "actual" debates and use of video recording and transcription. "At best," writes Liberman (2004:27), "indigenous Tibetan philosophy is engaged at the level of ideas, but never recognized as the actual *in vivo* social practices that compose real debating in the courtyard." (Georges Dreyfus, a brilliant Swiss-born debater who spent many years studying in India, has incorporated his intimate knowledge of the practice into his discussions of the genre [e.g., Dreyfus 2003, 2008], though again, this is no substitute, as Liberman rightly notes, for the close analysis of actual debate.)

Limitations of Liberman's work prevent it from being more useful than it might otherwise appear, however. He anchors his work in ethnomethodology, a sociological tradition from which Conversation Analysis (CA) emerged. CA would seem well suited for Liberman's project, since both Liberman and CA aspire to analyze transcribed recordings of naturalistic interaction in order to identify the local means by which members create meaning. CA seeks to induce, in as parsimonious a manner as possible, regularities from transcripts (e.g., facets of sequential organization like adjacency pairs). Liberman (2004:41) sets aside CA, though, arguing that CA's success has led to a tendency for it to rely on canned methods of analysis that risk obscuring truly *local* methods, which cannot be predicted in advance. He also hints at CA's overreliance on transcripts, which for some practitioners has led to a rather cavalier attitude toward fieldwork—namely that one doesn't need to do it (42). In a sense these are familiar critiques of CA (for a discussion of CA's "comparative" potential, see Sidnell 2007, 2009).

It is unclear whether Liberman's efforts to outdo CA in terms of a sensitivity to the local, tacit orderliness of interaction exceed what a competent CA practitioner could likely achieve with the same data. Liberman's transcripts are telling for what they omit. For an approach that aspires to reconstruct local methods, it is curious that the transcripts are in English, with no Tibetan (save for a few Tibetan expressions he considers pragmatic ready-mades). To the ethnomethodological sensibilities of CA, it would surely seem odd that Liberman's book provides little evidence for the ethnomethods he catalogues. An inventory of "organizational items" is provided, for instance, items that go by such captions as "because," "citations," "reversals," "ridicule," "calling for a definition," "stalls and digressions" (Liberman 2004:88–89). These are names for moves that monks do in debate. (Some of these items are named after the lexical item [purportedly] used to perform them, such as "because" and "it pervades.") At the very least, one wonders, How does one know a "stall" when one sees it? What local discursive criteria, evidenced in transcripts, permit one to speak of these organizational items and not others? Many of these core methodological—and, indeed, ethnomethodological— concerns do not seem clearly addressed in the book.

From the standpoint of other research traditions on language use, one cannot help but notice the scant attention paid to such resources as deictic expressions, discourse markers, lexicosyntactic repetition and parallelism, speech overlap, stance-taking and affectivity— not to mention matters of larger-scale textual organization in discourse. And when Liberman does venture into these waters, the results are not that convincing. To discursive phenomena such as cross-turn "repetition," for instance, he tends—as he does throughout the book—to attach pragmatic functions in a seemingly unprincipled manner: "Repetition gives the participants the opportunity to display understandings and have them validated"; "The repetitive and somewhat routine work of 'doing form' also provides the debaters time to think and work on their logical strategies"; "Also, it fills silence" (Liberman 2004:72). Later in the book, in a chapter dedicated to "rhymes and reason," he adds to the list, noting, for instance, that at the beginning of debate, "repeats provide the parties a way to get a rhythm going and to come into some sort of alignment" (124). (Notice that as the list of pragmatic functions of repetition grows, so does the gnawing question of how "repetition" can do all these things— a question that exposes the metonymic fallacy being committed here: it isn't repetition itself that is doing anything; Lempert 2008; see Agha 2007a.) Consider, similarly, his treatment of a more discrete, less configurational linguistic resource, the quotative clitic -s, which Liberman represents using the orthographic transcription of the verb *zer ba* ('to say') (Liberman 2004:105) (On quotative clitic usage in debate, see chapter 2 and Lempert 2007.) Liberman declares that *zer* means "so it is said" and that it "has the sense that what is said is undoubted, generally accepted wisdom and not merely the view of a particular thinker" (2004:105). Aside from the problem that the evidential gloss he provides is not a categorial meaning inherent to the form, but rather a meaning that emerges in a specific discursive environment, it is telling that Liberman attaches to *zer* a stable pragmatic effect: "By employing it," he continues, "a debater removes himself from his own statement." Here, as elsewhere, insufficient attention is paid to the conditions under which such effects become salient for participants in the interaction. Local orderliness feels as if it is imposed from without, not motivated from within, as one would expect of a project so carefully ethnomethodological.

In sum, while Liberman's book represents a valuable step beyond text-artifacts, and beyond the philological and Buddhist-studies frameworks that have informed the study of debate-based dialectics, it appears to fall short of its own objectives. Anthropologically, the work is also limiting for the way it both abstracts out this "dialectical practice" and sets it within a monolithic context of "culture," as the book's title, *Dialectical Practice in Tibetan Philosophical Culture,* suggests. Such monolithic characterizations of culture discourage us from appreciating the fraught place of debate-based learning in the Tibetan diaspora.

6. In Tibet, as French (1995:99–105) suggests, aspects of Buddhist debate were often freely incorporated into forensic proceedings, and monks who excelled at the practice were judged likely to be good legal representatives or judges.

7. I use "argument" for both senses of the term, namely "argument" as a propositional text consisting minimally of a premise and conclusion—a definition enshrined in most primers on logic; and "argument" in its pragmatic inflection, that is, as a (largely assertoric) speech act (or acts) in which claims are advanced and supported (O'Keefe 1982).

8. Paired terms for these speech-event roles include *snga rgol (ba) / phyi rgol (ba), rigs lam pa /dam bca' ba,* as well as more colloquial variants, such as *dri ba gtang mkhan / lan*

*rgyab mkhan* and *rtags gsal gtang mkhan / lan rgyab mkhan.* The English terms I use, "challenger" / "defendant," are not meant narrowly as *glosses* of any one of these pairs.

9. In speaking of "speech-event" roles, I distinguish between participant roles at a "speech-event" scale and at an "utterance-event" scale, a distinction introduced by Levinson (1988) and taken up by Irvine (1997).

10. *dge bshes ye shes dbang phyug.*

11. The *Collected Topics* primers used at both of Sera's monastic colleges are organized largely according to this tripartite structure. The older *Rato Collected Topics,* authored by Jamyang Chokla Wözer (*'jam dbyangs phyogs lha 'od zer*), is not organized this way but alternates instead between sections of debate and nondebate. Importantly, the ratio of debate to nondebate in the *Rato Collected Topics* is heavily weighted in favor of the former. Drepung Loseling's *Collected Topics* primer, composed by Jampel Trinlay Yonten Gyatso (*'jam dpal 'phrin las yon tan rgya mtsho*), is heavily weighted toward presentation. It is beyond the scope of this study to address the issue of variability across Geluk monastic colleges and monastic seats with regard to the study of the *Collected Topics.* While monks at Sera Mey take their own *Collected Topics* primer as primary, they sometimes supplement their study with the larger, *Rato* primer, since the latter is so rich in examples of debates. A final caveat: this isn't the only major principle that characterizes the textbook literature, another being the subdivision of textbooks into 'general meaning' (*spyi don*) and 'decisive analysis' (*mtha' dpyod*) commentaries.

12. *gzhan lugs 'gag pa rang lugs bzhag pa rtsod pa spong ba.*

13. In nine of the primer's initial thirteen lessons, the middle, nondebate section made up an average of only 16.7 percent of the lesson's total content. In the other four lessons, the nondebate section was more proportionate relative to the other two sections, consisting, on average, of 37.4 percent of the total content. If one considers the ratio of debate to nondebate in each lesson (that is, sections 1 and 3 collectively versus section 2), the disparity is even more glaring: debates amount on average to more than three times the length of the nondebate portion in each lesson. (The sizes of the lesson's internal sections were measured by line counts. To do so, the 1997 edition of Sera Mey's primer was used, since it was typeset by computer and was not a xylographic reprint. This ensured more regularity in the number of printed characters per line. Partial lines were assessed with fractional measurements, though no finer than .25. As mentioned above, two of the thirteen lessons lacked a final "dispelling objections" section. For these two cases, the size of section 1 [debate] was compared only with that of section 2 [nondebate].)

14. *gzhung mi mthun pa mang po yog red pa / 'di dre nang logs la ya mi mthun pa mang po cig yog red pa.*

15. *don dag cig pa red zer* [-s] *zer ya- bzo ya cig- bzo dgos kyi yog red pa.*

16. On this point, see Dreyfus 2003:211, but on forms of displacement, see Lempert 2007.

17. Indian Buddhism had privileged a probative style of argument loosely analogous to a syllogism, though the analogy breaks down especially when one considers the coda, where an example would be placed (Dreyfus 2003; Tillemans 2004).

18. A 'pervasion' (*khyab pa*), as Tillemans writes, is the "entailment between the reason . . . and the property to be proved" (1989:268). An elementary example is "If something is a color then it is necessarily red."

19. *khyad mtshar dra po mthong gi 'dug / khong tsho ga re byas na'i rtser rgyag kyi yin na zer* [-s] */ 'di bsam blo 'dra po.*

20. *khyad mtshar 'po mthong gi 'dug.*

21. *phyi logs la skad cha bshad* [*na*] */ rgya 'dre shor ba red pa.*

22. *khong khro dngos gnas ma red.*

23. I do not suggest that this biphasic emplotment of debate, that is, the movement from (esp. textbook-based) consensus to dissensus, is applicable to debate *tout court*. In this research I ended up not focusing primarily on the one-on-one sparring with a partner called *rtsod zla*, a style that characterizes much (but not all) of daily courtyard-based debating. This was a secondary focus. I trained attention primarily on the more formal, public 'defenses' (*dam bca'*), since these are more important ritual sites for the sympathetic effects central to this project. About the one-on-one style of sparring, Dreyfus (2003) notes that challengers don't necessarily begin with consensus, that is, with the dialogic construction of *shared* (especially textbook-based) propositions to which both parties are by default committed; the challenger could choose to begin with a position attributed to the addressee, the defendant. I did not find evidence of this in the one-on-one debates I witnessed and recorded, but this may well have been a function of my decision to limit observations of one-on-one debates to monks in the early years of socialization, thus excluding advanced debaters studying later topics like Middle Way philosophy. In the one-on-one debates I did witness and record, challengers would invariably begin with consensus. They would ask the defendant to restate definitions and divisions committed to memory, or would have him recite claims accepted in the textbook literature. As in debate defenses, though simpler and arguably less ritualized, the challenger thus began by dialogically constructing consensus.

Nor do I make an argument here about the distribution of this biphasic emplotment across sects and through history. In an essay that draws on texts by the famous Chapa Chökyi Senge, Hugon (2008:95), for instance, notes that "the initial stage of the argument starts with the statement of a thesis P under discussion," and that "the thesis P, which stands as the instigator's target, represents either an objection to the instigator's own position by a real or hypothetical opponent, or a philosophical tenet held by another philosopher." The starting thesis was thus not necessarily one upheld by the addressee, let alone by the speaker-addressee dyad whose views are to accord with monastic textbooks, which did not even exist as a basis for corporate allegiance at the time Chapa was writing.

24. *shes rab kyi pha rol tu phyin pa; prajñāpāramitā.*

25. If compared to Sera Mey before annexation by the PRC, India's Sera Mey has thirteen of the sixteen regional houses. The original sixteen were *gzhung pa, spom ra, tsha ba, yer pa, kong po, smar nyung, a ra, tsha rdor, the po, gtsang pa, gung ru, rong po, spo bo, min yag, rta 'on,* and *rgyal rong* (dbang phyug 1986:187–88). While in principle all regional houses should be visited by the candidate, in practice each candidate served as a defendant at eight of the thirteen. Monks from the five smallest regional houses—those with the least number of monks and the least adequate facilities for hosting debates—are folded into the larger houses during occasions like these.

26. Numerous second-order speaker-focal indexical effects are said to accrue to monks who pay deference this way. They accumulate merit, cleanse themselves of past nonvirtue, and so forth. Still, the first-order deference effect is undeniable: they index deference enti-

tlements in these beings, who are at least potentially accessible through their iconographic embodiment. To characterize these modes of deference as performed strictly for a monk's "own" edification would be to reduce the altar and its figures to mere props in a Protestantized scheme of individualistic self-development that would fail to resemble Buddhist practice, at least at places like Sera Mey for the majority of monks I witnessed. Still, the question of how Buddhist subjects orient toward material manifestations of these divine agents is a complex one, and beyond the scope of what I can discuss here.

27. Reincarnate lamas are not required to take debate examinations at Sera Mey. They are entitled to stand for the Rigchung debate regardless of their competence as measured through examinations and are automatically assigned the role of defendant. Further, reincarnate lamas are assigned topics deemed auspicious for their future role as instructors in the practice of Buddhism. Specifically, if there is only one reincarnate lama within the group of sixteen candidates, he is assigned the topic 'The Wheel of Dharma' (chos 'khor). If there are two, the second lama is assigned the topic '[Altruistic] Mind-Generation' (sems skyed). If there is a third, he is assigned 'The Three Refuges' (skyabs gsum).

28. During my fieldwork, Sera Mey's abbot, the late Venerable Geshe Losang Tharchin, was in residence in the United States. The abbot emeritus, who received his Geshe degree during the Buxa decade, presided over assemblies, delivered sermons, and the rest. He was, in short, the de facto abbot of Sera Mey during this period.

29. As Agha (1993) discusses, the primary auxiliaries yin, yod, and byung are all participant-indexing forms, while red, 'dug, and song are participant nonspecific. Though some maintain that there is an agreement system at work here (e.g., Denwood 1999), other linguists have considered this, following Hale (1980), a "conjunct–disjunct" pattern (DeLancey 1992, 1997) commonly found in Tibeto-Burman languages. (On the question of person marking and evidentiality in Tibeto-Burman, see especially Bickel 2000.) As Agha, DeLancey, and others have noted, and as Aikhenvald (2004:126) summarizes, these Tibetan auxiliaries may be used with the "wrong" person. Red and 'dug (labeled "disjunct," or "'participant'-nonspecific" in Agha's terms) can collocate with first-person arguments to motivate a range of interpretations, including "unintentional action, surprise, or irony" (Aikhenvald 2004:126). Conversely, the "conjunct" auxiliaries yin and yod (participant-indexing predicates, in Agha's terms) can collocate with third-person arguments, yielding quasi-evidential effects.

30. The challenger's questions during this entire initial phase are revealing. Of his twenty-eight questions, only three are WH questions. Of the remaining twenty-five questions, seven are confirmation-seeking questions (CSQs) formed with the nomic auxiliary yog red. In most of the remaining cases, the interrogative mood is signaled through a terminal rise in pitch. Later, one finds a higher frequency of explicit WH and YN questions. The challenger's avoidance of pointedly interrogative constructions allows him to avoid disrupting the defendant's self-positioning as knowledgeable.

31. This idiom is a delocutionary construction (Benveniste 1971), in this case, an utterance type specific to the debate register. It is derived from the tripartite consequence sequence, specifically, from the thal-clause (i.e., 'it [absurdly] follows that . . . '), denoting opposition to an unstated proposition, ascribed by default to the defendant.

32. skyabs 'gro gi mtshan nyid ga re gzhag.

33. da sgra bshad lab red da.

34. Analogies with other words and expressions have been attested but were not salient in my data (e.g., Perdue 1992:125 n. 1; Sierksma 1964). Perdue (1992), for example, cites two distinct glosses. The first, which he found to be "predominant" (Perdue 1992:125 n. 1) was 'finish', from *tshar* (tsāā). The second is 'amazing', from *mtshar* (tsāā, hence homophonous with *tshar*). Dreyfus (2003:381 n. 44) cites a longer expression from which *tshar* may be derived, *rtsa ba'i dam bca' tshar* ('[Your] root thesis [is] finished!'). I do not suggest that *ngo tsha* is the correct etymology. I am interested only in the stereotypical indexical force of this taunt, together with rationalizations of it.

35. When I asked monks to gloss the third taunt (*dpe cha 'gal* . . . ), they often did so by way of a narrative, especially if they had been steeped in Sera Mey's curriculum for at least a few years. This narrative describes a debate that allegedly transpired between Sera's founder, Jamchen Chöje Sakya Yeshe, and one of Tsongkhapa closest disciples, Khedrup. As monks at Sera Mey would invariably add at the start of this story, Jamchen Chöje was less intellectually accomplished than Khedrup—or, more charitably, he was 'humble' (*sems chung*)—and excelled instead as a meditator. Khedrup, by contrast, was typically cast at the outset as a brilliant scholar and prolific author but one prone to arrogance. Tsongkhapa, they explained, once instructed Jamchen Chöje and Khedrup to face off against each other in debate, but before the debate began, Tsongkhapa saw that Jamchen Chöje would lose, so to prevent his humiliation and cure Khedrup of taking pride in his punditry, Tsongkhapa secretly coached Jamchen Chöje. He laid out beforehand what he should argue, point by point, then assigned Jamchen Chöje the role of challenger. Khedrup, in turn, was to sit as the defendant. With Tsongkhapa's help, Jamchen shored up scriptural citations, and Khedrup couldn't respond. It was during such moments of paralysis that Jamchen is said to have taunted Khedrup by asking him whether he had in fact read the works (*phyag dpe*) of his own lama, Tsongkhapa. This narrative aspires to fix metapragmatically the significance of the *phyag dpe dgal* taunt. It remotivates the taunt's register-specific force by describing an exemplary and originary use of it.

36. Some well-schooled informants describe a specific scenario for appropriate '*khor gsum* use. Citing oral commentary from Geshe Kensur Lekden, Hopkins notes that it is used when "the reason, the pervasion of the reason by the predicate of the consequence, and the opposite of the consequence have been accepted" (1996a:444; see also Perdue 1992:58). In the color example cited earlier, for example, the defendant first claimed that all colors were necessarily red. The challenger responded by pointing out an absurd consequence, that "it follows that the color of a white religious conch is red, because of being a color." Few would deny that red is a color, hence the defendant cannot reject the "reason" clause (i.e., he cannot reject the final clause "because of being a color"); nor can the defendant reject the pervasion that all colors are red, since that was, in fact, his original claim or 'root claim' (*rtsa ba'i dam bca'*). He has no exit. Naturally, such explanations cannot be used to explain the patterning of this taunt in discourse, as Dreyfus (2003:50) suggests: "In practice, the expression ['*khor gsum*] is used to signal any mistake in the respondent's answer and not just the ones that satisfy to [*sic*] these three criteria."

37. A word on method is in order. As Kendon (1990:211) writes, the extension of the transactional space is "measured in terms of the location and orientation of their *lower bodies.*" Since challengers move frequently, a relatively discrete behavioral reference point was

needed. I selected the spatial positioning of challengers during the clap sequence, because this was frequently cited by participants as the most important kinesic sequence. Because the clap sequence itself elapses over several seconds and often spans several feet, I chose to assess the challenger's position at one moment in this sequence, namely when the hand-clap first becomes audible. To assess proxemic changes, the central aisle was first provisionally divided into roughly equal zones. As I reviewed the video data, I then adjusted the number and spatial extension of each zone to reflect actual, salient patterns. Since challengers often did not occupy the same position within each zone, fractional measures were used (no finer than .5). When multiple challengers occupied different positions, a mean was calculated. To assess the distance between challengers and defendant, I relied on anchor points contiguous with the challengers' feet or lower bodies, such as adjacent pillars or seated monks on the edges of the video frame. A fixed video camera was used throughout.

38. The defendant's and challengers' speech-articulation rates were compared across the debate for intonation units ranging from one to four phonemic syllables. For each length category, the defendant's mean rate was slightly lower.

39. *da go ya zer ci kyang yog ma red.*

40. *tsha de ga 'dras tsha.*

41. *nga mgo skor gyi ma red.*

42. The tight link between ethno-logic and demeanor in Buddhist debate stands out as remarkable only when one first presumes a separation between denotational and interactional planes of textuality. Once split, such cases of "parallels" surface as empirical surprises, reminders that we continue to labor under a referentialist regime and fail to appreciate how rituals of argumentation—not just Buddhist debate, to be sure—have a multiplex orderliness that neither an exclusive focus on ethno-logic nor a disregard for it can hope to illuminate.

43. In his *Theory of Communicative Action* (1984), Habermas suggested that the drive to reach consensus on criticizable validity claims—whether in everyday interactions or in formalized disputes—was part of a salutary, world-historical process of societal rationalization. Prior critics of societal rationalization, notably, the Frankfurt school theorists Horkheimer and Adorno, and Weber before them, failed to acknowledge, in Habermas's view, the existence of types of rationality other than the purposive and strategic; specifically, they neglected to appreciate "communicative rationality," which Habermas feels is the "original mode" of language use, on which all others are "parasitic" (1998:122). The centrality of argumentation in the *Theory of Communicative Action,* and its preliminary essays, was informed by Habermas's earlier study (1996) of the emergence and transformation of the bourgeois public sphere. From the early 1980s, Habermas extended his work on argumentation into the domain of "discourse ethics," where he rejects the monological Kantian exercise of the categorical imperative (in which one deliberates in solitude about which norms are generalizable to all) in favor of the dialogical enterprise of public argumentation (in which one publicly disputes competing normative claims with the aim of reaching consensus) (Habermas 1995, 1999; for a useful critique, see Ferrara 1990). In these discussions, the universal procedural presuppositions of the ideal speech situation again play a significant role, for they serve as an anchor that enables Habermas to avoid being swept away by the relativism of situationalist ethics.

CHAPTER 3. DEBATE AS A DIASPORIC PEDAGOGY

1. To the extent that revival suggests a temporal rupture, it is perhaps most applicable to the Geluk monastic seats of central Tibet, which did cease to function as centers of learning until the 1980s (see Goldstein 1998) (not to mention the many other functions they served that ceased and have not resumed). Goldstein's use of "revival" for the monastic seats is felicitous in this respect, even though this revival pales in comparison to the rapid growth of the now-sprawling Geluk monastic seats of South India. For the monastic seats in India, "revival" would be infelicitous, not only for the reasons outlined above, but also because there was no real temporal rupture, as there was in Tibet.

2. The text-artifacts analyzed in this chapter consist primarily of five volumes of public addresses delivered by the Dalai Lama in Tibetan (T. Gyatso 2000a and b). A secondary text used for comparative purposes was T. Gyatso 1996, which includes talks on education from 1960 to 1996.

3. 'jam dbyangs chos gling. In a one-page English-language overview that Jamyang Chöling offers visitors, the heading at the top of the page reads: "Jamyang Chöling Institute." Like Dolma Ling and other institutions, it thus invites comparison with the well-established Institute of Buddhist Dialectics. Elsewhere on the page it refers to itself as "Jamyang Choling Nunnery."

4. byang chub chos gling.

5. tshad ma rnam 'grel; Pramāṇavārttika.

6. snga 'gyur mtho slob mdo sngags rig pa'i 'byung gnas gling (Ngagyur Nyingma Institute, Higher Buddhist Studies and Research Centre).

7. During my fieldwork, debate had not been adopted by primary and secondary Tibetan schools in any serious way, but the Tibetan Government-in-Exile's Department of Education (bod gzhung shes rig las khungs) had published a series of readers on 'Buddhist philosophy and dialectics' (nang chos dang rigs lam) in the early 1990s, readers presumably intended for classroom use. In these readers, one finds excerpts from the Collected Topics and Minds and Awareness primers, which are studied extensively at the Geluk monastic seats by way of monastic debate. How these readers are actually used is another matter. The presence of dialectics in school primers has a long history in exile, in fact. As early as December 1959, a meeting was held that led to the creation of a textbook committee in 1960 (Office of H.H. the Dalai Lama 1969:248–49). The committee began work, and in 1962 it authored a series of primers (slob deb) for the first through fifth class. (A second edition of this set and a set of more advanced primers, for the sixth through eleventh class, appeared in 1965–66.) Of the religious topics that appear in the fourth class primer, one finds a topic from the Collected Topics (namely gzhi grub), but the topic includes only definitions and divisions; there is no debate, nor does the traditional three-part chapter structure of 'reject, posit, defend' ('gag gzhag spong gsum) appear. The fifth class primer, however, introduces students to debate-logic or rigs lam. This primer, the last of the set published in 1962, features considerable material from the Collected Topics and uses the traditional chapter structure, which is rich in debate. In addition, the end of the fifth primer includes topics that the Dalai Lama has said are vital for refugees, namely 'tenets' (grub mtha') of both Buddhist and non-Buddhist philosophical systems. (Only the two

lower tenet systems are presented in the fifth; the more advanced tenet systems appear in the higher primers. And in later primers topics like the four noble truths and the two truths appear, subjects that the Dalai Lama has also promoted.)

8. One prior student from the Central Institute in Sarnath reported that debate was practiced weekly, not daily, when he was there, and hence its use was rather minimal relative to that at the monastic seats. In an interview, a senior Geshe at Sarnath said in no uncertain terms that debate at the institute was very weak relative to that in the south.

9. *rdzongs dkar chos sde*. In a report published by the Information Office of His Holiness the Dalai Lama in 1981 (Information Office 1981), it is recorded that this monastery had a mere thirty-eight monks. According to informants the monastery was founded in 1972 with twenty-two monks and currently has around ninety monks.

10. The Dalai Lama appears to allude to traditional presentations of 'Awareness and Knowledge' (*blo rig*), the second major topic studied by Geluk monks in the philosophical curriculum. The five "sense consciousnesses" (eye, ear, nose, tongue, body) differ from "mental consciousnesses" in terms of 'basis' (*rtan*). Lati and Napper write: "Sense consciousnesses are produced in dependence upon an uncommon empowering condition which is a physical sense power—eye, ear, nose, tongue, or body sense power—which is clear matter located within the sense organ—eye, ear, nose, tongue, and throughout the body; mental consciousnesses are produced in dependence on a mental sense power—a former moment of consciousness" (1980:33). The "clear"-ness mentioned here is likely this "clear matter" said to support the sense faculties.

11. This Buddhist notion has been used as evidence of a scientific sensibility (Lopez 2008).

12. *rig gsar* has been corrected to *rigs gsar*. In this reading, a parallel is drawn between Tibet's indigenous 'scientists' (*rigs gsar mkhan tsho*) and the West's 'scientists' (*tshan rig pa*), which in turn maps on to a divide between that which is outer, material, and hence empirically observable, and that which is inner, immaterial, and incapable of being known through sheer force of observation. This divide—and the division of labor it entails between Tibetan Buddhism and the West—becomes a familiar one in the Dalai Lama's representation of Buddhism as a kind of "inner science." The gloss of the English term 'science' as *rigs gsar* was proposed in the twentieth century by Gendun Choepel (1994a:5; 1994b:167). I thank Tenzin Dargye for directing my attention to this gloss. An alternative reading as *rig gsar*, rather than *rigs gsar*, would be 'revolutionary' or 'innovative', hence 'innovative people' (*rig gsar mkhan*).

13. This address was apparently preserved and reconstructed through notes (*snying bsdus zin thor bkod pa*).

14. *'dzam gling yongs la chos kyi gnas lugs khyab spel thub pa zhig byed dgos* (T. Gyatso 2000a:vol. 1, p. 19).

15. *rgya gar ba dang / phyi rgyal khag gi rogs rma la brten nas deng 'dri dpe cha ba tshos chos 'chad rtsod byed rgyu'i dus skabs yod thog tu khyed rnam pas blo rgya che tsam dang / blo rgya gsar pa zhig gis rig pa'i rtsal bton te dus bstun gyi chos yang dag par 'chad pa dang / rtsod pa la 'bad brtson gnang na dus rabs nyi shu pa'i skabs kyi dpe cha ba'i mtshan don mtshungs la / nang pa'i chos ni rigs pa khungs dag dang ldan pa ngo 'phrod de / pha rol pos rang cag bod rigs spyi dang / bye brag chos lugs slob gnyer ba rnams la brtsi mthong je cher 'gro rgyur bod kyi spyi don la'ng phan khyad shin tu che ba yod* (T. Gyatso 2000a:vol. 1, p. 45).

16. *de ltar thub na pha rol pos thog ma do snang byed pa dang / bar du the tshom gyis brtag pa / mthar yid ches kyis ma bskul dwang bas kun nas bslangs te dam pa'i chos la don gnyer byed pa 'ong nges / de ltar byung na spyir ma gyur sems can spyi don rgya cher sgrub thub pa dang / yang sgos rang tsho'i da lta'i dmigs yul gcig pu bod rang dbang rang btsan bskyar gso dang / chos srid lugs gnyis bzang po dar khyab yun gnas 'byung bar khyad gnad shin tu chen po yod* (T. Gyatso 2000a:vol. 1, pp. 40–41).

17. See Goldstein (2007:491–522) for a detailed historical discussion of the Dalai Lama's trip to Beijing.

18. Melvyn Goldstein, personal communication. I make no historical argument here about how the Dalai Lama learned this expression, nor can I comment on the precise indexical associations it had for the Dalai Lama in the mid-1960s. That said, as noted, two primary interdiscursive sources for this expression seem likely: (1) the theosophical and more broadly Buddhist-modernist use of "blind faith" to define Buddhism in contrast to religions like Christianity; and (2) the Chinese Communist *mi xin,* for which *rmongs dad* was the Tibetan translation. In theosophical literature—a literature that, again, had an enormous impact on the shape of Tibetan Buddhist modernism—one finds frequent talk about Buddhism as a religion that eschews "blind faith," a point echoed in Buddhist-modernist literature generally. Though more research is needed, this usage seems to correspond most closely to the way the Dalai Lama has tended to use the expression. In English more generally, the trope of "blind faith" is a familiar one and is attested, for instance, in seventeenth- and eighteenth-century works like those of Scottish Presbyterian and nonconformist Samuel Rutherford (Rutherford 1649:135). The expression's use as an assault on a mode of religiosity, Roman Catholicism in particular, is evident in Enlightenment works like those of Anglican reformer Benjamin Hoadly.

The second source for *rmongs dad* is the Chinese Communist inflection of *mi xin,* a neologism from the late Qing that helped introduce a new, modern, Protestant-inflected category of "superstition" (Yang 2008; Liu 1995). To the extent that the Tibetan expression 'blind faith' (*rmongs dad*) was felt to index Chinese Communist discourses about religion, this would have motivated an additional vector of addressivity, in the sense that the Dalai Lama's remarks form a (partial) "rejoinder" to Communist voices that had indicted religion as blind faith. I say "partial," because at least in this address he does chide the Tibetan populace for succumbing at times to blind faith, a tendency that needs to be cured by a new regime of reason. From other uses of this expression in his talks, it is clear that the Dalai Lama does not fault Buddhism *itself* for this tendency, because Buddhism differs from religions precisely in that it discourages blind faith. For other Tibetan speakers and writers, leftist resonances of *rmongs dad* certainly did continue in exile, as evidenced, for instance, in a 1972 political cartoon from the Darjeeling-based exile newspaper *Tibetan Freedom.* The cartoon depicts Mao confiscating Buddhist art in his right hand and pawning it off with his left, in exchange for cash from foreign countries. He advises a cowering Tibetan on his right to avoid 'blind faith' (*chos dang rig gzhung rnying pa 'di tshor* rmongs dad *ma byas par rtsa gtor btang na nga'i bsam blo'i gsar brje pa yag shos shig yin la . . .* ). The figure of Mao animates the expression 'blind faith' through a represented speech construction. In the Dalai Lama's addresses, I found no such obvious correlation between voices of Chinese Communists and the expression *rmongs dad.*

19. Though he eschews blind faith, the Dalai Lama has not expressed unqualified enthusiasm for Geluk-style philosophical study. On many occasions, even in addresses to the Geluk monastic seats of South India, he has cautioned monks against the worldly aspects of intellectual life, like the lure of symbolic capital, which may manifest itself as attachment to the prestigious "Geshe" degrees (see, for example T. Gyatso 2000a:vol. 3, p. 456). In addition to the risk of careerism, two other dangers are frequently mentioned by the Dalai Lama: the risk of sectarianism and the risk of pedantry.

20. *rig pa* was corrected to *rigs pa*.

21. *rgyu mtshan gang yang ma brjod par bla ma dang / sangs rgyas rtsa ba chen po yin zer ba sogs byas pas nam zhig rang gri rang la 'dzugs nyen yod* (T. Gyatso 2000b:vol. 1, p. 68).

22. *rig lam* was corrected to *rigs lam*.

23. *rig pa* was corrected to *rigs pa*.

24. The first syllable of the oft-recited mantra of Avalokiteśvara.

25. In an address from January 1988, the Dalai Lama even extends blind faith in religion to blind faith in "freedom"; that is, Tibetans must actively strive to bring about Tibetan independence, rather than passively long for it (T. Gyatso 2000a:vol. 2, p. 419).

26. *deng sang bod lung pa'i nang rgya mis chos dad rang mos shig sprad yod.*

27. *phyag 'tshal skor sbyong byed pa de 'dra tsam la chog shes kyis mgo 'khor na mi 'grigs.*

28. A few examples, with the 'firm'-ness trope bolded:

> 20 May 1960. In encouraging young Tibetan refugees in his audience to persevere in India, the Dalai Lama says:
>
> *phyi'i dka' sdug gang byung yang nang gi bsam blo 'gyur med **brtan po** sdod thub kyi red.* (T. Gyatso 2000b:vol. 1, p. 9)
>
> No matter what external hardships befall [you], [your] mind inside will be able to remain **firm** without wavering.
>
> 26 March 1983. After citing the destruction of monasteries and temples in Tibet, the Dalai Lama states:
>
> *de 'dra'i byed las kyi rkyen pas bod mi'i sems nang ha cang sdug bsngal dang / mi dga' ba chen po zhig byung ba yin dus bod nang gi mi mang gi sems shugs ha las pa'i **brtan po** zhig dang / shugs chen po zhig bsdad yod pa red.* (T. Gyatso 2000a:vol. 2, p. 138)
>
> As a result of such actions, acute anguish and intense dislike [of the Chinese] have arisen in the minds of Tibetans. At the [same] time, the resolve of the people inside Tibet has remained unbelievably **firm** and powerful.
>
> 29 April 1988.
>
> *nga tsho rgya gar nang la bsdad yod kyang bod nang la bod mi'i lta ba de bsdad e yod / mi rigs kyi sems shugs **brtan po** bsdad e yod / chos dad 'gyur ba phyin mi yong ngam.* (T. Gyatso 2000b:vol, 1, p. 466)
>
> Though we have been residing in India, has the viewpoint of the Tibetans inside Tibet remained the same? Has the resolve of [our] people remained **firm?** [Our] religious faith hasn't undergone change, right?

18 January 1995. After noting how Tibetans inside Tibet have withstood Chinese discrimination and oppression, he adds:

> *khyed rang tshos dngos gnas drang gnas lhag bsam dang / sems shugs ri btsugs pa nang bzhin **brtan po** dang / 'gyur ba med par bsdad pa la rjes su yi rangs yod.* (T. Gyatso 2000a:vol. 3, p. 246)
>
> I am delighted that you have truly kept your loyalty and resolve **firm** and unwavering like a mountain.

I am grateful to Jermay Reynolds of Georgetown University's Linguistics Department for building on my initial work on *brtan po* during his term as my doctoral research assistant in the fall semester of 2008. Reynolds looked quantitatively across all tokens of this and several closely related characterological terms in a five-volume corpus of the Dalai Lama's published addresses.

29. This was corrected to ergative *gis,* consistent with *phra mos* in the subsequent line (T. Gyatso 2000a:vol. 2, p. 368).

30. *yin na yang so so'i chos kyi khyad chos rnams shes dgos rgyu gnad 'gag chen po yod.*

31. On rescaling, see, for example, Briggs 2004; Mansfield 2005; Moore 2008; Agha 2007b; Lempert 2012b.

32. In the 28 January 1964 public address cited earlier, the Dalai Lama alluded to the debate-based philosophical curriculum when he called on every Tibetan refugee to learn the "three modes" of logical proof. Young Geluk monks learn the three modes when they begin their socialization into debate by way of the *Collected Topics* primer. In a nonsectarian (*ris med*) spirit, the Dalai Lama also advocated the study of a book by Gampopa of the Kagyu sect, and one by Longchenba of the Nyingma sect. Yet he goes on to place special emphasis on the study of tenets, noting two famous Geluk authors, Jangya Rolpe Dorje (*lcang skya rol pa'i rdo rje;* 1717–86) and Jamyang Sheyba (*'jams dbyangs bzhad pa;* 1648–1722) (T. Gyatso 2000b:vol. 1, pp. 71–72; see Hopkins 1996b). The 'tenet' (*grub mtha'*) or doxographical literature offers readers a synoptic view of Buddhist philosophical schools together with certain non-Buddhist schools of Indian philosophy (Hopkins 1996). The schools of thought surveyed in the tenet literature are evaluated according to a graded logic of "higher" and "lower." Through studying and debating the lower schools, monks are to gradually come to appreciate the pinnacle of Buddhist schools, the Middle-Way Consequentialist School. Extreme materialist, nihilist, and other positions can be found in the non-Buddhist schools from India. On a number of occasions, the Dalai Lama has found analogues of these positions in the contemporary world—such as scientists who try to reduce "mind" to brain-based neural activity, or theistic faiths like Christianity, which believe that a deity created the world—which explains why he has pressed Tibetans to study this genre of philosophical literature. The study of tenets is held to have special relevance today. It provides Tibetans with resources to defend themselves against competing truth claims in exile. In an address from 1999 in which he advocates the tenet literature, the Dalai Lama is quick to add that one should study other philosophical positions not in order to refute them per se, but to understand what makes Buddhist claims distinctive (*dgag pa rgyag rgyu'i don du min par / khyad par gang yod pa de dag nga tshos shes pa byed dgos;* T. Gyatso 2000a:vol. 3, p. 661).

33. Anonymous 1989. Sources used for information on the revival of this event include Anonymous 1985; Anonymous [Jang Guncho Committee] 1985, 1987; Anonymous 1988a and b, 1990.

## CHAPTER 4. PUBLIC REPRIMAND IS SERIOUS THEATRE

1. I report here only normative discourses about the disciplinarian's authority. The idioms of deference described here do not mean that monks literally feared the disciplinarian or that he was always in character, as it were. In fact, part of what many monks seemed to find so endearing about Geshe-la in his role as disciplinarian was the way he would alternate between moments of sternness and moments of levity and even lively humor—the latter being, in my opinion, Geshe-la's forte. Paying deference through an idiom of "fear" is not limited to the disciplinarian, either. It applies to other high-ranking monastic officials. At Sera, I was once inside a phone center when some monks outside spotted the abbot on the circumambulation route. In an instant, the center was besieged by monks who scrambled for cover and huddled inside till the abbot passed.

2. For some remarks on corporal punishment in Tibet before 1959, see French 1995:321–23. On shifting orientations toward corporal punishment in exile schools, see Nowak 1984.

3. In an interview the disciplinarian stated that either the abbot or the disciplinarian may deliver *tshogs gtam*, but others may not, since that could lead to a lack of consensus. The fewer the people, the more consistent the message. For a comparison with forms of punishment in Tibet before annexation, see French 1995:315–25.

4. I do not wish to suggest that the form of *tshogs gtam* practiced here is identical to *tshogs gtam chen mo*, a genre that Cabezón (1997) has discussed for the college of Sera Jey. Cabezón glosses *tshogs gtam chen mo* as the 'Great Exhortation'. As described in chapter 5, the Great Exhortation is a fixed recitation delivered by the disciplinarian several times a year in a highly marked register of Tibetan. Unlike the Great Exhortation described by Cabezón, the *tshogs gtam* practice I analyze here is highly improvisational and is not rigidly scheduled.

5. Wortham and Locher (1996), for example, distinguish five categories of "textual devices" frequently used to produce voicing effects in discourse (viz. reference and predication, pronouns, epistemic modalization, evaluative indexicals, and reported speech constructions). As Wortham later clarifies (2001:38–40), however, this inventory of relatively discrete "devices" is best used only as a heuristic for identifying voicing effects.

6. *nga yin bsam pa byed dgos kyi yog red.*

7. *khyod dang khyod zer [-s] lab dgos red da* (Cabezón 1997).

8. A word about their backgrounds: Chögyel has had substantial schooling, while Trinley hasn't. Trinley's father is a pastoralist, and mother an apronmaker. The issue of social reproduction rears its head here, it would seem. Later, I pressed Geshe-la on the reason Chögyel is 'not smart', and the response was simply that he faired poorly in debate (which suggests, again, that at least at Sera this is the premier intellectual exercise).

9. See chapter 5 for a sustained discussion of *tshogs gtam* versus *tshogs gtam chen mo*. Geshe-la had the Jey text in his possession when he authored his own, which suggests that he may have drawn partly on it.

10. Monks who fail these exams are eventually shuttled into monastic jobs (as cooks, drivers of monastery-owned vehicles, agricultural laborers, etc.). Though monastic leaders often frame such labor as invaluable acts of service and remind monks that one can lead a virtuous life without being a scholar, these remarks often seem to ring hollow. At a monastery that prides itself on its rigorous training in Buddhist philosophy, symbolic capital accrues to those who perform well in the philosophical curriculum.

11. There is no matrix clause here to frame the discourse as represented speech or thought, but explicit frames are only a special case. Who is the implied "author" here, in the sense of the agent framed as bearing responsibility for the denotational content of the reported segment? If the disciplinarian himself were the author, he would be absurdly asserting that derelict monks who fail to show up for exams—monks who were topicalized in prior discourse—do not "need" to fulfill their duties. He holds, of course, the opposite view: they *do* need to fulfill their duties. Also noteworthy is the shift from honorific to nonhonorific verb use. It is considered a gross violation of etiquette to use honorific forms for oneself, which again suggests that the disciplinarian is representing an alter's speech, albeit in a quasi-direct manner.

12. In two earlier essays that included passages from this reprimand (Lempert 2005, 2006), I had transcribed this as 'shut [your] ass' (*rkub tshum a*). After additional transcription sessions with several mother-tongue speakers, 'stick [it up your] ass' (*rkub tshugs a*) emerged as the clearest reading. A few other relatively minor corrections were made in the transcription.

13. The line in Tibetan reads: *ji srid nam mkha' gnas pa dang / 'gro ba ji srid gnas gyur pa / de srid bdag ni gnas gyur nas / 'gro ba'i bsngal sel bar shog* (Shantideva 1990:234).

14. Other semiotic resources include voice dynamics like pitch, loudness, and speech rate, and there are countless discursive effects that may help register affect, some of which are noted above. On the problematic of recognizing emotion in and through language, see especially Wilce 2009.

15. These are grouped together impressionistically because they tend to co-occur and correlate with the voice of the derelict monk and the larger character zones in which this voice occurs.

16. About the event's right periphery: a "braking" effect occurs toward the reprimand's close, a half minute shy of the disciplinarian's parting prayer. There is a succession of three substantial pauses (2.1 seconds, 3.5 seconds, and 2.7 seconds, respectively), then a brief, 5-second bout of apparent dysfluency, then a long pause of 4.4 seconds, after which the disciplinarian resumes with the discourse marker 'then' (*de nas*), signaling a transition of some kind. In the 15 seconds or so that follows this discourse marker, pauses between utterances tend to become progressively longer, as if to "slow" the reprimand (the lengths: .15, .30, .26, .14, .81, .92). Next comes a stretch of talk with interutterance pauses around .18 seconds, soon after which he caps the reprimand with his closing dedication. Voice quality is mostly modal during this "braking" phase, albeit with some tenseness.

17. *gdong rdza ri las nag pa / sems gangs ri las dkar ba.*

18. The figurative "darkness" of the *rdza ri* or "craggy," "rocky" mountain turns on the fact that it fails to reflect light and thus from afar looks "dark" relative to gleaming moun-

tains blanketed with snow. This type of mountain may be contrasted as well with verdant, grass-covered hills (*spang ri*).

19. *dper na / dgon po dang chos rgyal de tsho drag po zhib po zhig red pa / oh 'di nang bzhin byed thub dgos kyi yog red.*

## CHAPTER 5. AFFECTED SIGNS, SINCERE SUBJECTS

1. Such bidirectional influence was surely already motivated by the legacy of Tibet's former Ganden Phodrang government's (*dga' ldan pho brang*) official state ideology, its fusion of "religion" and the "secular," captioned famously by the phrase *chos srid gnyis 'brel* ('religion and political affairs joined together') (Goldstein 1989:2; see Cüppers 2004). The present Dalai Lama has continued to use this and related expressions (e.g., *chos srid zung 'brel, chos srid gnyis ldan*) with Tibetan audiences in India, even if the institutional configuration indexed by such expressions has obviously changed.

2. For the literature on this international campaign, see, for example, Smith 1996; Goldstein 1999:75; Shakya 1999:412–16.

3. Discussions of the international campaign of the 1980s often list toward two extremes. Some overstate the discontinuity, like Goldstein (1999), who stresses discontinuity with past strategies and gives considerable weight to the role played by foreign experts in shaping the new campaign. The Five Point Peace Plan emerged from a series of strategy sessions in 1985–87 in Dharamsala, and while the packaging of the plan's points (note the apparent oppositional symmetry with the earlier, five-point policy of rapprochement extended by Hu Yaobang in 1981; Goldstein 1999:68–75) was new, the proposal must be disassembled into its component points for the distinct histories to be appreciated. The environmental component, for instance, is the newest and most discontinuous, as Huber's (1995) work suggests. The "Zone of Peace" (as proper noun or common noun), and indeed the ideal of Tibet's future demilitarization, do not appear to have had a very long history. (This, despite positions like that of Powers [1998:192], who seems to suggest that this proposal existed in the exile government's first constitution from 1963; it does not appear in that document. More extravagantly, Thurman [2008] implies that one can trace a direct line of descent from the Fourteenth Dalai Lama's proposal for a zone of peace to his seventeenth-century predecessor, the Fifth Dalai Lama.)

Key of course has been the "human rights" element, which has a particularly intricate history. There is no space here to address this element, but suffice it to say that, as Mountcastle (2006:91) remarks, it is wrong to suggest that human rights did not figure prominently as a strategy for Dharamsala before the international campaign of the 1980s. An appeal to human rights violations in Tibet was evident, albeit to a much lesser degree, in the early years of exile. The Dalai Lama's annual statements of 10 March (e.g., 1961, 1962, 1963, 1964) include appeals to such rights, for instance. In his letters to the UN secretary-general in 1959 and 1961, the focus was on Tibet's legal status, on proving its sovereignty prior to the PLA's invasion in 1949 and the atrocities that had occurred since Tibet's illegal occupation. It is better to view the appeals to human rights in 1959 and the early 1960s as a concession on the part of Tibetans in their bid to shore up support from UN member states. Knaus (1999) has written of the repeated pressure applied by the United States to Tibetans in Dharamsala to avoid using the incendiary language of independence and occupation and instead frame their cause in terms of human rights violations.

4. Variants of this aphorism include 'stick' (*rgyug pa*) for 'whip' (and with genitive case marking, *pa'i*). In the form cited here, the trope is an equestrian one, as *rta lcag* becomes a riding crop, and pupils are akin to beasts of burden.

5. *dge phrug 'di rang dbang med par bskur thub pa yod pa byed.*

6. *nga tsho'i bod pa'i gshis ka 'di yog red.* The nomic auxiliary *yog red,* indicating generally known truths, should be noted.

7. *phrug gu spyod pa yag po med na rdung rogs byed zer* [-s].

8. *phyi rgyal yin na pe sha nyes pa gtong wi red pa / 'dir pe sha nyes pa btang na pe sha sprod ya yog ma red pa.*

9. The names adopted by Tibetan monastic institutions, especially in their English-language brochures and on their websites, merit a study unto itself. In English translation, most prefer to use the descriptors "institute," "college," and "university." It is not only self-consciously modernized institutions like the Institute of Buddhist Dialectics in Dharamsala or the Central Institute of Higher Tibetan Studies in Sarnath that claim these as monikers; even institutions that have not attempted any far-reaching reforms (e.g., admitting nuns or nonclergy, abolishing privileges traditionally accorded to reincarnate lamas) have often discursively positioned themselves as modern, secular institutions of higher education. In its English brochure (undated but acquired in 2000) Nechung Monastery in Gangchen Kyishong, for example, declares itself an "Institute of Buddhist Studies." So does the "Kirti Institute for Higher Tibetan Studies," located up the hill from Nechung, in Mcleod Ganj. Even more frequent are the terms "college" and "university," which are predicated of a great number of Tibetan Buddhist monastic and submonastic institutions. On one multilingual sign found at India's Sera Jey, the English reads: "Sera Jey Monastic University for Advanced Buddhist Studies." These institutions are not to be confused with some now-defunct European medieval Scholasticism or contemporary Roman Catholic monasteries or even with theological seminaries. Instead, these schools are discursively positioned in English at least as parallel (and hence not subordinate) to the hegemonic figure of the modern Western academy that they (partially) emulate, wherein "Buddhist studies" now enjoys a measure of legitimacy. Though not investigated here, these patterns of institutional self-characterization are likely linked to the emergence of Tibetan Buddhist studies in Europe and the United States, and the complex ties that exist between academic scholarship and Geluk monk scholars.

10. *kho rang su yin na yang tshogs gtam tshig gcig pa rkyang rkyang lab ya gcig.*

11. *gnas tshul ga re dang 'brel ba yin na'i de dang 'phrod nas nga tsho mtshan nyid kyi tshogs gtam dang gcig pa gcig rkyang red.*

12. As a metapragmatic descriptor (a term used to frame speech as a certain kind of action)), 'advice' may, of course, euphemistically mask forms of interactional violence. The same may be said of the term *tshogs gtam* itself, whose literal meaning is 'assembly' (*tshogs*) 'talk' (*gtam*). I am interested here only in the relative stereotypical semantic value of these two lexical items: *tshogs gtam* was consistently glossed by my interlocutors at both Sera and Dharamsala as 'to scold' (*bshad bshad gtong*). Neither 'advice' (*slob gso rgyag*) nor its honorific equivalent (*bka' slob gnang*) has such a valence. In terms of their stereotypical semantic value, the metapragmatic descriptors *tshogs gtam gtong* and *slob gso rgyag* differ considerably.

13. *tshogs gtam / tshogs gtam zer na nga tsho la dmigs gsal zhe drag yog ma red / gal che shos 'di [sgrig rang khur].*

14. *so so gi slob sbyong gi thog la dus tshos 'phro brlag [ma] gtong rog byed zer [-s] / gal che shos 'di slob sbyong dus tshos 'phro brlag ma gtong zer [-s].*

15. It is possible that the ideal of communicative "directness," especially in events of constructive criticism, may draw partly on socialist rituals of criticism with which older Tibetans would have been familiar. When this ideal of directness is considered in concert with others reforms, its liberal-democratic affinities come to the fore, however.

16. *tshogs gtam chen mo gtong stangs nang bzhin byed dgos ma red zer.*

## CONCLUSION

1. The field I mean here includes monasteries of all Tibetan sects, even though Sera is a Geluk institution that does not aspire to be 'nonsectarian' or 'ecumenical' (*ris med*).

2. I concentrate narrowly here on the positioning of monasteries vis-à-vis a single interactional practice, debate. As should be expected, many other practices and policies help constitute the dimensions and topography of the field of Buddhist education, from the standardized, intermonastic Geluk exams (*dge lugs rgyugs 'phrod*) to the annual, monthlong Jang Kunchö (*ljang dgun chos*) debates held in the south to the network that ties monastic colleges of the big three (especially by way of shared 'monastic textbooks', or *yig cha*) to smaller, loosely affiliated monasteries spread throughout the subcontinent. As for the Institute of Buddhist Dialectics, one should not forget its proximity to the Dalai Lama's residence and the Tibetan Government-in-Exile, both of which have helped position Dharamsala as the moral center of the exile community, even if this center overlaps only partially with the field of Buddhist education. The Central Institute of Higher Tibetan Studies in Varanasi has a more complex placement relative to places like Sera and the institute in Dharamsala. As noted, it is furthest from "traditional" monasteries like Sera and far more self-consciously modernized than the institute. In curricular design and legal status, it was from the start more integrated into the state system of higher education.

3. *wā Na [ṇa] dbus bod kyi chos mtho'i gtsug lag slob gnyer khang.*

4. The trope employed here likens historical events to a linear sequence found in countless forms of Tibetan Buddhist practice, a sequence involving a primary division into 'preliminary' (*sngon 'gro*) and 'actual' (*dngos gzhi*) sessions.

5. Disrobing and returning to lay life are reported to be less stigmatized than they had once been (S. Gyatso 2003:233–36).

6. I have records only for Mey but suspect that analogous patterns exist for Jey, and for the other major Geluk monasteries of India. Mey's records, which I copied by hand, are preserved in ledgers. They have a number of limitations. Of all 2,266 entries recorded from 1978 to my fieldwork in 2000, 1,398 indicate place of origin. As noted below, place of origin is not registered with any regularity until the 1990s. The units used to indicate place of origin also vary. For recent Tibetan refugees from Tibet, for instance, some entries state current province or district name; others list only the traditional Tibetan toponym, like Amdo (*a mdo*) or Kham (*khams*). A key limitation of this record keeping is that the records register the date

of arrival but not that of departure. For none of the entries are names of monks provided, which makes registering departures from the monastery difficult. In some cases, monks who have left the monastery are indicated by a strike-through or $X$ next to their name, but this is rare. Consequently, one cannot glean reliable information about Sera Mey's population from these records alone. Here, I use these data only as a window onto the relative proportion of recruits drawn from Tibetan settlements in India. As for Sera's pre-1980 population, according to some reports, recruits did come from India but did not tend to stay beyond adolescence. Instead, they treated the monastery as akin to a secular school; monks tended to enter young and then return after a few years. Shifts in the average age of recruits may suggest support for this. Age is noted in all but 102 of the 2,266 entries. The average age for the entire 1978–2000 period is 18, but a jump occurs in 1983—the year in which new arrivals from Tibet were reported to have begun arriving. The average age for the years 1978–82 was 11.7 (12.7, 10.1, 9.7, 12.3, and 13.6, respectively). In 1983 the average age of all recruits jumped to 20.8. From 1983 onward, the lowest average age for any given year was 16, and that average occurred for only two years—1984 and 1999 (for 1999, this was due to a wave of young recruits from Nepal). For the 1983–2000 period, the average age increased to 19.2.

7. Cabezón (2008:2877) suggests several factors that may be affecting the flow into Indian monasteries from areas in eastern Tibet, including low limits placed on monastic enrollment in the TAR's monastic seats (Sera is capped at 550 official monks) and a "patriotic re-education" campaign launched in 1996 called the 'Strike Hard Campaign' (rdung rdeg tsha nan), which expelled some 20 percent of the monastic seats' population just a year after it was introduced. Though research is needed, flow from Tibet into the monastic seats (and elsewhere) is reported to have slowed after the fallout of the 2008 protests in Tibet, so that the monastic seats have redirected their recruiting efforts elsewhere (José Cabezón, personal communication).

8. The flow of new refugees from Tibet to Sera (and to other monasteries in India) is said to have intensified especially in the wake of the Dalai Lama's massive Kalachakra initiations in Bodhgaya in both 1985 and 1990. These are reported spikes in Sera's population that I cannot confirm using the records available. At least for the Mey college, for which I have copies of official records, 1983 appears to mark the beginning of a demographic shift. No clear spikes in the total number of recruits occurred in 1985 and 1990, but these facts alone do not refute the oft-mentioned influence of the Kalachakra initiations on Sera's growth.

9. This number alone may suggest that Sera's rough, official estimate of 4,500 monks may be somewhat exaggerated.

10. Indirect evidence of this may be found in the 1998 demographic survey's table on monastic population by age and sex in south India (Central Tibetan Administration-in-Exile [India], Planning Council 2000:218). Over 4,000 monks fall within the 20–29 age range (20–24 range: 2,029 monks; 25–29: 2,030 monks), with fewer in the 15–19 age range (1,044) and 30–39 range (1,199). The 40–59 age range is strikingly low: 290 (40–49: 150; 50–59: 140). The 60+ range is higher, at 650, most of whom, it can be presumed, were born in Tibet and were affiliated with monasteries before exile. The low number for the 40–59 range may hint at low recruitment from South Asian exile communities during the period extending from the early 1970s to the early 1980s, before the monastic seats expanded.

11. *gra* was corrected to *grwa*.

12. M. L.: *rgya gar ba la bskyes pa'i da grwa pa zhe drag nyung nyung red zer gyi 'dug.*
Geshe: *zhe* drag *nyung nyung / zhe* drag *nyung nyung / dpe mi srid nyung nyung.*

13. *da drug tsam da / da ga se da / yar 'gro mar 'gro / . . . ga re lab dgos red da . . . / dbyin ji skad . . .* time pass *lab kyi 'dug ga.*

14. This is not to suggest that this asymmetry can be explained purely by some attitudinal shift toward monasticism, or that Tibetans have, correlatively, been excluded from avenues of secular education, especially the network of Tibetan Children's Village boarding schools and the CTSA schools. Much could be said about emerging "secular" challenges to debate and other Geluk institutions from within the monastic seats. Though debate remains the premier intellectual practice at Sera, new literacy practices have made inroads and compete with debate for importance. Pen-and-paper exams on philosophical topics, which demand skills in Tibetan composition, were introduced in the 1980s. While most of my interlocutors at Sera considered written exams less important than debate-based exams, the former are still an alternative mode of evaluation that has the potential to displace or at least diminish debate's status.

15. See Nowak 1984 for another discussion of this editorial and the controversy it sparked.

# REFERENCES

Adams, Vincanne. 1998. "Suffering the Winds of Lhasa: Politicized Bodies, Human Rights, Cultural Difference, and Humanism in Tibet." *Medical Anthropology Quarterly* 12 (1):74–102.

Agha, Asif. 1993. *Structural Form and Utterance Context in Lhasa Tibetan: Grammar and Indexicality in a Non-configurational Language.* Edited by S. Belasco. Monographs in Linguistics & the Philosophy of Language. New York: Peter Lang.

———. 1996. "Tropic Aggression in the Clinton-Dole Presidential Debate." *Pragmatics* 7 (4):461–97.

———. 1998. "Stereotypes and Registers of Honorific Language." *Language in Society* 27:151–93.

———. 2005. "Voice, Footing, Enregisterment." *Journal of Linguistic Anthropology* 15 (1):38–59.

———. 2007a. *Language and Social Relations.* Cambridge: Cambridge University Press.

———. 2007b. "Large- and Small-Scale Forms of Personhood." Paper presented at the Annual Conference of the American Anthropological Association, Washington, DC.

Agha, Asif, and Stanton E. F. Wortham. 2005. "Discourse across Speech Events: Intertextuality and Interdiscursivity in Social Life." Special issue, *Journal of Linguistic Anthropology* 15 (1):1–150.

Aikhenvald, Alexandra Y. 2004. *Evidentiality.* Oxford Linguistics. Oxford; New York: Oxford University Press.

Anonymous. 1976a. "Buddhist School of Dialectics." *Tibetan Review* (August):7.

———. 1976b. "Dalai Lama: More on Universal Responsibility." *Tibetan Review* 11 (4):21–22.

———. 1976c. "Modern Education for Monks?" *Tibetan Review* 11 (12):7–8.

———. 1976d. "Suppression by Lama Teachers." *Tibetan Review* 11 (6–7):22.

———. 1977. "Special Report: Tibetan Settlements in Bylakuppe, South India." *Tibetan Review* (April):12–14.

———. 1985. "'jang dgun chos kyi dge skul." *shes bya* (April):19.

———. 1988a. "'jang dgun chos thengs bzhi pa tshugs pa." *shes bya* (January):25.

———. 1988b. "Jang Gunchoe Opened to All Sects." *Tibetan Bulletin* 19 (4):16.

———. 1989. "'jang dgun chos kyi dge skul." *shes bya* (April):25.

———. 1990. "gdan sa gsum gyi 'jang dgun chos lhan tshogs nas 'byor ba." *shes bya* (February):25.

Anonymous [Jang Guncho Committee]. 1985. "'jang dgun chos phyir 'then gsal bsgrags." *shes bya* (October):17.

———. 1987. "rigs lam gyi blo 'byed pa'i 'jang dgun chos legs grub byung ba." *shes bya* (May):14.

Arnold, Daniel Anderson. 2005. *Buddhists, Brahmins, and Belief: Epistemology in South Asian Philosophy of Religion*. New York: Columbia University Press.

Asad, Talal. 1993. *Genealogies of Religion: Discipline and Reasons of Power in Christianity and Islam*. Baltimore: Johns Hopkins University Press.

Bakhtin, Mikhail M. 1981. *The Dialogic Imagination*. Translated by C. Emerson and M. Holquist. Edited by M. Holquist. University of Texas Press Slavic Series 1. Austin: University of Texas Press.

———. (1963) 1984. *Problems of Dostoevsky's Poetics*. Translated by C. Emerson. Minneapolis: University of Minnesota Press.

Bakhtin, Mikhail M., Michael Holquist, and Caryl Emerson. 1986. *Speech Genres and Other Late Essays*. 1st ed. University of Texas Press Slavic Series 8. Austin: University of Texas Press.

Barnett, Robert. 2001. "'Violated Specialness': Western Political Representations of Tibet." In *Imagining Tibet: Perceptions, Projections, & Fantasies*, edited by T. Dodin and H. Räther. Boston: Wisdom Publications.

Bauman, Richard, and Charles L. Briggs. 2003. *Voices of Modernity: Language Ideologies and the Politics of Inequality*. Cambridge: Cambridge University Press.

Bechert, Heinz, and Richard Gombrich, eds. 1984. *The World of Buddhism*. London: Thames and Hudson.

Benveniste, Emile. 1971. *Problems in General Linguistics*. Miami: University of Miami Press.

Bernstein, Anya. 2010. "Religious Bodies Politic: Rituals of Sovereignty in Buryat Buddhism." PhD diss., Department of Anthropology, New York University.

Bhabha, Homi K. 1994. "Of Mimicry and Man: The Ambivalence of Colonial Discourse." In *The Location of Culture*. London; New York: Routledge.

Bickel, Balthasar. 2000. "Person and Evidence in Himalayan Languages." Special issue, *Linguistics of the Tibeto-Burman Area* 23 (2).

bla-ma, Ta'-la'I. 1962. *ngos kyi yul dang ngos kyi mi dmangs* [Autobiography of the 14th Dalai Lama]. Dharamsala.

Blo bzang rgya, mtsho, and Gareth Sparham. 1998. *Memoirs of a Tibetan Lama*. Ithaca, NY: Snow Lion Publications.

Bose, Shesadri Prosad. 2008. *Colonial India, Predatory State: Emergence of New Social Structure in Jalpaiguri District, 1865–1947*. Kolkata: Readers Service.

Bose, Subhas Chandra, and Madan Gopal. 1978. *Life and Times of Subhas Chandra Bose, as Told in His Own Words*. New Delhi: Vikas.

Bourdieu, Pierre. 1977. *Outline of a Theory of Practice*. Translated by R. Nice. New York: Cambridge University Press.

———. 1991. *Language and Symbolic Power*. Cambridge, MA: Harvard University Press.

———. 1996. *The State Nobility: Elite Schools in the Field of Power*. Stanford, CA: Stanford University Press.

Brenneis, Donald Lawrence. 1988. "Language and Disputing." *Annual Review of Anthropology* 17:221–37.

Briggs, Charles L. 1983. "Questions for the Ethnographer: A Critical Examination of the Role of the Interview in Fieldwork." *Semiotica* 46 (2–4):233–61.

———. 2004. "Theorizing Modernity Conspiratorially: Science, Scale, and the Political Economy of Public Discourse in Explanations of a Cholera Epidemic." *American Ethnologist* 31 (2):164–87.

Burnouf, Eugène, Katia Buffetrille, and Donald S. Lopez. 2010. *Introduction to the History of Indian Buddhism, Buddhism, and Modernity*. Chicago; London: University of Chicago Press.

Cabezón, José Ignacio. 1994. *Buddhism and Language: A Study of Indo-Tibetan Scholasticism*. Edited by F. E. Reynolds and D. Tracy. SUNY Series, Toward a Comparative Philosophy of Religions. New York: State University of New York Press.

———. 1997. "The Regulations of a Monastery." In *Religions of Tibet in Practice*, edited by D. S. Lopez. Princeton, NJ: Princeton University Press.

———. 2008. "State Control of Tibetan Buddhist Monasticism in the People's Republic of China." In *Chinese Religiosities: Afflictions of Modernity and State Formation*, edited by M. M.-h. Yang. Berkeley: University of California Press.

Central Tibetan Administration. 1968. *The Plight of the Tibetan Monk Community of Buxa Lama Ashram*. Dharamsala: Council of Cultural and Religious Affairs of H.H. the Dalai Lama.

Central Tibetan Administration-in-Exile (India). Dept. of Religion and Culture. 1998. *The Worship of Shugden: Documents related to a Tibetan Controversy*. Dharamsala: Dept. of Religion and Culture Central Tibetan Administration.

———. Planning Council. 2000. *Tibetan Demographic Survey 1998*. Vol. 1. Dharamsala: Planning Council, Central Tibetan Administration.

Chakrabarty, Dipesh. 2000a. *Provincializing Europe: Postcolonial Thought and Historical Difference*. Princeton Studies in Culture/Power/History. Princeton, NJ: Princeton University Press.

———. 2000b. "Translating Life-Worlds into Labor and History." In *Provincializing Europe: Postcolonial Thought and Historical Difference*. Princeton, NJ: Princeton University Press.

Chang, Kun, and Betty Shefts Chang. 1964. *A Manual of Spoken Tibetan (Lhasa Dialect)*. Seattle: University of Washington.

———. 1967. "Spoken Tibetan Morphophonemics: p." *Language* 43 (2):512–25.

Childs, Geoff H. 2004. "Culture Change in the Name of Cultural Preservation." *Himalaya* 24 (1–2):31–42.

———. 2008. *Tibetan Transitions: Historical and Contemporary Perspectives on Fertility, Family Planning, and Demographic Change*. Brill's Tibetan Studies Library. Leiden; Boston: Brill.

Childs, Geoff, Melvyn C. Goldstein, Ben Jiao, and Cynthia M. Beall. 2005. "Tibetan Fertility Transitions in China and South Asia." *Population and Development Review* 31 (2):337–49.

Choepel, Gedun. 1994a. *dge 'dun chos 'phel gyi gsung rtsom*. Edited by h. k. bsod nams dpal 'bar. Vol. 1. Lhasa: bod ljongs bod yig dpe rnying dpe skrun khang.

———. 1994b. *dge 'dun chos 'phel gyi gsung rtsom*. Edited by h. k. bsod nams dpal 'bar. Vol. 2. Lhasa: bod ljongs bod yig dpe rnying dpe skrun khang.

Chopra, Pran Nath, Yashwantrao Balwantrao Chavan, and India Ministry of Home Affairs. 1969. *Who's Who of Indian Martyrs*. New Delhi: Ministry of Education and Youth Services.

Council for Religious and Cultural Affairs. 1986. "The Re-establishment of the Tibetan Monasteries in Exile." *Chö-yang* 1 (1):49–66.

Crapanzano, Vincent. 1990. "On Dialogue." In *The Interpretation of Dialogue*, edited by T. Maranhão. Chicago: University of Chicago Press.

Cüppers, Christoph. 2004. *The Relationship between Religion and State (chos srid zung 'brel) in Traditional Tibet: Proceedings of a Seminar Held in Lumbini, Nepal, March 2000*. LIRI Seminar Proceedings Series. Lumbini: Lumbini International Research Institute.

Das, Veena. 2000. "Violence and the Work of Time." In *Signifying Identities: Anthropological Perspectives on Boundaries and Contested Values*, edited by A. P. Cohen. London: Routledge.

dbang phyug, ye shes. 1986. *Ser smad thos bsam nor gling grwa tshang gi chos 'byung lo rgyus nor bu'i phreng ba*. Bylakuppe: Sermey Printing Press.

———. 1997. *blo gsal rigs lam mig 'byed*. Bylakuppe: Sermey Library.

DeLancey, Scott. 1992. "The Historical Status of the Conjunct/Disjunct Pattern in Tibeto-Burman." *Acta Linguistica Hafniensia: International Journal of Linguistics* 25:39–62.

———. 1997. "Mirativity: The Grammatical Marking of Unexpected Information." *Linguistic Typology* 1:33–52.

Denwood, Philip. 1999. *Tibetan*. London Oriental and African Language Library, vol. 3. Amsterdam; Philadelphia: John Benjamins.

Dhondup, K. 1978. "'Lamaism' is an Appropriate Term: Interview with Tsultrim Kesang." *Tibetan Review* 13 (5) (May):18–19, 27.

Diehl, Keila. 2002. *Echoes from Dharamsala: Music in the Life of a Tibetan Refugee Community*. Berkeley: University of California Press.

Dorje, T. 1976. "Non-Tibetan Teachers Inefficient." *Tibetan Review* (October):34.

Dreyfus, Georges B. J. 1997a. *Recognizing Reality: Dharmakīrti's Philosophy and Its Tibetan Interpretations*. SUNY Series in Buddhist Studies. Albany: State University of New York Press.

———. 1997b. "Tibetan Scholastic Education and the Role of Soteriology." *Journal of the International Association of Buddhist Studies* 20 (1):31–63.

———. 1999. "The Shuk-Den Affair: Origins of a Controversy." *Journal of the International Association of Buddhist Studies* 21:2.

———. 2003. *The Sound of Two Hands Clapping: The Education of a Tibetan Buddhist Monk*. Berkeley: University of California Press.

———. 2005. "Where Do Commentarial Schools Come From? Reflections on the History of Tibetan Scholasticism. *Journal of the International Association of Buddhist Studies* 28 (2):273–97.

————. 2008. "What Is Debate For? The Rationality of Tibetan Debates and the Role of Humor." *Argumentation* 22:43–58.

Dreyfus, Georges B. J., and Sara L. McClintock, eds. 2003. *The Svātantrika-Prāsaṅgika Distinction: What Difference Does a Difference Make?* Studies in Indian and Tibetan Buddhism. Boston: Wisdom Publications.

Duranti, Alessandro. 1997. *Linguistic Anthropology.* Edited by S. R. Anderson et. al. Cambridge Textbooks in Linguistics. Cambridge: Cambridge University Press.

Durkheim, Émile, and Marcel Mauss. 1963. *Primitive Classification.* Chicago: University of Chicago Press.

Edwards, Jane Anne. 2001. "The Transcription of Discourse." In *The Handbook of Discourse Analysis,* edited by D. Schiffrin, D. Tannen, and H. E. Hamilton. Malden, MA: Blackwell Publishers.

Edwards, Jane Anne, and Martin D. Lampert. 1993. *Talking Data: Transcription and Coding in Discourse Research.* Hillsdale, NJ: Lawrence Erlbaum Associates.

Evans-Pritchard, E. E. 1965. *Theories of Primitive Religion.* Oxford: Clarendon Press.

Ferrara, Alessandro. 1990. "A Critique of Habermas's *Diskursethik.*" In *The Interpretation of Dialogue,* edited by T. Maranhão. Chicago: University of Chicago Press.

Fleming, David. 1996. "Can Pictures Be Arguments?" *Argumentation and Advocacy* 33 (Summer):11–22.

Forsee, Aylesa. 1959. *Frank Lloyd Wright, Rebel in Concrete.* Philadelphia: Macrae Smith.

Foucault, Michel. 1973. *The Order of Things: An Archaeology of the Human Sciences.* New York: Vintage Books.

————. 1979. *Discipline and Punish: The Birth of the Prison.* New York: Vintage Books.

Frazer, James George. 1963. *The Golden Bough: A Study in Magic and Religion.* Vol. 1. New York: Macmillan Publishing.

Frazer, Michael L. 2010. *The Enlightenment of Sympathy: Reflective Sentimentalism in the Eighteenth Century and Today.* New York: Oxford University Press.

Frechette, Ann. 2002. *Tibetans in Nepal: The Dynamics of International Assistance among a Community in Exile.* Studies in Forced Migration 11. New York: Berghahn Books.

French, Rebecca Redwood. 1995. *The Golden Yoke: The Legal Cosmology of Buddhist Tibet.* Ithaca, NY: Cornell University Press.

Gelek, Karma. 1976. "Letters: Ideal Leadership of Dalai Lama and Lama Teachers." *Tibetan Review* 11 (10):36, 42.

Gluckman, Max. 1954. *Rituals of Rebellion.* Manchester: Manchester University Press.

————. 1963. *Order and Rebellion in Tribal Africa: Collected Essays, with an Autobiographical Introduction.* London: Cohen & West.

Goffman, Erving. 1961. "Role Distance." In *Encounters: Two Studies in the Sociology of Interaction.* New York: Bobbs-Merrill.

————. 1967a. *Interaction Ritual: Essays on Face-To-Face Behavior.* New York: Anchor Books.

————. 1967b. "The Nature of Deference and Demeanor." In *Interaction Ritual: Essays on Face-to-Face Behavior,* edited by E. Goffman. New York: Anchor Books.

————. 1981. "Footing." In *Forms of Talk,* edited by E. Goffman. Philadelphia: University of Pennsylvania Press.

———. 1983. "The Interaction Order." *American Sociological Review* 48:1–17.

Goldbert, Margaret. 1985. "Argumentation and Understanding: A Study of Tibetan Religious Debate." PhD diss., University of Illinois, Urbana-Champaign.

Goldstein, Melvyn C. 1989. *A History of Modern Tibet, 1913–1951: The Demise of the Lamaist State.* Berkeley: University of California Press.

———. 1998. "The Revival of Monastic Life in Drepung Monastery." In *Buddhism in Contemporary Tibet: Religious Revival and Cultural Identity,* edited by M. C. Goldstein. Berkeley: University of California Press.

———. 1999. *The Snow Lion and the Dragon: China, Tibet, and the Dalai Lama.* Berkeley: University of California Press.

———. 2007. *A history of Modern Tibet.* Vol. 2, *The Calm before the Storm, 1951–1955.* Berkeley: University of California Press.

Goldstein, Melvyn C., T. N. Shelling, and J. T. Surkhang, eds. 2001. *The New Tibetan-English Dictionary of Modern Tibetan.* Berkeley: University of California Press.

Goldstein-Kyaga, Katrin. 2003. "The Tibetan Culture of Non-Violence—Its Transmission and the Role of Education." In *Culture and Education,* edited by B. Qvarsell and C. Wulf. Münster; New York: Waxmann.

Gombrich, Richard Francis, and Gananath Obeyesekere. 1988. *Buddhism Transformed: Religious Change in Sri Lanka.* Princeton, NJ: Princeton University Press.

Goodwin, Marjorie Harness. 1990. *He-Said-She-Said: Talk as Social Organization among Black Children.* Bloomington: Indiana University Press.

Gouldner, Alvin Ward. 1971. *The Coming Crisis of Western Sociology.* New York: Avon.

Grootendorst, R., and F. H. van Eemeren. 2004. *A Systematic Theory of Argumentation: The Pragma-dialectical Approach.* Cambridge; New York: Cambridge University Press.

Gross, Ernest. 1961. "Tibetans Plan for Tomorrow." *Foreign Affairs* (October):136–42.

Gyatso, Lobsang. 1973. "School for All Sects." *Tibetan Review* 8 (9–10):32.

———. 1976. "Lama Teachers More Competent." *Tibetan Review* 11 (6–7):24–25.

———. 1978a. *A Brief History of the Buddhist School of Dialectics (Dharamsala).* Translated by Anonymous. Dharamsala: Imperial Printing Press.

———. 1978b. *rigs lam slob gra'i lo rgyus.* Dharamsala: Imperial Printing Press.

———. 1987. *Institute of Buddhist Dialectics: Prospectus.* Translated by G. T. Wangdag. Edited by M. E. Poulton. Dharamsala: The Translation and Publication Bureau of the Institute of Buddhist Dialectics.

Gyatso, Sherap. 2003. "Of Monks and Monasteries." In *Exile as Challenge: The Tibetan Diaspora,* edited by D. Bernstorff and H. v. Welck. Hyderabad: Orient Longman.

Gyatso, Tenzin. 1990. *Freedom in Exile: The Autobiography of the Dalai Lama.* New York: HarperCollins Publishers.

———. 1996. *shes yon lam skor gyi bka' slob phyogs bsgrigs (1960–1996).* Dharamsala: Sherig Parkhang.

———. 2000a. *srid zhi'i rnam 'dren gong sa skyabs mgon chen po mchog nas rgya che'i bod mi ser skya mang tshogs la blang dor byed sgo'i skor stsal ba'i bka' slob phyogs bsdebs.* 3 vols. Tibetan Information Office. New Delhi: Paljor Publications at Creative Advertisers.

———. 2000b. *srid zhi'i rnam 'dren gong sa skyabs mgon chen po mchog nas slob grwa khag sogs la she yon slob sbyong byed sgo'i skor stsal ba'i bka' slob phyogs bsdebs bzhugs so.* 2 vols. Delhi: Tibetan Information Office. New Delhi: Paljor Publications at Creative Advertisers.

Gyatso, Tenzin, and Jeffrey Hopkins. 1985. *The Kalachakra Tantra: Rite of Initiation for the Stage of Generation.* London: Wisdom Publications.

Habermas, Jürgen. 1984. *The Theory of Communicative Action: Reason and the Rationalization of Society.* Translated by T. McCarthy. Vol. 1. Boston: Beacon Press.

———. 1995. *Justification and Application: Remarks on Discourse Ethics.* Translated by C. P. Cronin. Cambridge, MA: MIT Press.

———. 1996. *The Structural Transformation of the Public Sphere: An Inquiry into a Category of Bourgeois Society.* Translated by T. Burger. Cambridge, MA: MIT Press.

———. 1998. "Social Action, Purposive Activity, and Communication (1981)." In *On the Pragmatics of Communication,* edited by M. Cooke. Cambridge, MA: MIT Press.

———. 1999. *Moral Consciousness and Communicative Action.* Translated by C. Lenhardt and S. W. Nicholsen. Cambridge, MA: MIT Press.

———. 2001. "Truth and Society: The Discursive Redemption of Factual Claims to Validity." In *On the Pragmatics of Social Interaction: Preliminary Studies in the Theory of Communicative Action.* Cambridge, MA: MIT Press.

Hacking, Ian. 1984. "Language, Truth, and Reason." In *Rationality and Relativism,* edited by M. Hollis and S. Lukes. Cambridge, MA: MIT Press.

Hale, Austin. 1980. "Person Markers: Finite Conjunct and Disjunct Verb forms in Newari." In *Papers in South-East Asian Linguistics,* no. 7, edited by R. Trail. Canberra: Pacific Linguistics (A-53).

Hanks, William F. 1989. "Text and Textuality." *Annual Review of Anthropology* 18:95–127.

Hansen, Hans V., and Robert C. Pinto. 1995. *Fallacies: Classical and Contemporary Readings.* University Park: Pennsylvania State University Press.

Harding, Harry. 1992. *A Fragile Relationship: The United States and China since 1972.* Washington, DC: Brookings Institution.

Harrer, Heinrich. 1954. *Seven Years in Tibet.* 1st American ed. New York: Dutton.

Haviland, John B. 1996. "Text from Talk in Tzotzil." In *Natural Histories of Discourse,* edited by M. Silverstein and G. Urban. Chicago: University of Chicago Press.

———. 1997. "Shouts, Shrieks, and Shots: Unruly Political Conversations in Indigenous Chiapas." *Pragmatics* 7 (4):547–73.

Herzfeld, Michael. 1997. *Cultural Intimacy: Social Poetics in the Nation-State.* New York: Routledge.

Hill, Jane. 1997. "The Voices of Don Gabriel: Responsibility and Self in a Modern Mexicano Narrative." In *The Dialogic Emergence of Culture,* edited by D. Tedlock and B. Mannheim. Urbana: University of Illinois Press.

Hopkins, Jeffrey. 1983. 1996a. *Meditation on Emptiness.* Boston: Wisdom Publications.

———. 1996b. "The Tibetan Genre of Doxography: Structuring a Worldview." In *Tibetan Literature: Studies in Genre,* edited by J. I. Cabezón and R. R. Jackson. Ithaca, NY: Snow Lion Publications.

———. 1999. *Emptiness in the Mind-only School of Buddhism.* Vol. 1 of *Dynamic Responses to Dzong-ka-ba's "The Essence of Eloquence."* Berkeley: University of California Press.

———. 2002. *Reflections on Reality: The Three Natures and Non-natures in the Mind-only School.* Vol. 2 of *Dynamic Responses to Dzong-ka-ba's "The Essence of Eloquence."* Berkeley: University of California Press.

Horkheimer, Max. 1974. *Critique of Instrumental Reason: Lectures and Essays since the End of World War II.* New York: Seabury Press.

Horkheimer, Max, and Theodor W. Adorno. 1994. *Dialectic of Enlightenment.* New York: Continuum.

Huber, Toni. 1995. "Green Tibetans: A Brief Social History." In *Tibetan Culture in the Diaspora: Papers Presented at a Panel of the 7th Seminar of the International Association for Tibetan Studies, Graz 1995,* edited by Frank J. Korom. Vienna: Verlag der Österreichischen Akademie der Wissenschaften.

Hugon, Pascale. 2008. "Arguments by Parallels in the Epistemological Works of Phya pa Chos kyi seng ge." *Argumentation* 22:93–114.

Hume, David. 2000. *A Treatise of Human Nature.* Edited by David Fate Norton and Mary J. Norton. Oxford Philosophical Texts. Oxford: Oxford University Press.

Information Office. 1981. "Tibetans in Exile, 1959–1980." Dharamsala: Information Office, Central Tibetan Secretariat.

International Commission of Jurists (1952–). Legal Inquiry Committee on Tibet. 1960. *Tibet and the Chinese People's Republic: A Report to the International Commission of Jurists.* Geneva: International Commission of Jurists.

Irvine, Judith T. 1997. "Shadow Conversations: The Indeterminacy of Participant Roles." In *Natural Histories of Discourse,* edited by M. Silverstein and G. Urban. Chicago: University of Chicago Press.

Irvine, Judith T., and Susan Gal. 2000. "Language Ideology and Linguistic Differentiation." In *Regimes of Language,* edited by P. V. Kroskrity. Santa Fe, NM: School of American Research.

Jackson, David. 1994. "The Status of Pramāṇa Doctrine according to Sa skya Paṇḍita and Other Tibetan Masters: Theoretical Discipline or Doctrine of Liberation?" In *The Buddhist Forum,* volume 3 (1991–1993), *Papers in Honour and Appreciation of Professor David Seyfort Ruegg's Contribution to Indological, Buddhist, and Tibetan Studies,* edited by T. Skorupski and U. Pagel. London: School of Oriental and African Studies, University of London.

Karlström, Mikael. 2004. "Modernity and Its Aspirants: Moral Community and Developmental Eutopianism in Buganda." *Current Anthropology* 45 (5):595–619.

Karmay, Samten G. 1977. "Religion: A Major Cause of Tibetan Disunity." *Tibetan Review* 12 (5):25–26.

Keane, Webb. 1997. "Religious Language." *Annual Review of Anthropology* 26:47–71.

———. 2001. "Voice." In *Key Terms in Language and Culture,* edited by A. Duranti. Malden, MA: Blackwell.

———. 2002. "Sincerity, 'Modernity,' and the Protestants." *Cultural Anthropology* 17 (1):65–92.

———. 2007. *Christian Moderns: Freedom and Fetish in the Mission Encounter.* The anthropology of Christianity 1. Berkeley: University of California Press.

Keenan, Thomas. 2004. "Mobilizing Shame." *South Atlantic Quarterly* 103 (2/3):435–49.

Kendon, Adam. 1990. *Conducting Interaction: Patterns of Behavior in Focused Encounters.* Cambridge; New York: Cambridge University Press.

Knaus, John Kenneth. 1999. *Orphans of the Cold War: America and the Tibetan Struggle for Survival*. 1st ed. New York: PublicAffairs.

Krull, Germaine. 1968. *Tibetans in India*. [Bombay]: Allied Publishers.

Kusari, Abani Mohan. 1981. *West Bengal District Gazetteers: Jalpaiguri, Gazetteer of India*. Calcutta: Barun De, Honorary State Editor, West Bengal District Gazetteers.

Lahiri, Abani, and Ranajit Dasgupta. 2001. *Postwar Revolt of the Rural Poor in Bengal: Memoirs of a Communist Activist*. Calcutta: Seagull.

Lati, Rinbochay, and Elizabeth Napper. 1980. *Mind in Tibetan Buddhism: Oral Commentary on Ge-shay Jam-bel-sam-pel's Presentation of Awareness and Knowledge, Composite of All the Important Points, Opener of the Eye of New Intelligence*. Valois, NY: Gabriel/Snow Lion.

Latour, Bruno. 1993. *We Have Never Been Modern*. Translated by C. Porter. Cambridge, MA: Harvard University Press.

———. 2005. *Reassembling the Social: An Introduction to Actor-network-theory*. Clarendon Lectures in Management Studies. Oxford; New York: Oxford University Press.

Lempert, Michael. 2005. "Denotational Textuality and Demeanor Indexicality in Tibetan Buddhist Debate." *Journal of Linguistic Anthropology* 15 (2):171–93.

———. 2006. "Disciplinary Theatrics: Public Reprimand and the Textual Performance of Affect at Sera Monastery, India." *Language & Communication* 26 (1):15–33.

———. 2007. "Conspicuously Past: Distressed Discourse and Diagrammatic Embedding in a Tibetan Represented Speech Style." *Language and Communication* 27 (3):258–71.

———. 2008. "The Poetics of Stance: Text-Metricality, Epistemicity, Interaction." *Language in Society* 37 (4):569–92.

———. 2012a. "Indirectness." In *Handbook of Intercultural Discourse and Communication*, edited by S. F. Kiesling, C. B. Paulston, and E. Rangel. Malden, MA: Wiley-Blackwell.

———. 2012b. "Interaction Rescaled: How Monastic Debate Became a Diasporic Pedagogy." *Anthropology and Education Quarterly*.

Levinson, Stephen C. 1988. "Putting Linguistics on Proper Footing: Explorations in Goffman's Concepts of Participation." In *Erving Goffman: An Interdisciplinary Appreciation*, edited by P. Drew and A. Wootton. Oxford: Polity Press.

Lévi-Strauss, Claude. 1968. *Structural Anthropology*. London: Allen Lane.

Liberman, Kenneth. 1992. "Philosophical Debate in the Tibetan Academy." *Tibetan Journal* 17 (1):36–67.

———. 1996. "'Universal Reason' as a Local Organizational Method: Announcement of a Study." *Human Studies* 19:289–301.

———. 1998. "Can Emptiness Be Formulated? A Debate from a Gelugpa Monastic University." *Tibet Journal* 23 (2):33–48.

———. 2004. *Dialectical Practice in Tibetan Philosophical Culture: An Ethnomethodological Inquiry into Formal Reasoning*. New York: Rowan & Littlefield Publishers.

———. 2008. "Sophistry in and as Its Course." *Argumentation* 22:59–70.

Liu, Lydia He. 1995. *Translingual Practice: Literature, National Culture, and Translated Modernity—China, 1900–1937*. Stanford, CA: Stanford University Press.

Locke, John. 1959. *An Essay concerning Human Understanding*. New York: Dover Publications.

Locke, John, and Robert Hebert Quick. 1902. *Some Thoughts concerning Education*. Cambridge: Cambridge University Press.

Lopez, Donald S. 1988. *Buddhist Hermeneutics*. Honolulu: University of Hawaii Press.

———. 1995. *Curators of the Buddha: The Study of Buddhism under Colonialism*. Chicago: University of Chicago Press.

———. 1997. *Religions of Tibet in Practice*. Princeton Readings in Religions. Princeton, NJ: Princeton University Press.

———. 1998. *Prisoners of Shangri-La: Tibetan Buddhism and the West*. Chicago: University of Chicago Press.

———. 1999. *Asian Religions in Practice: An introduction*. Princeton Readings in Religions. Princeton, NJ: Princeton University Press.

———. 2002. *A modern Buddhist Bible: Essential Readings from East and West*. 1st Beacon Press ed. Boston: Beacon Press.

———. 2008. *Buddhism and Science: A Guide for the Perplexed*. Chicago: University of Chicago Press.

Lukken, Gerard, and Mark Searle. 1993. *Semiotics and Church Architecture: Applying the Semiotics of A. J. Greimas and the Paris School to the Analysis of Church Buildings*. Kampen, Netherlands: Kok Pharos Pub. House.

Maher, Derek F. 2010. "Sacralized Warfare: The Fifth Dalai Lama and the Discourse of Religious Violence." In *Buddhist Warfare*, edited by M. K. Jerryson and M. Juergensmeyer. Oxford; New York: Oxford University Press.

Mahmood, Saba. 2001. "Feminist Theory, Embodiment, and the Docile Agent: Some Reflections on the Egyptian Islamic Revival." *Cultural Anthropology* 16 (2):202–36.

Makley, Charlene E. 2007. *The Violence of Liberation: Gender and Tibetan Buddhist Revival in Post-Mao China*. Berkeley: University of California Press.

Mansfield, Becky. 2005. "Beyond Rescaling: Reintegrating the 'National' as a Dimension of Scalar Relations." *Progress in Human Geography* 29 (4):458–73.

Maurer, Bill. 2005. *Mutual Life, Limited: Islamic Banking, Alternative Currencies, Lateral Reason*. Princeton, NJ: Princeton University Press.

McGranahan, Carole. 2010. *Arrested Histories: Tibet, the CIA, and Memories of a Forgotten War*. Durham, NC: Duke University Press.

Mertz, Elizabeth. 2007a. *The Language of Law School: Learning to "Think like a Lawyer."* Oxford; New York: Oxford University Press.

———. 2007b. "Semiotic Anthropology." *Annual Review of Anthropology* 36:337–53.

Mertz, Elizabeth, and Richard J. Parmentier, eds. 1985. *Semiotic Mediation: Sociocultural and Psychological Perspectives*. Edited by E. A. Hammel. Language, Thought, and Culture: Advances in the Study of Cognition. New York: Academic Press.

Migyur, Tsering. 1976. "Schools Need Strict Discipline." *Tibetan Review* 11 (10):34.

Mills, Martin A. 2003. "This Turbulent Priest: Contesting Religious Rights and the State in the Tibetan Shugden Controversy." In *Human Rights in Global Perspective: Anthropological Studies of Rights, Claims, and Entitlements*, edited by R. Wilson and J. P. Mitchell. London; New York: Routledge.

mkhas-grub, dge-'dun bstan-pa dar-rgyas. 1995. *phar-phyin spyi-don rnam-bshad rnying-po rgyan gyi snang-ba*. Vol. 1. Bylakuppe: Sera Monastic University.

Moore, Adam. 2008. "Rethinking Scale as a Geographical Category: From Analysis to Practice." *Progress in Human Geography* 32 (2):203–25.

Mountcastle, Amy. 2006. "The Question of Tibet and the Politics of the 'Real.'" In *Contemporary Tibet: Politics, Development, and Society in a Disputed Region*, edited by B. Sautman and J. T. Dreyer. Armonk, NY: M. E. Sharpe.

Need, David Norton. 1993. "The Guru's Mandala: Interpretation, Authority, and Culture." Master's thesis, University of Virginia, Charlottesville.

Newland, Guy. 1996. "Debate Manuals (*Yig cha*) in dGe lugs Monastic Colleges." In *Tibetan Literature: Studies in Genre*, edited by J. I. Cabezón and R. Jackson. Ithaca, NY: Snow Lion Publications.

Ngawang Lobsang Yishey Tenzing, Gyatso. (1962) 1997. *My Land and My People: The Original Autobiography of His Holiness the Dalai Lama of Tibet*. New York: McGraw-Hill.

Norbu, Dawa T. 1976. "The State of Tibetan School Education." *Tibetan Review* 11 (4):3–5.

Norbu, Jamyang. 1986. *Warriors of Tibet: The Story of Aten, and the Khampas' Fight for the Freedom of Their Country*. New ed. A Wisdom Tibet Book, Yellow Series. London: Wisdom Publications.

———. 1997. "Non-violence or Non-action? Some Gandhian Truths about the Tibetan Peace Movement." *Tibetan Review* (September):18–21.

———. 1998. "Rite of Freedom: The Life and Sacrifice of Thupten Ngodup." http://www .phayul.com/news/article.aspx?id = 6853&t = 1.

———. 2004. *Shadow Tibet: Selected Writings, 1989 to 2004*. New Delhi: Bluejay Books/ Srishti Publishers & Distributors.

Nowak, Margaret. 1984. *Tibetan Refugees: Youth and the New Generation of Meaning*. New Brunswick, NJ: Rutgers University Press.

Ochs, Elinor. 1979. "Transcription as Theory." In *Developmental Pragmatics*, edited by E. Ochs and B. B. Schieffelin. New York: Academic Press.

Office of H.H. the Dalai Lama. 1969. *Tibetans in Exile, 1959–1969: A Report on Ten Years of Rehabilitation in India compiled by the Office of H.H. the Dalai Lama*. New Delhi: Bureau of H.H. the Dalai Lama.

O'Keefe, Daniel J. 1982. "The Concepts of Argument and Arguing." In *Advances in Argumentation Theory and Research*, edited by R. J. Cox and C. A. Willard. Carbondale: Southern Illinois University Press.

Onoda, Shunz o. 1992. *Monastic Debate in Tibet: A Study on the History and Structures of bsdus grwa Logic*. Wiener Studien zur Tibetologie und Buddhismuskunde 27. Vienna: Arbeitskreis für Tibetische und Buddhistische Studien Universität Wien.

Ortner, Sherry B. 1994. "Theory in Anthropology since the Sixties." In *Culture/Power/History: A Reader in Contemporary Social Theory*, edited by N. B. Dirks, G. Eley, and S. B. Ortner. Princeton, NJ: Princeton University Press.

Parmentier, Richard J. 1994. "The Semiotic Regimentation of Social Life." In *Signs in Society: Studies in Semiotic Anthropology*, edited by R. J. Parmentier. Bloomington: Indiana University Press.

———. 1997. "The Pragmatic Semiotics of Cultures." *Semiotica* 116 (1):1–114.

Perdue, Daniel E. 1992. *Debate in Tibetan Buddhism*. Edited by R. Jackson, A. Klein, K. Lang, and J. Strong. Textual Studies and Translations in Indo-Tibetan Buddhism. Ithaca, NY: Snow Lion Publications.

Powers, John. 1998. "Human Rights and Cultural Values: The Political Philosophies of the

Dalai Lama and the People's Republic of China." In *Buddhism and Human Rights,* edited by D. Keown, C. S. Prebish, and W. R. Husted. Richmond, UK: Curzon.

———. 2004. *History as Propaganda: Tibetan Exiles versus the People's Republic of China.* New York: Oxford University Press.

Ray, P. K. 1990. *Down Memory Lane: Reminiscences of a Bengali Revolutionary.* New Delhi: Gian Pub. House.

Reddy, William M. 2001. *The Navigation of Feeling: A Framework for the History of Emotions.* Cambridge; New York: Cambridge University Press.

Rigzing, Chhime. 1976. "Lamas as Stopgap Teacher." *Tibetan Review* 11 (10):34–35.

Robbins, Joel. 2001. "God Is Nothing but Talk: Modernity, Language, and Prayer in a Papua New Guinea Society." *American Anthropologist* 103 (4):901–12.

Roemer, Stephanie. 2008. *The Tibetan Government-in-Exile: Politics at Large.* Routledge Advances in South Asian Studies 10. London; New York: Routledge.

Rogers, Katherine, and Byams-pa-rgya-mtsho Phur-bu-lcog. 2009. *Tibetan Logic.* Ithaca, NY: Snow Lion Publications.

Rorty, Richard. 1993. "Human Rights, Rationality, and Sentimentality." In *On Human Rights: The Oxford Amnesty Lectures 1993,* edited by S. Shute and S. Hurley. New York: Basic Books.

Rutherford, Samuel. 1649. *A free disputation against pretended liberty of conscience.* London: Printed by R.I. for Andrew Crook.

Sacks, H., Emanuel A. Schegloff, and Gail Jefferson. 1974. "A Simplest Systematics for the Organization of Turn-Taking for Conversation." *Language* 50 (4):696–735.

Said, Edward. 1978. *Orientalism.* New York: Vintage.

Sangay, Lobsang. 2003. "Tibet: Exiles' Journey." *Journal of Democracy* 14 (3):119–30.

Santideva. 1996. *The Bodhicaryavatara.* Translated by K. Crosby and A. Skilton. Oxford: Oxford University Press.

Schiffrin, D. 1984. "Jewish Argument as Sociability." *Language in Society* 13:311–36.

Schlagintweit, Emil. 1863. *Buddhism in Tibet illustrated by literary documents and objects of religious worship. With an account of the Buddhist systems preceding it in India.* Leipzig [etc.]: F. A. Brockhaus.

Shakya, Tsering. 1999. *The Dragon in the Land of Snows: A History of Modern Tibet since 1947.* London: Pimlico.

———. 2001. "Who Are the Prisoners?" *Journal of the American Academy of Religion* 69 (1):183–89.

Shantideva. 1990. *byang chub sems dpa'i spyod pa la 'jug pa.* Dharamsala: Serig Parkhang.

Sidnell, Jack. 2007. "Comparative Studies in Conversation Analysis." *Annual Review of Anthropology* 36:229–44.

———. 2009. *Conversation Analysis: Comparative Perspectives.* Studies in Interactional Sociolinguistics. Cambridge: Cambridge University Press.

Sierksma, F. 1964. "*Rtsod-pa:* The Monachal Disputations in Tibet." *Indo-Iranian Journal* 8 (2):130–52.

Silverstein, Michael. 1981a. "The Limits of Awareness." In *Working Papers in Sociolinguistics,* no. 84. Austin: Southwest Educational Development Laboratory.

———. 1981b. "Metaforces of Power in Traditional Oratory." Lecture, Department of Anthropology, Yale University, February.

———. 1997. "The Improvisational Performance of 'Culture' in Real-Time Discursive Practice." In *Creativity in Performance*, edited by R. K. Sawyer. Greenwich, CT: Ablex.

———. 2004. "'Cultural' Concepts and the Language-Culture Nexus." *Current Anthropology* 45 (5):621–52.

Silverstein, Michael, and Greg Urban. 1996. *Natural Histories of Discourse*. Chicago: University of Chicago Press.

Smith, Warren W. 1996. *Tibetan Nation: A History of Tibetan Nationalism and Sino-Tibetan Relations*. Boulder, CO: Westview Press.

Sperling, Elliot. 2001. "'Orientalism' and Aspects of Violence in the Tibetan Tradition." In *Imagining Tibet: Perceptions, Projections, & Fantasies*, edited by T. Dodin and H. Räther. Boston: Wisdom Publications.

Stasch, Rupert. 2011. "Ritual and Oratory Revisited: The Semiotics of Effective Action." *Annual Review of Anthropology* 40.

Stoler, Ann Laura. 2004. "Affective States." In *A Companion to the Anthropology of Politics*, edited by D. Nugent and J. Vincent. Malden, MA: Blackwell.

Stoller, Paul. 1995. *Embodying Colonial Memories: Spirit Possession, Power, and the Hauka in West Africa*. New York: Routledge.

Tambiah, Stanley Jeyaraja. 1981. *A Performative Approach to Ritual*. London: British Academy.

———. 1995. *Magic, Science, Religion, and the Scope of Rationality*. Cambridge: Cambridge Univesity Press.

Taussig, Michael T. 1993. *Mimesis and Alterity: A Particular History of the Senses*. New York: Routledge.

———. 1999. *Defacement: Public Secrecy and the Labor of the Negative*. Stanford, CA: Stanford University Press.

Taylor, Charles. 1989. *Sources of the Self: The Making of Modern Identity*. Cambridge, MA: Harvard University Press.

Thurman, Robert A. F., ed. 1981. *The Life and Teachings of Tsong Khapa*. Dharamsala: Library of Tibetan Works & Archives.

———. 2008. *Why the Dalai Lama Matters: His Act of Truth as the Solution for China, Tibet, and the World*. New York; Hillsboro, OR: Atria Books; Beyond Words Pub.

Tibetan Centre for Human Rights and Democracy. 1997. *The Next Generation: State of Education in Tibet Today (1997)*. http://www.tchrd.org/publications/topical_reports/next_generation_education-1997/.

Tillemans, Tom J. F. 1989. "Formal and Semantic Aspects of Tibetan Buddhist Debate Logic." *Journal of Indian Philosophy* 17:265–97.

———. 2004. "Inductiveness, Deductiveness, and Examples in Buddhist Logic." In *The Role of the Example (dṛṣṭānta) in Classical Indian Logic*, edited by Shoryu Katsura and Ernst Steinkellner. Wiener Studien zur Tibetologie und Buddhismuskunde 58. Vienna: Arbeitskreis für Tibetische und Buddhistische Studien Universität Wien.

Toulmin, Stephen Edelston. 1958. *The Uses of Argument*. New York: Cambridge University Press.

Tournadre, Nicolas, and Rdo-rje. 2003. *Manual of Standard Tibetan: Language and Civilization; Introduction to Standard Tibetan (Spoken and Written) followed by an Appendix on Classical literary Tibetan*. Ithaca, NY: Snow Lion Publications.

Trilling, Lionel. 1972. *Sincerity and Authenticity*. Cambridge, MA: Harvard University Press.

Tshewang, Geshe. 2003. *sbag sa chos sgar gyi byung ba nor bu'i phreng ba*. Sidhpur: Norbulingka Institute.

Tylor, Edward B. 1913. *Primitive Culture: Researches into the Development of Mythology, Philosophy, Religion, Language, Art, and Custom*. Vol. 1. London: John Murray.

Uhmann, Susanne. 1992. "Contextualizing Relevance: On Some Forms and Functions of Speech Rate Changes in Everyday Conversation." In *The Contextualization of Language*, edited by P. Auer and A. Di Luzio. Amsterdam; Philadelphia: John Benjamins.

Urban, Greg. 1994. "Repetition and Cultural Replication: Three Examples from Shokleng." In *Repetition in Discourse: Interdisciplinary Perspectives*, edited by B. Johnstone. Norwood, NJ: Ablex.

———. 1996. "Entextualization, Replication, and Power." In *Natural Histories of Discourse*, edited by M. Silverstein and G. Urban. Chicago: University of Chicago Press.

———. 2001. *Metaculture: How Culture Moves through the World*. Minneapolis: University of Minnesota Press.

Urban, Greg, and Kristin Smith. 1998. "The Sunny Tropics of 'Dialogue'?" *Semiotica* 121 (3–4):263–81.

Waddell, L. Austine. 1895. *The Buddhism of Tibet or Lamaism, with its Mystic Cults, Symbolism and Mythology, and in its Relation to Indian Buddhism*. London: W. H. Allen.

Walton, Douglas N. 1995. *A Pragmatic Theory of Fallacy*. Tuscaloosa: University of Alabama Press.

Wangyal, D. 1976. "Poisonous View." *Tibetan Review* 11 (10):32.

Warner, Michael. 1993. "The Mass Public and the Mass Subject." In *The Phantom Public Sphere*, edited by B. Robbins. Minneapolis: University of Minnesota Press.

Wilce, James M. 2009. *Language and Emotion*. Cambridge: Cambridge University Press.

Wittrock, Bjorn. 2000. "Modernity: One, None, or Many? European Origins and Modernity as a Global Condition." *Daedalus* 129 (1):31–60.

Woolard, Kathryn A. 1998. "Language Ideology as a Field of Inquiry." In *Language Ideologies: Practice and Theory*, edited by B. B. Schieffelin, K. A. Woolard, and P. V. Kroskrity. New York: Oxford University Press.

Wortham, Stanton. 2001. *Narratives in Action*. New York: Teacher's College Press.

Wortham, Stanton, and M. Locher. 1996. "Voicing on the News: An Analytic Technique for Studying Media Bias." *Text* 16:557–85.

Wylie, Turrell V. 1959. "A Standard system of Tibetan Transcription." *Harvard Journal of Asiatic Studies* 22:261–67.

Yang, Mayfair Mei-hui. 2008. Introduction to *Chinese Religiosities: Afflictions of Modernity and State Formation*, edited by M. M.-h. Yang. Berkeley: University of California Press.

Yelle, Robert A. 2003. *Explaining Mantras: Ritual, Rhetoric, and the Dream of a Natural Language in Hindu Tantra*. New York: Routledge.

Zhabs-drung, Tshe-brtan. 1986. *Bod rgya tshig mdzod chen mo*. 3 vols. Beijing: Nationalities Publishing House.

# INDEX

Adams, Vincanne, 3
addressivity, 86–87, 94, 96, 100, 110–11, 113–14, 124–25
Adorno, Theodor, 77, 180n43
advice (bka' slob gnang), 12, 91–92, 143, 144, 149, 189n12
affect, 110, 124–25, 126
afflictive emotions (nyon rmongs), 124, 126
aggression, 55, 70, 125, 126
Agha, Asif, 13, 48, 64, 75, 110, 178n29
Aikhenvald, Alexandra Y., 178n29
altar areas and deities, 59
analogical punishment (Foucault), 147, 149
anger: afflictive emotions (nyon rmongs), 124, 126; aggression, 55, 70, 125, 126; dissimulated anger, 125, 126; histrionic anger, 5, 110, 114, 124–26, 127, 149; indirection, 113–14; semiotic resources to express, 187n14; in tripartite text structure, 124–25, 126; voice reflecting, 117–18
aphorisms, 111–12, 113, 125, 187–88n18
argumentation: consequence mode of, 54–55, 64, 68; denotational textuality, 48, 49, 50, 53, 57, 75, 123, 180n42; mimetic sympathy, 75, 76, 78, 103; proposition in, 35–36, 48–50, 53; studies of, 47–49, 77, 175n7, 176n17, 180n43; symmetry in, 10, 77, 78. See also debate (rtsod pa); demeanor
Autonomists (rang rgyud pa, svātantrika-mādhyamika), 54

autonomy: advice (bka' slob gnang), 12, 143, 144, 149, 189n12; communicative autonomy, 151–53; Dalai Lama on, 9, 133, 153, 154; of the disciplined subject, 10, 12, 16, 127–28, 134, 144–46, 147, 149; as expected by foreign spectators, 10, 140; in face-to-face interactions, 10, 13, 82, 100, 102; Five Point Peace Plan, 3, 7, 132–33, 188n3; Habermas on, 78; at Institute of Buddhist Dialectics, 127–28, 143–44, 156; of the liberal subject, 3, 10, 16, 156; Tibetans on, 10, 13, 16, 127–28, 140; Tibet question, 131–33
Avalokiteśvara, 10
"Awareness and Knowledge" (blo rig), 182n10

Bakhtin, Mikhail, 6, 85, 86, 87, 109, 117, 166–68
Barnett, Robert, 7
Bauman, Richard, 12
Benjamin, Walter, 10
Bentham, Jeremy, 109
Bhabha, Homi, 153–54
Bickel, Balthasar, 178n29
biphasic emplotment of debate, 57, 177n23
blind faith (rmongs dad): in Chinese Communist propaganda (mi xin), 96, 183n18; cultivation of answerability, 91, 96; popular religion, 86, 91, 97, 98–99, 149; reason as antidote to, 90–91, 95–97, 98, 99, 100; use of expression, 183n18
Bodhgaya, 91
Bön order of monks, 47, 102, 171n6

183n18; Buddhism as inner science, 2, 150, 153, 182n12; criticism of, 133; on debate's dissemination, 89–90, 155; in defense of Buddhism, 6, 86, 91–94, 180n10; deference paid to, 90; democratization initiatives, 7, 129, 130, 170n4; on educational reform, 91, 93–94, 95–100, 158, 181–82n7; on empty ritual, 86, 91, 97, 98, 149; encourages his followers to spread the dharma, 93–94; Enlightenment ideology of, 3; on the Great Exhortation (*tshogs gtam chen mo*), 148–49; international campaign of, 3, 7, 131, 132–33, 188n3; Kalachakra initiations, 191n8; meeting with Mao Zedong, 94–95; Middle Way, 133; on modernity, 2, 3, 6, 85–86, 91–92, 95, 182n10; on monastic recruitment, 160–62; nonviolence promoted by, 3, 133, 159; on philosophical study, 100–101, 184n19, 185n32; on propitiation of Dorje Shugden (deity), 22; on public reprimand (*tshogs gtam*), 147–49; on the Tibet question, 3, 131, 132–33; urges Tibetans to clarify Buddhism to wider world, 91–92, 93–94, 180n10; valorization of reason by, 1–2, 3, 85, 87, 90–94, 96–100. See also CTA (Central Tibetan Administration of His Holiness the Dalai Lama); Geluk sect; Institute of Buddhist Dialectics

*dam bca'*, 26, 47, 50, 57, 177n23. *See also* Rigchen debates; Rigchung debates

Dargye, Tenzin, 182n12

Das, Veena, 23

data recording, xix

debate (*rtsod pa*): argumentation, 35–36, 47–49, 53, 64, 68, 175n7, 176n17; challenges to textual ideology during, 26, 36–38, 41; citation phase of, 34, 61, 62–64, 65f4, 66–67, 70; colors debate, 51–52, 54–55, 56, 176n18, 179n36; commencement of, 50, 65–66, 66f5; *Commentary on Valid Cognition* (Dharmakīrti), 101–2; consensus building in beginning of, 37, 50, 57, 61–64, 68–69, 75–76, 177n23; curricular texts defended during, 36–38, 41; *dam bca'*, 26, 47, 50, 57, 177n23; defined, 37, 47, 82; evolution of debate-based study, 45–46; expansion of, 80, 83, 88–89, 100–104, 181–82n7; first impressions of, 55–56, 103; gestures during, 32, 50, 55, 60, 69t2; as illiberal, 5, 13, 43, 82; instruction for, 51–52, 176n11, 176n13, 185n32; language of competition in, 30–32; mimetic power of, 40, 75,

103; outline phase, 64, 66; performance evaluation in, 30–31; plot summary, 36–38; propositions in, 35–36, 48, 53; reciprocation during, 74–75; refuge (*skyabs 'gro*) as debate topic, 58, 62–64, 67–68, 71; repetition in, 65, 67, 73, 175n5; Rigchen debates, 28, 41; Rigchung debates, 28, 57–58, 59–60, 178n27; as ritual, 38–41; seating during, 59–60, 60f3, 61; shift from -*s* to *byas* framing, 67–68; sports compared with, 31–32; transactional space, 59–60, 60f3, 61, 70–71, 179–80n37; tripartite structure of, 51–52, 124–25, 126, 176n11, 176n13; unsettling of, 65–66, 68–69, 70, 71; as zero-sum contest, 31–32, 82. *See also* challenger (in debate); defendant (in debate); textbooks (*yig cha*)

debate examinations, 178n27

defendant (in debate): challenger's treatment of, 36–37, 53, 56; college ideology threatened by performance of, 36, 37; consequences evaluated by, 55; deceleration of responses, 72, 73–74, 74t3, 180n38; definitions offered by, 67–68; demeanor of, 37–38, 50, 71, 73, 82, 102–3; firm-ness (*brtan po*) exhibited by, 102–3; knowledgeability, 37, 53, 59, 61, 65, 66, 67–68, 71, 73; reconstruction of source citation, 34, 61, 62–64, 65–66; reconstruction of textbook source clause, 64, 65f4; reincarnate lamas as, 59, 178n27; seating for, 59, 61; speech-articulation rates, 71–74, 74t3, 180n38; on the topic of refuge, 58–59; as tradition's envoy, 59; transactional space, 59–60, 60f3, 61, 70–71, 179–80n37; unflappability of, 37, 50, 69, 73, 82, 102–3

deference, 32–33, 59, 82, 90, 118, 177–78n26, 186n1; exhibited during public reprimand (*tshogs gtam*), 107–8, 186n1; honorifics, 53, 116, 122–24, 187n11

DeLancey, Scott, 178n29

demeanor: of challenger, 60–61; commitment to doctrinal tradition reflected in, 32–35, 37–38, 50–51; of defendant, 37–38, 50, 73, 82, 102–3; indexicality of, 48, 50, 64–66, 65, 66f5, 75; knowledgeability, 50–51, 59, 65, 66, 68, 73; poise, 73, 74; signaling of, 64–65, 178n29; speech-articulation rates, 71–74, 180n38; of unflappability, 37, 50, 69, 73–74, 82, 102–3

demeanor indexicality, 48, 50, 64–65, 65–66, 66f5, 75

Democracy Day, 129

TEXT
10/13 Sabon

DISPLAY
Sabon

COMPOSITOR
Integrated Composition Systems

INDEXER
Nancy Zibman

CARTOGRAPHER
Bill Nelson

PRINTER AND BINDER
IBT Global

CPSIA information can be obtained at www.ICGtesting.com
Printed in the USA
LVOW07s0727150915

454161LV00001B/3/P